Ananda

Ananda

Happiness Without Reason

ACHARYA PRASHANT

HarperCollins *Publishers* India

First published in India by HarperCollins *Publishers* 2022
4th Floor, Tower A, Building No. 10, Phase II, DLF Cyber City,
Gurugram, Haryana – 122002
www.harpercollins.co.in

2 4 6 8 10 9 7 5 3 1

P-ISBN: 978-93-5629-219-2
E-ISBN: 978-93-5629-220-8

Typeset in 12/15 Arno Pro at
Manipal Technologies Limited, Manipal

Printed and bound at
Thomson Press (India) Ltd

MIX
Paper
FSC FSC® C010615

This book is produced from independently certified FSC® paper
to ensure responsible forest management.

Contents

Part III
What do the Scriptures Say?

Introduction

This book was spoken first and written later.

As a Vedanta philosopher and teacher, Acharya Prashant has been interacting with diverse audiences for over a decade. Though the questioners come from varying backgrounds, each of these interactions is usually in the form of a question that the teacher responds to. The length of each such interaction varies from ten minutes to as much as an hour. Every chapter of this book is essentially based on one such interaction. This means that each chapter, though coming from a single centre, exhibits the response of the speaker to very different people and their peculiar life-queries. The questioners are spaced apart across years, continents, genders, and everything else that makes a human being distinct from the other. As a result, the readers get an enriching kaleidoscopic perspective as they go through the range of human conditions, confusions and questions – all related to a certain want of inner clarity, peace and joy.

What is that one fundamental thing for which we go about toiling all our lives – sacrificing, negotiating, scheming, praying? Very intuitively we might answer – happiness. But do we really know what happiness is? Are we always clear on what makes us happy? And if everybody wants happiness, what is the source of all the misery in our lives?

There is no dearth of literature on happiness, both in material and spiritual circles, claiming to answer the fundamental questions about happiness. However, most of these works paint a fuzzy image of happiness, beautiful in words but generally not useful. The more divine the words, the more unattainable the happiness they point to.

As the readers go through the first few chapters of this book, they realize how they might have been blindsided by the usual pursuit of happiness. Acharya Prashant brings down this seemingly 'holier than thou' pursuit to a level field. The reader gets to see happiness as an ornamental sculpture in the backyard of sadness, just pleasure in play with pain. Saddened by this duality-stricken drama of life, man is constantly on the lookout for happiness that is unconditional, without reason. This happiness without reason is classically called 'Ananda' or Joy.

Each chapter in the book follows a line of enquiry initiated by seekers about the trials and tribulations they encounter in their daily lives - petty to profound. The questions revolve around human experiences like pleasure, pain, laughter, excitement, peace and contentment. The discussion that follows is often ruthless in the sense that it shatters common misconceptions about happiness, sadness, and related jargons like 'loving unconditionally' and 'living in the present'. The latter chapters of the book draw heavily from Vedantic seers and celebrated saints. Touching upon deeper questions on pure Joy, these chapters reveal to the readers something immense: they *already* have what they are looking for. Although, 'reveal' might be an oxymoron – how do you reveal something that is the default? And if one already has it, how does it remain veiled?

A word of caution: Because of the vast differences among seekers and their queries, the responses of the teacher too are customised and not standardised. At some places, therefore, the responses in one chapter may be apparently contradictory to the responses in another chapter. We hope that our discreet readers will be able to appreciate the differences as various roads leading to the same core.

Part I

———•———

Ananda Is Contentment in Which Happiness Is No Longer Needed

1

Do Your Pleasures Really Please You?

> *IF YOU WANT TO PLEASE YOURSELF, FULFIL YOUR DEEPEST DESIRES, NOT THE FLIMSY ONES. YOU WANT TO LOVE, AND YOU WANT TO LOVE THE HIGHEST. THAT'S THE REAL PLEASURE THAT YOU WANT. SO, FIRST OF ALL, BECOME CAPABLE OF LOVING THE HIGHEST, AND THEN FALL IRREVOCABLY IN LOVE.*

Listener: Sir, please explain the futility of chasing bodily pleasures. Looking back, my love for pleasures has always been above everything. There is a very strong feeling of missing out when I don't act on my urges.

Acharya Prashant: Futility does not lie in chasing pleasures. Futility lies in chasing futile pleasures. Do your pleasures really succeed in pleasing you? It doesn't look that way. Have you ever really been pleased by anything? What kind of pleasures are you talking of then? Why should you even call them pleasures? Call them illusions.

Being a pleasure-seeker is your natural state. Man, for substantial reason, has been called a manifestation of Joy. Have you seen all these sannyasis from various orders? They address themselves with names such as Turiya Ananda, Atma Ananda, Brahm Ananda and Keval Ananda. There is one thing common in their names: Ananda. Have you never wondered why all of them necessarily have the term 'Ananda' in their names? It doesn't matter what comes before that word; even after everything, 'Ananda' remains.

So, it is all right if you love pleasure. Ananda is something that you must love. It is the holiest thing to love. Being a pleasure-seeker is an act of piousness. But we are not pious people. Why? Not because we seek pleasure, but because we hate pleasure. What is it to be a pleasure-hater? It is to be a chaser of incomplete pleasures. Do not say that you are satisfied by momentary pleasures; instead, state that you hate eternal pleasure and that is why you are gratified by momentary pleasures.

Had you really been a lover of pleasure, why would you make peace with these trivial things that you call pleasurable? Some psychedelics, some drugs, some excitement, some women, some booze—that is your pleasure, right? High-speed driving, somehow managing a room in a posh hotel, walking into it with a woman— that is what your definition of pleasure is. How does the bedsheet look after the night? How is the morning after the rampage? How does the bottle look now? What does it give you the next day but a hangover? You call that pleasure?

After five minutes of sex, you turn your back to her and start snoring and she starts farting. Is that pleasure? Seriously? Moreover, after all the orgasmic heights, you rush to the washroom and she hears the flushing of the water in the toilet. What pleasure are the two of you getting? Soon after, you come back and crash like a log, and the next morning your mouth is stinking. Is that pleasure? Broken beer bottles—is that pleasure? Merry made on somebody else's money—is that pleasure?

I am not denigrating it on moral grounds; I am disparaging it on the basis of its sheer incompleteness. It does not give you pleasure. I am not against your pleasures; I am against your hollow pleasures. Why don't you chase the highest pleasures? Why not? Yes, life has to be pleasurable. So why not aim for a higher pleasure? Why must you seek the lowest kind of pleasures, and that too when you know that they don't succeed in fulfilling you?

Remember who you are. Once consciousness is out of you, you are nobody. They will not even keep your ashes. Dogs will dig your bones, if any remain. So, remember who you are. Had you just been the body, why would they have buried you in the ground, or burned your body?

Who are you, then? Let the funeral ground clearly tell you who you are. Are you the body? If you are the body, why is the body burned away after a particular date? Who are you? You are somebody else who is in the body, who uses the body, who speaks through the body, but who is certainly not the body. If you are somebody else, then will the pleasures of the body satisfy you?

You are X, and X has a body. So, should X give pleasure to the body or to himself? If you want to be happy—which you would want to achieve, let's say, by being drunk—do you put beer in your car's radiator? When you want to have a good time, you fill yourself up with beer, not your car, right? This is because you are not the car; you *have* the car. So the car's pleasure is not your pleasure. When you want to have pleasure, it is not the car you go out and please, or do you?

So, when you want to have pleasure, why do you want to give pleasure to your body? Why don't you give it to yourself? Instead of giving pleasure to yourself, you keep giving pleasure to your body and your bodily tendencies. How will that satisfy *you*? The body, after all the pleasures that it has had, will finally turn into ashes. Give pleasure to yourself, not to the body.

What does pleasing oneself really mean? For that, you have to know who you are. You are the one who sits in the body and seeks through the body. You are one who wants to know, who wants to understand, who wants to love, who wants to really seek and reach. That is what you want.

So, if you want to please yourself, kindly fulfil your deepest desires, not the flimsy ones.

You want to love, and you want to love the highest. That's the real pleasure that you want. So, first of all, become capable of loving the highest, and then fall irrevocably in love with it. That is the pleasure you really want.

You want to know and understand because that is the nature of your consciousness. So go ahead, figure out, find out, know and understand. And the pleasure of understanding is beyond comparison.

All the fun and merrymaking will never give you what you really want. Have some real fun, like an adult, not like a baby. An adult must have grown-up pleasures. Booze and sex are for kids.

> " The body, after all the pleasures that it has had, will finally turn into ashes. Give pleasure to yourself, not to the body. "

(Advait BodhSthal, 2019)

2

Pleasures of Instant Gratification and Suffering

"" WHEN THE ENTIRE POPULATION HAS GONE INSANE, YOU
WILL HAVE INSANE LEADERS. WHEN YOU HAVE INSANE
LEADERS, VERY CATASTROPHIC DECISIONS WILL BE MADE
CONTINUOUSLY.   ""

Listener: The humanity of today has more entertainment available to itself than ever before. All kinds of virtual platforms and services encourage us to seek short-lived and repeated pleasures by offering us instant gratification in various ways. The need to wait has reduced, and so has our patience. What do you have to say on this?

Acharya Prashant: First of all, I will describe the situation you have pointed at.

There is no need for any kind of spirituality if all is hunky-dory. If we are doing well and life is smooth and natural, we need not make any efforts towards betterment. What brings a person towards Truth, which is what is called spirituality, is suffering. When you are suffering, you are forced to acknowledge that there is something wrong in the way you think and operate.

Today, as you said, there are ample means of gratification, and the suffering is not allowed to last: you are given an easy escape from reality. You operated wrongly, rather you *exist* wrongly, so you suffered. But a thousand and one means exist within your easy access to block your suffering, to anesthetize you. Not that your suffering would be gone that way, but you would be numbed down. The experience of suffering would be covered under a deceptive layer of pleasure, so the incentive to introspect and change the inner fundamentals would be reduced.

When you do this repeatedly, the suffering gets internalized more and more and goes deeper, because you are not allowing it to come to the surface. What do I mean by the surface? The surface denotes the level, the place at which your suffering can become available for experience. There is this table before me. All that is available for my eyes to experience is the surface of the table. Even if I know that the whole thing (table) is here, all I experience is the surface.

So, we have a dirty escape option. If the table is cluttered, or dirty, or soiled, or spotted, what do I do? I cover it with some cloth. To my eyes, with all their limitations, the dirt or the problem will no longer be visible or available to be experienced. That is what most of our progress throughout our history has been about: not about solving, really solving problems, but about obfuscating them.

We have been on a spree to invent ways, methods, very clever mechanisms to just hide our problems. But the problem is not gone; it is just going in and in, deeper and deeper. It is now reaching your core; it will *become* your core. And it will be a very bad situation because on the surface, on the skin you will be all right, but within you will be all dirty. That is what is happening, and a more common name for this situation is neurosis.

Now you see why we are seeing a deluge of mental health cases over the last few decades. It is an epidemic. Mankind was never as terribly diseased mentally as it is today. And this is not my subjective opinion, please do consult the statistics and the research papers. The average stress and anxiety levels measured numerically today in several groups are way higher than what they were even at the time of the world wars, and we are many times more prosperous today than we were ever in our history.

We have conquered disease, we have conquered natural unpredictability, we want to colonize the moons and planets, and we want to beat death. But inwardly we are getting more and more rotten every passing year. That is precisely because of the availability of easy means of gratification. Life just showed the mirror to you, exposed to you how rotten you are, and what do you do? You switch on the TV, you rush to the nearest shopping mall, you call up your boyfriend or girlfriend—easy means to please yourself all around, abundant. Pick up the bottle and pour yourself a drink, play a video game. What is this gaming industry all about?

Don't you ever wonder why man needs so much entertainment today? It should be obvious. We have never needed as much entertainment as we do today, and we have never been as mentally sick as we are today. These two go together.

Now, this will lead to an explosion. This will lead to a situation where the bulk of mankind is mentally sick—we are already there actually. What will that result in? A series of poor decisions at the aggregate level. An entire country might decide it does not want its rivers. A comity of nations might decide that it values economic progress more than the environment. What are you seeing in the climate change deliberations? Please, tell me. Why are they failing again and again?

Had the group of leaders been sane, they would have said that we want to control the carbon footprint and it does not matter what economic costs we will have to bear. But the leaders have been just dragging their feet for the last several decades, and we are continuously making the wrong kind of decisions. How are these leaders affording such pathetic decisions? It is because they are propped up by a democratic system in which the entire demography, the whole voter base is neurotic. Don't you see how people vote?

When the entire population has gone insane, you will have insane leaders. When you have insane leaders, very catastrophic decisions will be made continuously. So, everyone says, 'We need to mine out the minerals. It doesn't matter that we will have to wipe out an entire forest for that. Hack down the forest, we want the minerals.' If you just sit down and think about it, you will realize that nobody but a mad culture, a mad population can make such decisions.

All of this is very intimately linked to the fact that you can entertain yourself quite easily, and also to the fact that nothing entertains you. So, TikToks (popular mobile application) were one minute long, whereas the reels are fifteen seconds. Because nothing succeeds in entertaining you, you want something else very quickly. You just can't stick to one thing because you very well know that thing is bound to fail.

We are heading towards a mass catastrophe. To top that, our role-models, our corporate poster boys, the global icons are declaring, 'Why care for the Earth? We can colonize Mars!' And that leaves you with an even lesser incentive to save the planet. This is collective madness.

But you know, in the larger scheme of things, the continuation or disappearance of this one species called Homo sapiens hardly matters. My concern is the kind of suffering this mad species is going to inflict upon all other life forms before it itself is obliterated. Obviously, mankind is heading towards deep disaster, but it is also carrying millions of other species towards extinction in the process. We just have to see the number of species that are becoming extinct per day—per day! This is not in the natural scheme of things; it is all man-made. We are doing it because we are mad.

So, fine. It is probably just natural justice that we pay for our sins, but it really saddens me that the entire planet has to pay for our misdeeds.

" WE HAVE CONQUERED DISEASE, WE HAVE CONQUERED NATURAL UNPREDICTABILITY, WE WANT TO COLONIZE THE MOONS AND PLANETS, AND WE WANT TO BEAT DEATH. BUT INWARDLY WE ARE GETTING MORE AND MORE ROTTEN EVERY PASSING YEAR. THAT IS PRECISELY BECAUSE OF THE AVAILABILITY OF EASY MEANS OF GRATIFICATION. "

(IIT Bombay, 2021)

3

Pleasure and Pain, Happiness and Sadness

" WHO ARE YOU? THE OLD, TIMELESS TENDENCY TO
ASSOCIATE WITH THE BODY AND TREAT THE BODILY
HAPPENINGS AS ITS OWN. "

Listener: Sir, you have said:

'All the things that we associate with pleasure, with pain, with hurt, are all concepts that we have been indoctrinated into. Remove these concepts, and then show me where is pleasure and where is pain. When you remove them, there is just life—simple, total and joyful.'

Can you please elaborate what you mean by this? When I feel hunger, how is hunger a concept? When my fingers get burnt in fire, I feel pain. How is pain a concept?

Acharya Prashant: Pleasure and pain here are in the context of happiness and sadness, celebration and suffering, good and bad.

So, you are saying, 'When I feel hunger, how is hunger a concept? When my fingers get burnt in fire, I feel pain. How is pain a concept?'

No, pain is not a concept. Hunger, too, is not a concept. Pain is felt by the body. Have you seen how instantaneous the body's reaction to pain is? The moment the fingers get burnt, the body knows what to do. Or does the body ask you what to do? The body knows what to do. The body does what it should.

The body is a self-contained and self-sufficient mechanism designed with the objective of self-preservation and self-proliferation. These are the two objectives of the design of this body, and the body knows that. When these objectives are defeated, the body calls that situation as pain. When these objectives are furthered, the body calls that situation as pleasure.

Look into pleasure and pain, go deep into them, and you will find that all instances of pleasure are happenings that somehow help you stay alive in a bodily way, and all instances of pain threaten your bodily existence. So, there is something wrong somewhere in the body which you cannot even know of; the head starts paining, you get a headache. Because the headache would be noticeable to the conscious part of the brain, the headache would come as a conscious happening to the brain, and it would then be forced to respond to the headache; the brain would then be forced to take care of the body.

Pain and pleasure are bodily. They are *of* the body and *to* the body. They are not to *you*. So, what do you have to do with the pain? Nothing. When there is pain, the body knows what to do, and when there is pleasure, the body knows what to do.

What is a concept, then? The body cannot have concepts; the body is not so literate. The body is a beast, and beasts do not live in concepts. Who has a concept, then? You.

You are the primal tendency to associate with the body. Who are you? The old, timeless tendency to associate with the body and treat the bodily happenings as its own. So, if there is pain to the body, you say, 'Oh, I am in pain!' And if there is pleasure to the tongue, you say, 'I am so happy!' If the shoulder gets hurt, you say, 'I am hurt!' That is the definition of you—the very, very old tendency to consider the body as itself. And this is a concept. It is a concept because it can be removed. One can get rid of this concept.

Mind you, you can never get rid of your property, but you can get rid of your concepts. The body's property is to get burnt when in fire. And it doesn't matter what kind of enlightenment you enter into— the body will get burnt when in fire. That will not change. But your association with bodily happenings can change, and that is a concept. It is called a concept precisely because it can be changed, it can be dropped. Properties cannot be dropped. And if something can be dropped, surely it is not an essential property; it is merely a concept.

So, if a Buddha's body is threatened with burns, he would let the mind-body complex do what it must. In a condition where there is a risk of physical elimination, the brain knows what to do. Does the brain not have intellect? What else is the intellect for? Does the brain not have memories? Does the brain not have the capacity to analyze, arrange, organize, plan, find a way out? The brain knows all these things.

So, what would the Buddha do? He would just let the brain do what it must. What would the common man do? He would start crying, 'I am burning, I am burning!' and would make his condition worse, pathetic, and would ultimately actually get burned. That is the difference between the conceptless Buddha and the man who is carrying the concept that 'I am the body'. In a burning house, the Buddha would not say 'I am burning'; the Buddha would let the expert take over. Who is the expert? The body-brain complex is the expert. It takes over and it finds out a way.

And if the body-brain complex cannot find out a way, surely the ego-tendency never can. The ego-tendency only knows attachment—foolish attachment. The ego-tendency does not even have intellect, let alone intelligence. Where does the intellect reside? In the brain. The brain has intellect. Ego has no intellect and, obviously, ego has no intelligence. Ego knows only panic. Ego knows only foolishness.

So, in a burning house, the common man would panic foolishly, and all kinds of thoughts would start coming to him: 'What will happen to my kids if I get burnt down? If help doesn't arrive within two minutes, I am gone!' and so on. Do any of these thoughts help the body survive? No. We know the kind of foolishnesses man is capable of in adverse situations. Panic kills more people than calamities. And who is panicking? Does the body ever panic? No, it is the 'I'-sense that panics.

The Buddha is free of the 'I'-sense. The Buddha lets the body experience pleasure and pain and does not interfere. The Buddha lacks the concept that he must interfere in the matters of the body. He lets the body work—and when I say body, I include the brain. So, the Buddha does not interfere with the intellect. His intellect is free of 'I'. If he has thoughts, those thoughts are free of 'I'. Buddha is not thoughtless; it is just that his thoughts are not burdened with 'I'. He is not continuously thinking about himself. And what is the common man doing when he is thinking? He is always thinking about himself.

That is the difference between living concept-free and living conceptually. When you live conceptually, then all the things related to the body become your own. If you eat, you say, 'You know, this food will satisfy me.' The Buddha knows that the food will indeed satisfy, but not *you*. The food will offer satisfaction, but only to the stomach. And what does the common man think? He thinks that by having great food he will get a deep internal satisfaction. And that is why the common man is always frustrated: because that which he wants never comes.

15

The Buddha is never frustrated because he does not meddle with others' affairs. To him the body is an other. If the body wants food, let it have food. If the brain wants to think, let it think. And what does the brain want to think of? Let the intellect decide that. The brain does not need to think of *me*. My thoughts do not need to carry the 'I'.

So, there can be thoughts about this and that, but there need not be any thoughts about 'I' because the 'I' of a Buddha is not in need of any nursing. The 'I' of the Buddha is not threatened anymore. He does not have to continuously wonder about his safety, his progress, his accomplishment, or his fulfilment. So, he does not think about himself. The brain thinks, and the brain thinks of whatever it wants to think. The Buddha does not think, which means his thoughts are free of 'I'.

What is a concept, then? The most fundamental concept is that you are in danger, that you are unfulfilled, that you are lonely and therefore need company. The first company that you accord to yourself is that of the body, and that is how the child is born. Who is the child? The ego having assumed foolish company—that is called childbirth. The ego has chosen another useless partner—you celebrate it as childbirth. Now the ego will throughout the life of the child keep saying, 'It is me, it is me, it is me!'

The body is just a prakritik (natural) instrument. There are the hands, the eyes, the nose, the lungs and the brain—a complete apparatus in itself. It does not even need the support or interference of the 'I'.

But the 'I' is such a trespasser. It even likes to claim, 'I breathe', 'I sleep', 'I took birth'. Seriously? You *took* birth? Even that was done by you? Then what were your mother and father and the doctors and the five nurses doing? Upon being born, the two-kilogram thing is saying 'I took birth'. It took ten people to just get you out into the air, and you say 'I *took* birth'? And then he says 'I died', as if dying is a verb. 'I died!' It doesn't matter if the fellow has expired in coma; you still say he died. 'He died'? What did he have to do with the event of death? He was in coma!

That's the ego. It likes to attribute to itself that which is none of its business, and therefore it keeps suffering and getting disappointed. It is a meddler, poking its nose everywhere. It has one concept— it *is* the concept. What is the concept? 'I need'. And 'I need' can be extended with any suitable word: 'I need association', 'I need fulfilment', 'I need this', 'I need that'. The fundamental concept is that 'you need'.

Pleasure and pain are not concepts. They are material states of the body. Just by examining a person's brain, you can tell whether he is in pleasure or not. Just by introducing some material dopamine into your body, you can be induced to experience pleasure. These are material states.

Pleasure and pain are not concepts; they are material states. Happiness and sadness are concepts. The body feels pleasure, feels pain. The ego feels happy, feels sad. The ego in itself is a concept.

> " *THE BODY IS A SELF-CONTAINED AND SELF-SUFFICIENT MECHANISM DESIGNED WITH THE OBJECTIVES OF SELF-PRESERVATION AND SELF-PROLIFERATION. WHEN THESE OBJECTIVES ARE DEFEATED, THE BODY CALLS THAT SITUATION AS PAIN. WHEN THESE OBJECTIVES ARE FURTHERED, THE BODY CALLS THAT SITUATION AS PLEASURE.* "

(Advait BodhSthal, 2018)

17

4

Pleasures of the Consciousness versus Pleasures of the Body

“ *THE MORE PLEASURES YOU GIVE TO THE BODY, THE MORE BODY-IDENTIFIED YOU BECOME. THE MORE PLEASURES YOU GIVE TO THE CONSCIOUSNESS, THE MORE ALL YOUR IDENTIFICATIONS DISSOLVE.* ”

'Throw out concepts like "I am virtuous" or "I am a sinner". What is the entity that senses this? Body-consciousness will not lose its grasp on you with the thought that your well-being is the result of some spiritual activity. All you need is to keep observing yourself. Do not befriend anything that is visible to you. If you have to act at all, do only this: please your consciousness. It is very merciful. It will show you all that is, directly.'

~Nisargadatta Maharaj

Listener (L): How is it possible to please the consciousness without being pleased in return? The correlation between spiritual activities and the sense of well-being and peace seems obvious. Why are we being told to get rid of that? Kindly guide.

Acharya Prashant (AP): The pleasures of consciousness are not the pleasures of the body. The body has its pleasures, and consciousness has a totally different dimension of pleasure. That which pleases the body is not that which pleases consciousness, but the two become one because our consciousness is body-consciousness.

Consciousness not entangled with the body seeks a destination of a totally different nature. And as far as the body is concerned, it is seeking pleasures of its own kind. In some ways, the saint is also a pleasure-seeking individual, and so is a greedy or a lustful man. It is just that the pleasures that the two are seeking are widely separate.

Please the consciousness, not the body. And those who are in the business of pleasing the body, to them I say, I exhort and invite: try experiencing the pleasures of consciousness, you will forget all about the pleasures of the body. If pleasure is what you must have, then, in Nisargadatta Maharaj's parlance, have the pleasures of consciousness.

The pleasures of the body inflate the body, reinforce the body, and the pleasures of consciousness dissolve the consciousness. Such a great difference. The more pleasures you give to the body, the more body-identified you become. The more pleasures you give to consciousness, the more all identifications dissolve.

Usually I do not use the term 'pleasure' in the context of consciousness, but here because Maharaj is using that lexicon, so I am following him. The pleasures of the body are called sukha (happiness), the pleasures of consciousness are called Ananda (joy, bliss), and the two are very different.

In fact, when you are consciousness itself without its traps and identifications, and when you are trying to please consciousness alone, then that can result in displeasure to the body. And that is all right, because the quality of the pleasure of consciousness is far higher than the quality of pleasure of the body, so the latter can be compromised for the former.

Why does the consciousness need to be pleased? Because it is lonely. It usually gets attached to the body, but now you are saying, 'No, you will not have the body', so it has become even more lonely. You need to give it something better than the body. That is what is called pleasing consciousness: Give consciousness something better than the body to be with. This will greatly please consciousness and probably annoy the body, but that is okay. It is a good trade-off.

L: Can you give us an example?

AP: When you are sitting here listening to me, obviously I am not giving you a body-massage. But you are getting pleased, right? What is getting pleased? Not the body, but the consciousness. And the body is getting displeased. Look at him *(pointing at someone in the audience who is moving constantly)*! Forty-two times he has moved!

In giving pleasure to consciousness, even if the trade-off is that you will have to displease the body a little, it is all right. It is the cardinal mistake man makes—to place the pleasures of body higher than the pleasures of consciousness. Just don't make that mistake and everything will be okay.

L: Sir, does the negation of that which is not always bring you to that which is?

AP: It will not leave you to go to any point. You are saying, 'Sir, if I negate what is not, will it bring me to what is?' That which is not includes you as well. If that which is not is negated, will you still be left?

But that is the common expectation. 'After everything has been negated and cut down, I will survive, and I will then reach the Truth.' Once you are determined to cut down everything that is not, you will have to first of all slit your own throat. Firstly, you are not—who will then remain to reach the Truth?

Therefore, the Truth is not a destination. Forget the Truth; look at your own validity. Do you exist? And if you do exist, is it doing any good to yourself?

Ask the ego to do you a great favour—what? Leave! She leaves, you leave. Nothing remains. Peace! Nothing remains in context of what was existent earlier. Would there be something after you have gone? Maybe, maybe not. What is certain is that this question would not be there after you have gone.

The very need to be certain that even after your disappearance things will carry on is a mark of the ego still hanging around. It is only the ego that wants a certainty about the future, right? 'After I am gone, would there be bliss? After everything has been negated down, would there be Truth?' You are talking about the future. Who is concerned about the future? Exactly the entity which you are thinking of hacking down. If it has been hacked down, who will think about the future?

So, don't think about the future. Just see whether all this that is around you and within you needs to exist, whether it is doing you any good by its existence. It is a simple thing. Just look at what you have and what you are, and ask yourself, 'Is it doing me any good?' Full stop.

L: We know that there are five ways to get the pleasures of the body—through the five senses—and one gets the pleasures of consciousness at the feet of the Master and by reading scriptures. Are there any other ways to get pleasures of consciousness?

AP: What is pleasure of consciousness? Doubts receding; peace prevailing; complexities getting dissolved; all that which keeps

21

bugging you, nagging at you, frustrating you from within, subsiding. That is pleasure of consciousness.

So, the pleasure of consciousness lies in *not* being. Pleasure of consciousness is a pleasure of disappearance. Pleasure of consciousness is similar to the pleasures of sleep.

Why do you want to try out five or seven alternate ways of seeking pleasures of consciousness? You said, 'I know two ways of getting pleasures of consciousness: reading scriptures and listening to the Guru. Can you tell me five other ways?' Why? These two ways you want to abandon? If you know two ways, is that not sufficient? Why do you want five other ways?

But man is like this, you know. 'Can I have a few more options? I love him, I love him, I also love him. Let there be bounteous choice!' If man gets one option, he should be thankful for that and that should suffice for entire life. Why do you want fifteen? There are one hundred and fifty actually—but you do not need one hundred and fifty. And if you chase one hundred and fifty, you will probably not have even a single one.

Begin with what you have. Be grateful for what you already have. Stick to it. Maybe that will open the door for many others. But don't be in expectation of many others. Stick to what you have.

> " THE PLEASURE OF CONSCIOUSNESS LIES IN NOT BEING.
> THE PLEASURE OF CONSCIOUSNESS IS A PLEASURE OF
> DISAPPEARANCE. "

(Advait BodhSthal, 2019)

5

Learning the Best Laughter

" LAUGHTER IS INDEED BEAUTIFUL, BUT THERE IS NOTHING
UGLIER THAN LAUGHTER. AND CRYING IS, OF COURSE, A
MATTER OF SADNESS, AND THERE CAN BE NOTHING MORE
BEAUTIFUL THAN TEARS. IT DEPENDS ON WHERE YOUR TEARS
ARE COMING FROM. IT DEPENDS ON WHERE YOUR SMILE IS
COMING FROM. "

Listener (L): Why do people laugh?

Acharya Prashant (AP): Why do people laugh? Like anything else about life, this too is a good point to begin with. Since the root of everything is the same, it doesn't matter which leaf you put your finger on. If the inquiry is genuine, you will reach the root.

So, let's begin with laughter. Just like anything else that we engage in, laughter, too, can come from two very distinct points within us. There is a laughter that arises when one is pleased because one's desires are fulfilled. Have you seen this kind of laughter? You wanted something and you got it. You say, 'I am happy, pleased', and then you laugh.

It is this way that we usually laugh—after the satisfaction of a desire. There is a definite reason behind the laughter: fulfilment of the ego. The ego was feeling hard-pressed, incomplete, not satiated, and something happens which, at least temporarily, gives an impression to the ego that it has attained fulfilment. And one laughs and laughs.

But there is another kind of laughter, where you laugh not at the fulfilment of desire, not upon the satisfaction of the desire, but at desire itself. Now, there can be no reason behind this laughter. You are just looking at life, the desirous life as it is, and in looking at the contradiction and absurdity contained in it, you just feel like laughing.

There is no made-up joke which is a non-factual representation of our life. Our life itself is the biggest joke. But to be able to laugh at it, one needs a certain distance from it. That is why you find it difficult to laugh when the joke is on you; then, instead of it becoming a matter that pleases you, it becomes something that humiliates you. Have you not experienced this? If the joke is on you, everybody laughs and you cringe, isn't it?

A joke is nothing but the fact of our daily lives.

In the first kind of laughter, you laugh because you are attached to yourself. In the second kind of laughter, you laugh because you are witnessing yourself. The first kind of laughter has clear purpose and objective. The second kind is free of all purposes, objectives and limitations. It is laughter in freedom, freedom from oneself. 'I am no more obliged to carry my own weight. I am no more obliged to fulfil the ever-growing demand of this beast called the self.'

It is always hungry. It is always asking for something. When you put a little into its mouth it laughs, and after a while it again starts clamouring and asking and demanding and squirming. And if you don't please it, it cries. In fact, the more you feed it, the more energy it gets for crying. Crying requires a lot of energy. That energy comes from pleasure. Do you see this?

Laughter is wonderful when it is reasonless, purposeless and detached. When you can just laugh or just smile without having to depend on some kind of satisfaction, this is laughter in gratitude. When you can laugh without bothering for satisfaction, you are laughing in gratitude. Now you are saying, 'I am so fulfilled that I don't need to bother whether I am feeling satisfied or dissatisfied, hot or cold, happy or unhappy. I am still okay.' This okay-ness is, then, the laughter. There is no difference between this laughter and tears.

It doesn't matter whether you are laughing or crying. What matters is that you are crying or laughing from the right centre.

It is very difficult to tell whether the usual expression on the face of a saint is a gentle smile or gentle remorse—it is pretty much the same, whether he is smiling or whether he is a little ponderous, a little heavy. None of these states are for himself. None of these states are self-centred states. When he is smiling, it is not because some of his needs have been fulfilled. And if he isn't smiling and looks a little burdened, the burden isn't a personal one. He is not burdened by the obligation to build a house for himself or get more respect for himself.

Kabir often says, 'Bhaye Kabir udas' (Brother Kabir is sad). Is Kabir unhappy for himself? No, he is unhappy for the world. And there are saints who laughed, laughed in abandon. Were they laughing because they had obtained something for themselves? No, they were laughing because something existential was now right. As such there is no difference, whether they laugh or cry.

There have been wise men who kept crying. There have been wise men who kept silent. There have been wise men who kept dancing, and there have been wise men who kept laughing. They are all operating from the same centre, which was not their personal centre.

So, laughter is indeed beautiful, but there is nothing uglier than laughter. And crying is, of course, a matter of sadness, and there can be nothing more beautiful than tears. It depends on where your tears are coming from. It depends on where your smile is coming from.

There can be nothing more hurtful than a smile. With one smile—better called as a smirk—you can wound and lacerate someone. Your smile can be a tremendous putdown. Without even uttering a word, you can shred someone psychologically just by using your smile. It is such a deadly weapon. And that same smile can be a balm that heals, something that puts you to rest.

Don't bother about what is happening through you. Just bother about where you are. If you are in the right place, then whatever happens through you will just be the right thing. Now you don't need to guard against yourself. Now you don't need to be cautious for yourself. Now you don't need to say that your laughter must be measured. You don't need to say that one must weep only at the right place, right occasions, in right quantities. Now you can weep an ocean. Now you can laugh your lungs out, or maybe just be quiet. How does it matter?

The way common morality looks at these things—laughing, crying—is quite amusing. It is amusing because it is so stupid. In personality-grooming classes, you are even told the extent to which your muscles should part around your mouth, the angles that the edges of your lips must make with your ears, and if your smile is anything beyond that or less than that, it is a socially inappropriate smile. This is nonsense.

But the fact is that all of us have internalized this nonsense, at least to some degree. Kids have not done that so far. Let children weep however they want to weep. You don't teach a fish to swim or a bird to sing—why must you teach a kid to laugh? They know what to do. Anything other than this would be a contrived smile, and who likes factory products? When something is coming so naturally, let it come. Just be careful about one thing: Where are you located?

If you are located right at the feet of the Truth or in the embrace of the Truth, you don't have to worry about what is happening to you, through you, or in the world. Whatever happens now will happen through the right doer, the perfect doer, the Truth itself.

Surrender to That. When you surrender to That, the Truth joins in your laughter. When you surrender to That, Joy flows in your tears.

So, worry only about that and forget all else. But instead of that, we worry about everything and forget the thing that is most important. Our ways are so convoluted, absurd and inverted. The Truth knows how to laugh and when to laugh.

L: How do we know that we are at the feet of Truth?

AP: You can't know that. But you can surely know when you are trying to depend too much on your own feet. Is that not very obvious? When you are worrying about what will happen to you, when that happens, are you depending on the Truth or on yourself?

L: On ourselves.

AP: So, do not worry about the Truth. Just be careful that you do not become too large for yourself. The smaller you are, the more you are immersed in the Truth. The more you have this feeling of 'I', 'me', 'myself', 'what to do?', 'what will happen to me?', 'how to take care of my future?', the more you are occupied with such concerns and thoughts, the more it is certain that you are away from the Truth. So worries, planning, speculation, gossip are all sure-shot signs that you are forgetting something very important; rather, you are remembering a lot of rubbish, which is one and the same thing.

Truth is not something that you can detect. Truth is not something that you can know. Truth is not an experience. You will never be able to know the Truth. But the separation from Truth, the perceived distance from Truth can always be known through your suffering. The more you suffer, the more it is certain that you take yourself to be the ego. Otherwise, you can't suffer.

So, your internal churning, the whole agony, the divisions, the inner conflicts, they are all proofs of a disloyal life. They all are proofs of a defiance, of rebellion against the Truth. 'I will not surrender to the Ultimate, I will defend for myself. I am somebody, I have a certain power, certain capability. Why can't I go out and make it big?' And this, of course, you can know because this is consciousness. All of this is experience and is very well within the scope of your cognition. So, you can know this, and the moment you detect this, you must know that you are slipping.

Forget about the Truth. Look at your life. You know you are going to slip and that your intention is to not slip. When the occasion of slipping becomes a joke for you, you know very well that you have recovered. You have actually stood up if you can laugh at yourself when you slipped. That is such a beautiful laughter: 'Oh, I slipped again—ha ha ha!'

Now, this is an impersonal laughter. Now, you are not taking yourself too seriously. Now, you are not thinking that you are someone who can't slip. You are saying, 'Of course, I am full of imperfections. Of course, I will slip', and then you laugh at the ego which thought that it can't slip. This laughter is so beautiful.

> **LAUGHTER IS WONDERFUL WHEN IT IS REASONLESS, PURPOSELESS AND DETACHED. WHEN YOU CAN JUST LAUGH OR JUST SMILE WITHOUT HAVING TO DEPEND ON SOME KIND OF SATISFACTION, THIS IS LAUGHTER IN GRATITUDE.**

(Himachal Pradesh, 2016)

6

How to Reclaim Your Happiness?

> **HIGHER HAPPINESS IS NOT DIFFICULT TO GET. PROBABLY IT IS MORE AVAILABLE THAN YOU CAN IMAGINE. IT IS AVAILABLE, BUT NOT IN THE SHAPE, FORM OR NAME YOU WANT IT TO HAVE.**

Listener: Sir, I fail to understand how I could reclaim happiness. How can I be happy when I have so little control over my tendencies? How can I be happy when I can see that time is running out and I have failed to live gracefully? How can I be happy when I know that if this continues, my life has gone to waste?

Acharya Prashant: You ask this question while remaining unhappy. That is why you are asking, 'How can I be happy?'

How will you reclaim higher happiness if you continue to clutch the lower one? If I am asking, 'How can I be happy?' what is my current state? I am unhappy. So, you are clutching unhappiness and then asking, 'How do I be happy?' Otherwise, why would you ask?

For sure you are unhappy. If you are unhappy, what does it mean? This is your state *(holds out his arm and clenches his fist)*: four fingers and one thumb fiercely clutching unhappiness, and with an innocent face you are asking the teacher, 'How can I be happy?' Can you please relax first *(unclenches his fist)*? Now let us talk—but now there is no need to talk because the unhappiness itself is gone.

How will you ever embrace higher happiness if you have already embraced four kinds of lower happiness? Imagine a person who is already in embrace with four lowly people, and he is asking, 'How do I embrace the higher one? He is standing out there.' Well, he is available. Are *you* available? Who are you in embrace with? And how many of them? Four of them.

These four don't come to you uninvited or unsolicited; you cooperate. Withdraw that cooperation, withdraw your consent. These four will retreat out of shame. The energy which their embrace has is actually just the reciprocal of the energy you put in embracing them. Have you ever experienced that? Somebody comes to embrace you, and initially it is just a formal embrace. He puts his arms around your shoulders and probably wants to be done with it. But you are in some mood and decide to hug him tightly, and if you are hugging him tightly for a while, what does he do? He reciprocates by hugging you almost equally tightly.

So do not say, 'All these lowly ones are embracing me so tightly. How do I get rid of them?' First of all, relax your embrace. They are just reciprocating. They are, in a sense, your mirror images. You leave them, and they will leave you. You do not want to leave them. Additionally, you want to enjoy the righteous pleasure that comes with saying, 'Oh, but I am a victim! They are the ones who are surrounding me and dominating me.' They are not. They are just responding to the warmth of your feelings. You are so warm towards them, and they are nice, civilized people—how can they remain cold?

Higher happiness is not difficult to get. Probably it is more available than you can imagine. It is waiting. Don't look out for it when you are in a passionate embrace with falseness. You won't find it in the way you imagine it to be. It is available, but not in the shape, form or name you want it to have. It is there in a disguised manner.

Do not ask for assurances. Do not ask for advanced guarantees. Do not say, 'Show me where higher happiness is first, and only then will I drop the lower happiness.' These kinds of assurances you cannot get. Grace says, first have the faith and the guts to drop the lowly things, and then see whether the higher comes to you. In fact, the moment you drop the lowly, the higher has already come to you. You do not even have to wait. Have some guts to live through uncertainty.

> " Do not ask for assurances. Do not ask for advanced guarantees. Grace says, first have the faith and the guts to drop the lowly things, and then see whether the higher comes to you. In fact, the moment you drop the lowly, the higher has already come to you. "

(Advait BodhSthal, 2020)

7

How to Be Happy without Depending on Others?

❝ Pursuit of happiness is a great way to pass time. You will keep doing and doing but never fully succeed, so you will always have more to do. **❞**

Listener (L): Sir, how can we be happy without depending on others?

Acharya Prashant (AP): First of all, one has to begin by seeing that the happiness that is obtained by depending on others has a certain transience about it. This helps us in disengaging from that kind of happiness. Otherwise, if one is certain that the source of happiness lies in others, then the very possibility, the very inspiration to seek differently does not arise.

So, we begin by honestly examining what we usually do. We seek happiness in this or that and we succeed in getting it, and then we continue seeking happiness, which means the success is incomplete and short-lived, even if it comes. We highlight the success as our achievement, and we downplay the failure as a law of life. So, if you obtain success, you have achieved happiness using your efforts. What you want to selectively remember is that you tried and succeeded in getting happiness. The fact that the happiness faded away is completely forgotten, or even if it is remembered, it is remembered as something unavoidable, something to do with some unjust universal law.

We have surrendered to the cycle. What is the cycle about? We will work hard to attain happiness, and then the happiness will wither away, and because it withers away, we again try hard to get more of the same happiness. And the cycle continues. We have made peace with this scheme of things. We have told ourselves this is the universal order, and success lies in incessantly chasing happiness, getting it for a while, losing it, reclaiming it, and losing it again.

That is how the ego, the 'I'-sense which all of us have, has defined success and satisfaction. What is the definition? After you lose happiness, go for it once again. Don't be demotivated. Even if you fully well know that the next round of happiness is going to be equally fleeting as the previous one, still invest yourself fully, remain harnessed and fully occupied in this endeavour.

And if you are fully occupied in this, there is no one available to observe what you are doing. When you have totally given yourself, committed yourself and surrendered to this cyclical process, then, of course, there is no possibility of examining this process. That is your definition of commitment and surrender: Once you tell yourself that you are sold out or beholden to something, you withdraw from yourself the right to question that thing. Suspicion would be treachery, so you keep all suspicion at bay and just keep following the cycle.

First of all, we need to be a bit curious, even suspicious. We need to keep our certainties aside. That is difficult because certainty is a mental rock on which you are standing. Firstly, it is a rock;

secondly, you are standing on that rock. So how will you displace it? To displace that rock is to displace yourself. And who wants to be displaced?

But we will have to ask ourselves if we are genuinely interested in exploring whether a quality of happiness that is independent of others exists. What has happiness that is dependent on others really given us except for allowing us to while away time? It is a good way to pass time—make it, break it, make it, break it, make it, break it! In this process nothing is obtained, but you are spared the agony of honestly looking at yourself. You are left with no resource, no time, no space to look at yourself because you are fully committed to the cycle of making and breaking.

Someone comes and says, 'Son, what are you doing?'

And you say, 'Don't interfere! I am involved in something very serious, very important—make it, break it, make it, break it!'

So you get the pseudo-satisfaction of doing something meaningful. You can conveniently wear a mask of seriousness on your face. You can tell yourself that you are not internally unemployed. You can tell yourself that you are an important person involved in some important work. That helps one's self-esteem, which is ego.

One says, 'I am on a very serious project these days'—and what is the name of the project? Make it, break it, make it, break it. 'Make it' would require your effort; 'break it' is inevitable, like a sandcastle.

Are you okay with this? If you are, then there is no point asking whether there is happiness independent of the world. Are you okay with remaining invested in this cycle?

There are obvious advantages of remaining absorbed in this process. The first and foremost, as we already said, is that you are left with no time, no energy, no space to question. Honestly look at yourself. You are so busy!

A fellow is huffing and puffing and running down the lane. I stop him and say, 'I have something important to tell you: you might be going down the wrong lane!'

He says, 'Don't waste my time. If I invest a minute in listening to you, I would be losing a minute of distance covered! Covering the distance is so very important. How can I idle around listening to your teachings?'

Observation requires energy; it is dangerous for the ego. The ego does not quite like honesty. Remaining occupied in the pursuit of happiness keeps you so busy that there is no space for inner honesty. That is a great relief to the ego.

Then comes time—the great enemy. If you have something seriously worthwhile to do in life, time is a friend. But if you are just loafing around and you fully well know you are just killing time, in that case time is obviously an enemy. Every passing moment reminds you that you are committing a crime against yourself. That is the situation of most people. They know fully well that they are wasting life, so the clock's tick-tock is actually the announcement of a perpetual sentence. Tick-tock, tick-tock… The judge is there constantly telling you that you have been condemned to an inner hell of total waste, so it becomes very important to just pass time.

Have you seen how people are addicted to TV, to gossip, to all kinds of methods that just somehow enable them to pass time? Pursuit of happiness is a great way to pass time. You will keep pursuing it but never fully succeed, so you will always have more to do.

So, if you realize that you do not want to remain with this continuous process you are currently committed to, something else opens up. Then you start seeing many things. You see that the things or persons that you use in order to fulfil yourself all belong to the same plane. Therefore, if one of them has failed to fulfil you, the other one cannot really succeed.

It is one thing to honestly experiment, and it is a totally different thing to foolishly hope. Hope and experimentation do not go together. You do not experiment with a certain hope. In fact, if you are hopeful while experimenting, the hope will distort the results of the experiments. You have already tried out various things, but you are still hopeful about several other infinite things. You can pass away your entire life trying them one after the other and you will still have something left to try out. Think about all the flowers in a garden. You smell one petal from one flower, then another petal from another flower and so on. How many flowers and petals are there? Not only are they practically infinite, but they also keep growing infinitely. Will you ever exhaust them?

It is strange, but this disillusionment is very central to Ananda or Joy. You cannot have Joy without disillusionment. If you are hopeful about the world, Joy won't be possible.

It is a strange thing, because usually we associate disillusionment with sadness, and here I am saying that Joy comes with disillusionment. In a way I am saying that Joy is accompanied by sadness. Yes, at least those who have been chasers of happiness will find that Joy has come to them along with sadness. Later on the sadness may or may not evaporate, but given that chasing happiness is our default state, Joy does come with sadness, and you have to be prepared for that.

You need to have an appetite for sadness. You cannot keep rejecting sadness and yet want Joy. Joy is not ordinary happiness. Joy is a very demanding kind of happiness; it is the kind of happiness that demands sadness.

And therefore, Joy has depth that happiness does not. Artists will say there is great Joy in the depth of tears. Great epics and lots of creativity have sprung forth from deep agony. In fact, agony is often a trigger to creativity.

You will find it strange to hear this, but the ego does not like Joy because Joy is expensive. Happiness is quite cheap—you can buy it at a burger outlet—but Joy requires you to sell happiness itself. And that is merely the first instalment.

The ego does not like Joy. Several people dislike their few glimpses of Joy. They hold themselves accountable and feel guilty for having tasted even a few drops of Joy.

Joy is not a socially sanctioned kind of happiness. Joy is deep, disruptive, rebellious. It takes you far away from everything and into yourself. It fulfils you but does not please you. It takes you really higher but at a great risk.

No feeling of attainment accompanies Joy, so the ego does not quite like Joy. The ego keeps on resisting Joy till the Joyfulness finishes off the ego itself—because Joy and ego cannot coexist for long.

Joyfulness is such a difficult thing. It is ours if we want it, but it is a difficult thing to want. The very declaration to oneself, 'Yes, I want that expensive thing' will require you to break your vows. Remember that we are all committed to the pursuit of happiness. So a lot of promises will need to be broken, and the ego will have more reasons to feel ashamed and guilty.

When you say that you will have happiness through someone, it is always a two-way thing: you will have happiness through the other person, and the other person will have happiness through you. When you decide that you don't see any merit in this exchange, you withdraw. But when you withdraw, your business partner will taunt you. You are the one who sees and declares that you do not want happiness through them anymore, but they are still convinced that they can have happiness through you. So when you withdraw from this arrangement, they will feel entitled to blame you, sue you.

Joy can land you in a court of law. And lawyers are expensive.

What is Joy?

To smile through a heartbreak, that is Joy.

You cannot have Joy if you are too afraid of heartbreaks. Obviously, when you fall in love with Joy later on, there won't remain any ego to break, but that comes much later. Firstly, you have to pass through agony—alone. Now that you are doing this one thing alone, you have a taste of aloneness. That is Joy.

L: I am currently living by myself and I spend most of my time alone. I feel lonely very often. Is this loneliness caused by the conditioning of my mind? When I feel lonely, I try to reach out to the divine, or at least try to feel like I am in His lap and that I don't need anybody else. But when I reach out, I don't feel any comfort. How can I endure this feeling of loneliness?

AP: You will have to just stay put. Theoretically, you have put your finger at the right point. You know what is going on, but this knowledge may prove insignificant. You will need to muster courage. You would now sense why it is so difficult to return to the centre: the farther you have receded, the more you have to give up in your return journey.

I read this piece of news recently about a case of burglary. There were two thieves who had somehow broken into a shop. One of them had managed to take a lot of stuff. The other one was probably a novice, so he had managed to gather much less. And then they both hear the siren of the police arriving. Now, the one who had pinched a little managed to throw the little that he had and run away; on the other hand, the one who had stolen much tried to somehow preserve what he had obtained and as a result could not escape quickly enough. He was caught.

The more you have gathered, the more difficult freedom becomes for you. That is just karmaphala (result of past action). Live through it.

L: Is it important to spend time mostly alone during the spiritual process?

AP: No. This is just a purification phase, merely transient. Once you get established in an inner aloneness, there is no danger in coming out, socializing and mingling. This is like a sadhana technique. Even classically, there has been this technique called ekantvāsa (living in solitude). It hurts, but you just have to live through it. Listen to songs, cultivate new hobbies, do a few things that you anyway cannot do in a crowd—learn to sing, paint or acquire a new area of knowledge. But don't buckle down. Don't feel so lonely or depressed or defeated that you start running towards some party or celebrations.

I have spoken a lot of times about how aloneness and loneliness are distinct, but you must also see that the dawn of aloneness is preceded by the darkness of loneliness, and for a while they co-exist. Does morning come to you in a flash? There is a period of transience that you have to live through. If you succumbed to that period, then the morning is not for you. And of course, as they say, it is darkest before dawn.

As long as you are living a socially adjusted and internally compromised life, as long as you are living resigned to your limitations, even your agony is limited. There won't be depth even in your sadness. You will cry for a while, and the moment somebody shows you a plum cake you are all right. Isn't that how we treat sadness? 'Oh, she is very sad today. All right, have this cake!' In fact, sometimes you are sad just because you want to have the cake.

So, even our sadness is shallow. But when you want to break away from this duality of happiness and sadness and all the filth that we somehow name as life, your agony is sharpened even deeper: it cuts through you spiritually. That is a great thing, because it actually cuts through the ego. But spiritually, even though it might be a great thing, it still hurts and hurts badly. You will have to live with that hurt. Don't succumb.

L: So, should we actually be thankful to the people who are causing the agony?

AP: If the agony leads to realization.

L: What is the state of Joy? Is it peace?

AP: It is being carefree. Happiness is a burden, is it not? Have you tried being happy for ten hours? See how you would feel. In fact, try smiling for an hour. You will need a face massage! It is one of the most irritating things to smile for the camera, is it not? That itself shows that the camera is not your nature.

L: But there are those who want to live like that.

AP: That is because we are living in sadness. So a temporary relief from sadness appears welcome. It is only in the backdrop of sadness that happiness appears attractive; otherwise both sadness and happiness are burdens.

You could say there is a scale of being burdened, one end of which you call as sadness and the other end you call as happiness. Even though the names of these two extremes are different, the name of the scale is just one—burden.

Joy is to be unburdened, carefree. Therefore, Joy is actually not a state.

L: What exactly is the sadness that is associated with the pursuit of happiness? What is the burden of the people who pursue happiness?

AP: Such people are not lying; it is just that their method succeeds only for a while. When the normal state of consciousness is such a burden, you might want to drink alcohol to get rid of that state. However, you cannot remain drunk forever. Sooner or later, you have to return to the normal state.

L: Is Joy the same for everyone?

AP: No, it depends on what you take yourself to be. If you take yourself to be a responsible person, the meaning of Joy or aloneness is to go beyond responsibility. If you think you are a clever or wise person, the meaning of aloneness is to go beyond cleverness. If you live in suspicion, Joy is freedom from suspicion.

Actually, Joy has no meaning. But if you want to give it a meaning, it can only be a negation of what you otherwise live as. Do not look for an independent meaning of Joy because no meanings are independent. A thing means something only in the context of its dual opposite. Joy is not a dualistic state. It does not quite have a meaning.

L: We still add meaning to it.

AP: Yes. And the meaning itself is a burden, is it not?

> " ONCE YOU TELL YOURSELF THAT YOU ARE SOLD OUT OR
> YOU ARE BEHOLDEN TO SOMETHING, YOU WITHDRAW
> FROM YOURSELF THE RIGHT TO QUESTION THAT THING.
> SUSPICION WOULD BE TREACHERY, SO YOU KEEP ALL
> SUSPICION AT BAY AND JUST KEEP FOLLOWING THE CYCLE OF
> HAPPINESS AND SADNESS. "

(Goa, 2019)

8

Live through Pain, Beautifully

> " PLAY THROUGH PAIN. PLAY IN PAIN. JUST KEEP PLAYING!
> PAIN IS LIFE. "

Listener (L): I have undergone two major surgeries and accidents in my life. I understand that I am identified with the body and that is the reason for my suffering. I have read many books and scriptures, and listened to the masters who say that 'I am not the body', but I do not know how to come out of this pattern.

Acharya Prashant (AP): You are bearing physical pain. Keep bearing it. You cannot avoid it. Stop resisting the pain. Bear it gracefully. Live beautifully in pain and then you will not suffer. When you shout about, throw your hands about, stamp your feet, complain like a petulant child, that is when suffering happens.

You were born a human being. You have come to a certain age. You have had accidents and surgeries, and now you have pain. What else do you expect? You were not born a human being to live painlessly. To be born is to be born in pain. Do you know how much pain your mother went through when you were born? What do you mean by complaining against pain?

Bodhidharma was asked, 'What is the greatest fortune?'

He said, 'The greatest fortune is not to be born at all.'

The greatest fortune is not to take birth at all because if you are born, pain is inevitable. Pain is a necessary accompaniment of living a human life.

Do not grudge, do not whimper, do not crib. Your very expectation is misplaced. You *will* have pain. Go to the great athletes and they will tell you how they play through pain. One tennis player is retiring, he has won multiple grand slams, and he says, 'Now one thing is certain: I won't wake up every morning in terrible pain!'

Who told you that you were born to rejoice and celebrate and have a gala time? Maybe the advertisers told you that. The Buddhas have never told you that you were born to be felicitated, decorated or rewarded. That is why in India it has been said since long that when you are punished, you are cursed to take birth. You know how most of the myths go? There was this great angel and she made a mistake, so she was cursed to take birth. And you have dozens of stories like this—'the Great Spirit was cursed to take birth because it made a mistake.'

That is what human birth is all about. You are here to bear. You are not here to have a party. Even if you have a party, you will … ?

L: Suffer.

AP: You will have a lot of pain. No, I didn't say suffer. I will come to that.

The very concept that life can be painless is false. Pain is due and legitimate. You will have pain. Now, live through it in a positive manner.

Now, what is suffering? Suffering comes only when you start espousing the flawed concept that life must be pain-free. When you start feeding that concept, when you start nourishing and identifying with the concept that life must be painless, you suffer— because when pain comes, you are shocked. You say, 'Life should have been painless. From where has this pain arrived? No, no, you go away. It is unjust! I was born to dance and now something unfair is happening. See, pain has arrived!' Now you will suffer.

Suffering is nonsensical. It is an ignorant resistance to pain. Welcome pain! You have no option, so better welcome it. Just live through it, play through it, as champions do.

Go and ask Roger Federer; he will say, 'I play through pain.' Ashish Nehra (ex-cricketer) retired, and he said, 'It isn't as if there was pain in my body. Sometimes I was searching for my body amidst all the pain. Pain is everywhere—where is the body?' He used to have a surgery every two days. You get the idea, right? He had so many surgeries and he kept playing till he was forty.

Play through pain. Play in pain. Just keep playing! Pain is life.

There is such great delight in playing through pain. If you don't have pain, then playing isn't as beautiful. If you can smile through tears and in tears—oh, what a beautiful smile it is! Only then is the smile really beautiful.

The lyricist might not even know what he has written, and he has written maybe for an entirely different context, but his lines make a lot of sense: 'Jab dard nahi tha seene mein, kya khaak maza tha jeene mein?' (When there was no pain in the heart, what was the joy in living?)

If you can embrace pain, then pain is your beloved. In our case, it is the other way round—our beloved is the pain. If you don't turn pain into your beloved, your punishment will be that your beloved will be the pain. It doesn't matter whether it is the beloved or the pain—do not resist. That is the way life is meant is to be.

You were not born a deity or an angel. You were born a human being. Kindly lower your expectations. Be a little grounded. And if you cannot be grounded, watch a moth rushing towards its incineration in a flame. It is designed to go through that pain, isn't it?

Ever seen a flame where insects jump into from all directions? That is how they are designed. And you are designed a human being.

Buddha said the first of the four noble truths is that life is suffering. Life is suffering because not only are you designed to have pain, but you are also designed to resist pain. Now, that is doubly harmful. You are designed to both have pain and resist pain, and that is called suffering.

Have pain and have a lot of depth in your being, so much depth that it can take in all the pain. Keep soaking in pain. If you can do that, you will find that something strange is happening: now you can rejoice because you are not really human. Had you been human, you would have resisted pain. When you do not resist pain, you are no more human, and if you are not human, you will not suffer as humans do. Instead, you are blessed with delight, and delight is not available to the so-called normal human. Why? Because they are rushing after delight. And how do they run after delight? By trying to avoid or resist pain.

If you resist pain, all you get is suffering. If you embrace pain, there is delight.

How is the day?

'Sir, really painful!'

That is the way it should be.

> " HAVE PAIN AND HAVE A LOT OF DEPTH IN YOUR BEING, SO
> MUCH DEPTH THAT IT CAN TAKE IN ALL THE PAIN. KEEP
> SOAKING IN PAIN. WHEN YOU DO NOT RESIST PAIN, YOU ARE
> NO MORE HUMAN, AND IF YOU ARE NOT HUMAN, THEN YOU
> WILL NOT SUFFER AS HUMANS DO. "

(Advait BodhSthal, 2019)

9

Joy that Remains Untouched by Defeat

> **HOW IS IT POSSIBLE THAT THERE IS SOMETHING WHICH IS THERE IN VICTORY AND ALSO IN THE OPPOSITE OF VICTORY, IN DEFEAT? THE ANSWER IS OBVIOUS: IT HAS TO BE SOMETHING WHICH HAS NOTHING TO DO WITH DEFEAT OR VICTORY.**

Defeat, my defeat, my solitude and my aloofness;
You are dearer to me than a thousand triumphs,
And sweeter to my heart than all world-glory.

~Khalil Gibran

Listener: How can defeat be sweet? How can there be joy in being shunned and scorned?

Acharya Prashant: There is no particular glory or joy in defeat. In fact, the moment one looks for glory or joy in particular events or happenings, joy has been constrained, localized, and hence lost.

The poet here is talking of defeat because man has taken defeat as abhorrent. Victory is likeable, and defeat is to be avoided and shunned. Victory is likeable because man associates joy with victory and the loss of joy with defeat. Whenever joy is thus made conditional, it is certain that there will be no joy in defeat nor in victory. And whenever there is Joy, it remains equally in victory and in defeat.

The problem that our mind faces with statements like the one I just made is that these statements do not subscribe to any particular definition of Joy. To really understand these statements, one will have to bow down to Joy rather than try to be a master of Joy.

What is meant by being a master of Joy? You are a master of something if you can find a way to get that thing. If you can define something and also know how to get that thing, you are a master of that thing.

Godliness and Joy are to be surrendered to, not fought with. Your victories will not bring you Joy. If your victories bring you joy, then it is a very shallow and tiny joy. You have earned it, you have won it; it is the result of your efforts. It cannot be bigger than you.

Man lives in duality. Man finds it comfortable to think that there are things and there are opposites of things. Such thinking enables all definitions, because to define anything is to limit it. To limit something is to create two: a thing and its opposite. That is what definitions do. To 'de-fine' is to make something finite. Obviously, the Infinite escapes all definitions, and that is where we start struggling; that is where we start feeling strangulated.

We start asking, how is it possible that there is something which is there in victory and also in the opposite of victory, in defeat? The answer is obvious: it has to be something which has nothing to do with defeat or victory. That something has to be simply unconditional, irrespective of everything. It is unconditional irrespective of your efforts, unconditional with respect to the result of the effort, and also unconditional irrespective of your response to the result. One has to live that deeply.

One tried—yes, there is something deeper than that. One lost—there is something deeper than that. One felt bad—still, there is something deeper than that; something deeper than the depths of thought, something deeper than the depths to which human perception can go, and hence something deeper than man's very existence, reach and penetration.

So, if the poet is singing of defeat, he is not really singing of defeat in particular. He is singing of the Joy that remains untouched by defeat. Hence, he is celebrating defeat. He is saying, 'Ah! To most people defeat is such a nightmare. But look at me: I have that which defeats even defeats! I have defeated defeat, and hence now I can celebrate defeat.'

This does not mean that now defeat is to be worshipped exactly as victory was worshipped previously. Victory appeared favourable; defeat appeared unfavourable. The poet is celebrating the fact that that which appeared unfavourable is no more unfavourable.

> " THE POET IS SINGING OF THE JOY THAT REMAINS UNTOUCHED BY DEFEAT. HENCE, HE IS CELEBRATING DEFEAT. HE IS SAYING, 'AH! TO MOST PEOPLE DEFEAT IS SUCH A NIGHTMARE. BUT LOOK AT ME: I HAVE THAT WHICH DEFEATS EVEN DEFEATS! I HAVE DEFEATED DEFEAT, AND HENCE NOW I CAN CELEBRATE DEFEAT.' "

(Uttarakhand, 2017)

10

Uneasy and Unhappy at Workplace?

> ❝ IT IS NOT THAT YOU HAVE COME TO DISLIKE THE TOTAL STRUCTURE IN WHICH YOU ARE TRAPPED. IT IS JUST THAT YOU DO NOT LIKE THE OTHER END OF DUALITY. YOU WANT TO KEEP YOUR PRIVILEGES; YOU WANT TO KEEP YOUR BENEFITS. ❞

Listener: Sir, I am a project manager in an IT firm. I have been a part of this industry for the last two to three years. However, I am not happy with the current project, and this is a continuous pattern with me. I often feel disempowered because of the lack of opportunities and start procrastinating. I am never at peace with myself. What should I do?

Acharya Prashant: So, you want to be a project manager with a reputed IT firm that gives you what you want. You have mentioned things that you don't like about your job, but you haven't mentioned about your salary cheque. Do you dislike that as well? You don't dislike that, do you? You want to keep that. And you also want other stuff tailored to your desires. It is not the whole package that you want to reject. It is not as if the place appears strange to you; you just want it to be more according to your desires.

The person is rejecting chicken butter masala not because he has compassion towards the bird but because the dish is not to his liking today. It is a little bland, and he wanted it to be spicier. But because he is rejecting chicken butter masala, he thinks that this is some kind of vairāgya, some kind of dispassion.

It is not that you have come to dislike the total structure in which you are trapped. It is just that you do not like the other end of duality. You want to keep your privileges; you want to keep your benefits. You would be carrying your visiting card, wouldn't you? It is an IT firm, you are a project manager—that is quite respectable, isn't it? You would be displaying your card with pride. Don't you see all that you are deriving from that job?

But you do not want to pay the price. You want to have food, and when the bill is served you complain about the heartlessness of the universe: 'See? They can't even feed a hungry man for free!' I am sure that if you are awarded a different project and a couple of things as per your desire, you wouldn't be asking these questions. In fact, chances are that if you are given a sufficiently high raise on the condition that you would be working till ten in the night on many days of the week, you wouldn't be found listening to me at this time. You are a project manager, and the vice-president comes and says you will have a twenty-five per cent hike if you can stay in the office on all days when that fellow Acharya speaks—would you be listening to me then?

You are not fed up of where you are. You are not fed up of who you are. You just want a higher price even as you are selling yourself. You don't want freedom. You are not saying you are not for sale. You are just saying, 'Give me a higher price!' What kind of a demand is that? Why don't you quit this job? Simple. Just quit. Take a break and work with me as a volunteer for a while.

Now do you see how greed clutches you? You just experienced a chill down your spine, didn't you? Admit that. It is such a favourite pass time to crib about the job, the boss, the project and the working conditions. I say, quit. But you won't quit because you are deriving a lot from that place.

In fact, it is *you* who is exploiting that place. You are not only deriving pleasure, money and security from there but you are also deriving the pleasure of cursing and abusing them. You are saying, 'I will take salary from you'—that is one pleasure—'and I will then magnify my pleasure by cursing you!' Why? Reject the damn cheque! Why do you stay there and receive that cheque?

I am not trying to hurt you. Please get the point. Nobody can enslave you or belittle you or trouble you without your consent. You have agreed to being troubled. And you accept trouble because trouble pays you richly. Why would you accept being troubled and then complain about it?

You are saying you are disempowered because of the lack of opportunities. Why must others provide you opportunities? Create opportunities for yourself. Your very being itself is an opportunity, don't waste it. Or would you keep complaining about lack of opportunities? Would you keep petitioning? Would you keep saying that the others are just not sensitive enough and magnanimous enough to give you opportunities?

Keep complaining—the universe is neutral to both commendations and complaints. It does not bother. You have been given a life and you have been given rights to run your life as per your wish. Yes, you have no rights to so-called situations, but you have all the rights over your responses to the situations—which means, you fundamentally have a lot of power. Either exercise that power or keep complaining. You decide. It is your life.

The scriptures put it so gracefully:

51

'The Atma becomes available to the one who expresses it.'

Now, that is strange and mysterious. The Atma becomes available to the one who *decides* to express it. Live by the Atma, and the Atma comes running to you. Oh, she can't literally come to you, it is a metaphor. She is yours only when you express her; otherwise, she is nowhere.

You can't experience Shiva except in the dance of Shakti. The expression is everything. Express it and you have it. And if you don't express it, it is nowhere. And that is where we lose the plot: we keep looking for the Truth within, without, or somewhere, but we don't *live* by the Truth.

Looking for the Truth is futile. Truth can be had only by living by the Truth, expressing the Truth. Truth must be there in the movement of your hand, even in your feeble gestures, in your twitches, in your glances. Truth expressed is Truth achieved. Otherwise, there is nothing called achievement of the Truth.

But look at us: we want to achieve the Truth and hide it like a dirty secret. We don't want to express it because we are afraid. 'If I express the Truth, what will fufi (aunt) say?' So, attain it and hide it—like teenagers hide pornography.

You have to shout it out loud. You have to announce it from the rooftop. You have to stand at the crossing and sing it, and only then do you get it. It is not as if you get it and then sing it; you sing it and *then* you get it. The expression is everything.

Live by the Truth and you will get more courage. The Truth keeps getting vast; the Truth keeps on expanding. It is an expanding infinity. I know that may sound like a contradiction, but accept it. Step into it and you will be emboldened to take an even deeper step. Keep watching from the fringes and you will just keep watching. Of course, then you can console yourself that you are a sākṣi (witness). If you don't dare to step into the waters, you say you are a witness.

You are young. You have talked of a few years of experience in some company. Don't be caught in these petty stories. Even if you must have troubles, have bigger troubles. Move towards bigger challenges, have bigger problems. What kind of problems are these? 'My manager is not appraising me rightly. I got an eight per cent hike, but I deserved a twelve per cent one! And they aren't putting me on the best project!'

You are a human. Do you know what it means to be a human? You are not just a professional inside the shirt and the trouser and the necktie and the identity card hanging from your neck. You are a human being. Don't forget that.

These professional organizations dehumanize you. You are not a human being there anymore, you become a professional; all you are is the profession. At 9 a.m., you are swiping, entering, sitting—there are metrics for everything—and you do not know why you are working, you do not know for whom you are working. You have no relation, no connection with the Total. All you know is your assignment, your paycheque and your career growth. Many a time, you don't even know the name of your client! All you know is that 'If I do this task, I will be paid some money, and after a while I will be paid more money. I will be rising up the career ladder!'

What is all this? Are you really a human?

> " LOOKING FOR THE TRUTH IS FUTILE. TRUTH CAN BE HAD
> ONLY BY LIVING BY THE TRUTH, EXPRESSING THE TRUTH.
> TRUTH MUST BE THERE IN THE MOVEMENT OF YOUR HAND,
> EVEN IN YOUR FEEBLE GESTURES, IN YOUR TWITCHES, IN YOUR
> GLANCES. TRUTH EXPRESSED IS TRUTH ACHIEVED. "

(Advait BodhSthal, 2017)

53

11

It Is Beautiful to Earn Pain

> **"** To the common man pain is incidental, uninvited.
> It comes as a surprise: 'Oh, the pain has come.
> From where? I didn't ask for it.' To the spiritual
> practitioner, pain is almost a target, pain is a value.
> He says, 'I want it. Bring it on!' **"**

People make all sorts of efforts to find peace and pleasure, but no one tries to earn pain. Says Nanak, listen, mind: whatever pleases God comes to pass.

~Guru Tegh Bahadur Ji, Guru Granth Sahib, Salok Mahalla 9

Listener: What is meant by earning pain?

Acharya Prashant: The constitution of the body is such that it is pleasure-seeking, and that is the guiding principle behind all bodily actions. Bodily actions include the impulses of the brain. So, that which you call 'natural' in a loose language is nothing but pleasure-seeking behaviour. When you say that something is natural, effectively what you are saying is that it is pleasure-seeking behaviour.

So, that is how your system is—it wants to have pleasure. What is the definition of pleasure? That which helps Prakriti (physical nature) further its agenda. Food pleases you because it gives energy to the body to continue; that is what Prakriti wants. Flattery pleases you because it provides the subtle body with the energy to continue. It will continue, it will stay motivated, it will further its goals.

So, what is pleasure, really? That which agrees with the agenda of your physical constitution is called pleasure. In getting that pleasure you get pain as well, and that pain makes pleasure even more necessary. So, you earn two units of pleasure, and along with two units of pleasure you also get two units of pain. What is the inference that your system draws from this? Two units of pleasure is not sufficient, because two units of pleasure came along with two units of pain and got nullified; the net was zero. So, now your system wants three units of pleasure. But very soon the system discovers that three units of pleasure have come along with three units of pain, so now you want four units of pleasure.

That is the cycle of human life—chasing pleasure, getting pain, and pain spurs you on to chase pleasure even more. This is not the pain that you have earned; this is the pain that has come as a bonus. What did you want? Pleasure—but the pain tagged along.

Had you had a choice, you would have said, 'I want only pleasure. Let's un-tag the pain. I don't want the pain that comes with pleasure. Can't we just separate the two? No, I don't want the combo; no, I don't want the one plus one offer. I only want the one that I want—pleasure.' So, we get pain without earning it or wanting it or choosing it. We get it as a compulsory attachment, a compulsory accompaniment of pleasure.

Guru Sahib is talking of something different here. He is talking of earning pain. He is saying, 'You already have had enough pain. That pain came to you as a compulsion, as helplessness. You didn't want it, but you were subjected to it. Now, can you *willingly* go for pain?' What does he mean? He means something quite radical.

Your system is designed to go only for pleasure. If you are being told to go deliberately for pain, you are actually being told to go against your system. In a practical way, he is teaching you a method of detachment, a way to get disidentified with the body.

Deliberately choosing pain has been a method in India and elsewhere since long. Spiritual practitioners, those who have really wanted to know and live life fully, have invited pain. Knowing fully well that the road they are taking would hurt them, they have still gone down those roads.

I repeat, to the common man pain is incidental, uninvited. It comes as a surprise: 'Oh, the pain has come. From where? I didn't ask for it.' To the spiritual practitioner, pain is almost a target, pain is a value. He says, 'I want it. Bring it on!' Not that there is some great virtue in pain. It is just that when you are choosing pain, you are denying the bodily compulsion of seeking pleasure; you are getting disidentified. And once you are disidentified, there is no need to seek pain either.

Have you noticed that a lot of progress, even in the material sense, happens only by inviting pain? Even in the loose sense, that which we call discipline is nothing but an invitation to pain. Is there discipline without pain? You have to get up at some point in the morning—doesn't that involve pain? Pleasure is to keep sleeping even after the alarm has rung. Is that not pleasurable?

All discipline is nothing but pain. It is a very well-directed pain, it is a very discrete pain, but nevertheless, all discipline involves pain. And progress, be it in the material or the spiritual realms, moves on discipline. So, all progress is nothing but the art of inflicting pain upon yourself—wisely, not randomly. You will get no progress by just slashing your wrist or holding a cigarette to your arm. Random or mindless pain will not help you. Although random and mindless pain will not help you, there can be no discipline without pain, and there can be no progress without discipline.

Pleasure is a pattern. In fact, all patterns become patterns of pleasure. Discipline is the determination to go beyond patterns. So, pleasure has to be transcended, which means your body, your prakriti (nature), your physical tendencies have to be transcended. That is what Guru Sahib is pointing at.

Have discipline. And what does having discipline involve? Be a disciple, be a shishya (disciple). Be a Sikh. Who is a Sikh? The one who can wisely, discreetly, deliberately choose pain. You cannot be a student if you cannot bear pain. You cannot be a student if you say, 'You know, I want to be handled in cotton and wool. I want to learn a lot from the teacher, but I don't want pain from the teacher.' Then you cannot be a Sikh, you cannot be a shishya; you cannot be a disciple because you do not have discipline.

" THERE IS NO GREAT VIRTUE IN PAIN. IT IS JUST THAT WHEN
YOU ARE CHOOSING PAIN, YOU ARE DENYING THE BODILY
COMPULSION OF SEEKING PLEASURE; YOU ARE GETTING
DISIDENTIFIED. AND ONCE YOU ARE DISIDENTIFIED, THERE IS
NO NEED TO SEEK PAIN EITHER. "

(Advait BodhSthal, 2019)

57

12

Ananda Is Contentment in Which Happiness Is No Longer Needed

> *JOY IS NOT HAPPINESS. JOY IS JUST AN INNER FULLNESS IN WHICH YOU DO NOT NEED HAPPINESS AND DO NOT INVITE SADNESS.*

Listener (L): Is being happy a choice?

Acharya Prashant (AP): You see, both these words, 'choice' and 'happiness', belong to the same domain. Whenever the mind says that it wants to make a choice, something is always chosen—selecting something and rejecting something, opting for something and discarding something. Whenever the mind says that it wants to make a choice, obviously the choice is intended to maximize happiness directly or indirectly.

All choices are aimed towards happiness. So, if you are asking whether it is a choice to be happy, the answer really is that all choices are made so that one may be happy. Even if you choose to be unhappy, in some way your happiness lies in being unhappy.

Every single choice that the mind makes is in the direction of happiness—the perceived direction of happiness. 'This is what I think would make me happy, so I choose this. This is what I think would make me unhappy, so I reject it.' So choice and happiness are in the same domain. Do you see how closely they are together?

You choose happiness. All right, that is what the intention is—to choose happiness. But what is it that happens? In spite of choosing happiness, deciding to be happy, trying to be happy, putting in efforts to be happy, does one remain happy? We choose happiness and we do not necessarily get happiness. Even if we do get happiness, does that happiness last? Is that your experience? Does the happiness become permanent? Is that what you have seen in life? In your life, or in the world around you, have you seen that? No.

So, our choices are frustrated. In spite of choosing one thing, we end up getting something else. Would it not be interesting to investigate why that happens? Should we go into that? In spite of wanting happiness, why do we not get happiness? Let me give you an example. It is a very common one but always useful because it tells us something important.

Two students are awaiting their examination results. One of the students is quite sure that she will pass; the other is uncertain and, therefore, tense. The next morning the results are going to be declared. One sleeps well and soundly on the eve of the results; the other one is anxious, worrying and thoughtful, not able to sleep, turning sides. The next morning both of them go to see their result—the relaxed one, who anyway knew that she would pass, and the tense one, who is having a harrowing time wondering what the result might be. Both of them go, and both of them discover that they have passed. Which of these two is going to become madly happy? Which of these two will go crazy with happiness? One was sure she would pass, the other was highly uncertain; in fact, she was probably thinking that she won't. Now, both indeed do pass the examination. Which of them experiences greater happiness?

L: The one who was tense.

AP: Right. We are investigating the nature of happiness here. For the same happening, one mind experiences more happiness than the other, right? Which mind experiences more happiness? The mind that was tense, which means unhappy.

Hence, to be happy you first of all need to be anxious. Do you see this? The deeper your unhappiness, the deeper your stress, the easier it is for you to move into happiness. Happiness is experienced only in the background of tension, sadness, misery, worries.

There are two persons, one very hungry and the other satisfied having eaten in the morning. Both of them are given a dish in the evening. Which of these two is going to feel happier eating the dish? Obviously, the hungry one.

Do you see how necessary it is to be unhappy before you can be happy? Which of these two wanted happiness more desperately, the one who was satisfied with her meals or the one who had had no meals for several hours? Which of these two really wanted to eat?

L: The one who was hungry.

AP: Do you see who wants happiness? The one who does not have happiness, the one who is sad.

Desire for happiness is a clear proof of unhappiness. And if you are unhappy, you will surely get happiness. The deeper your sadness, the more likely it is that you will soon be very happy. Do you see this? So, if you want to be happy, the trick is simple: become deeply sad. And soon you will find that you are experiencing heavenly happiness.

Happiness can be experienced only in the background of its dualistic opposite. This is the basic law of duality. All that the mind experiences is experienced only against its opposite. If you do not experience the opposite of something, then you cannot experience that thing either. This whole thing about happiness arises from unhappiness. The unhappier you are, the more desperately you will want to chase happiness.

Now, what do we do? I am asking you because it is a matter of choice. If you have two options—one, chase happiness, second, drop the question of happiness, drop the very topic of happiness—which one would you prefer? Remember, chasing happiness implies that you are unhappy. So, that is one option: chase happiness, which would mean that you will have to be unhappy at that point. The second is, the very question of happiness does not arise. What would that mean? If the desire to eat does not arise, what does that mean?

L: You are satisfied.

AP: Right, you are satisfied. Which of these two would you prefer? You can have a long discussion on how to get happiness—would you want that, or would you want to rather drop the question of happiness? Dropping the question of happiness means that you now do not need happiness; you are already full. And when you are full, that state is beyond happiness. It is contentment.

The contentment in which happiness is no longer needed is called Ananda or Joy. Joy is not happiness. Joy is just an inner fullness in which you do not need happiness and do not invite sadness.

Instead of asking for happiness, it is probably more important to investigate what all we do to make ourselves sad, to make ourselves feel as if happiness is lacking and we need to get it. Chasing happiness is not very important; what is important is to drop sadness. We clutch sadness and the result of that is happiness. You cannot be too sad for too long. You will either die or you will become very happy. Only two things can happen after deep sadness.

Let's say my shoes are tight. I am wearing shoes that are one size smaller than my feet, and I walk up to the railway station, walk down, and again walk up, and then walk down, and I do that all day. In the evening I come back and I remove the shoes. How do I feel? I feel heavenly pleasure! Finally relieved!

Instead of chasing pleasure, see how agony can be dropped. That is far better.

You see, we talk of happiness, but mankind is a lover of sadness. In a hundred ways we stick to sadness even though we talk of happiness as if we really want to be happy. Ask anyone to choose between happiness and sadness, and what would they say? Happiness. But then you look at the lives of people around you. What do you see them doing? Are their actions for happiness or sadness? The intention is happiness, but the action is towards sadness. And that is because we are not watchful of our thoughts and actions. We do not see how we are contributing to our sadness. And once we are sad, we say we want happiness.

Yes, let's rather not be sad. Let us use this opportunity to reflect on what we do to retain our sadness. What is sadness? Sadness is a feeling that something is missing. What all do we do to reinforce the feeling that something is missing from life, that something is wrong with life? If we can honestly go into that, that would be something far deeper and longer-lasting than happiness.

L: Why do we hold on to that sadness?

AP: We are born as limited beings. We just said that sadness is the feeling that something is missing from life. We are born as a limited body, and the mind has limited thoughts. Whenever the mind experiences limitations, it obviously feels that what is outside those limits is missing.

You see, I am this body. I will perceive anything outside of this body as missing. So, there is a beautiful jacket there, and here is the body. The body feels it is justified in saying that it is missing the jacket because it is outside the limits of the body. Similarly, the mind thinks and all thought is limited. Immediately it feels that it is missing something.

It is our nature not to stop before perfection. It is our nature not to settle for anything less than perfection. And given our physical and mental limitations, it is obvious that perfection is not available to this limited organism. So, you feel something is missing. You might be tall, but there are people who are taller. You might be beautiful, but there are people who are apparently more beautiful. You may have a sharp intellect, but there are people who have sharper intellects. You might be rich, but there are people who are richer. Your car may be big, but there are people who have jets.

So, wherever you are, there is always a limit, and beyond that limit is something that you do not have, so you feel it is missing. The element that 'I am missing something' is a direct product of being born. The moment you are born, it is guaranteed that you feel you are limited and hence deprived of something, missing something.

L: How can we stop feeling like we are always missing something or deprived of something?

AP: It is the nature of the mind to miss. It is not your nature. Human beings have a very special ability, and that ability is to be able to know the mind. If we were just the body, you would have been justified in saying that missing is our nature. If we were just the mind, we would again be justified in saying that missing is our nature.

But we have a great power, and that power is the ability to watch the functioning of the mind, to know how the whole thing moves. The moment you see how the whole thing moves, you are not that thing. So, now that thing may have a limitation, but you don't have a limitation because you are not that thing.

To be able to know what is really going on in your mind and life is to be able to go beyond that happening.

We can know; we can realize what is going on; we can see that the poor old mind is playing its old game. The moment you see that, you are no longer subjected to the limitations of the mind; then you say, 'Ah! It is the mind's limitations, not mine. The body is tired, not me. The body is getting old, not me. The mind is feeling anxious or passive or jealous or afraid, not me.' So, who had the limitations? The body had the limitations. Who had the limitations? The mind had the limitations. You have gone beyond the limitations.

The body and the mind will always have limitations. You may enhance your personal self as much as you want to, but remember that it would still be limited. The richest man on Earth would still find that his wealth can be summed up in one particular number, and that number is limited, it is not infinite. There can be a number greater than that number.

Whatever you have in this world will always give you only limitations and therefore sadness, because we have defined sadness as the feeling that there is something missing in life, that life is limited. The more you attach and associate yourself with stuff in the world, the more you are inviting sadness.

For example, you say that if you bring something to your house, you will get happiness. 'If this piece of furniture comes, I will be happy'—and indeed you are happy for a while. But very soon you discover that there is something better than that piece of furniture in the market, or worse still, in the neighbour's house. Now that same thing that was intended to give you happiness becomes a daily reminder of sadness. Don't you see that?

Look at how our relationships are. We often marry the best person possible. The marriage was intended to make us happy, but that same relationship often becomes the greatest source of misery for both the partners.

That which you choose as an agent of happiness turns out to be the harbinger of sadness because it is limited. Whatsoever is limited, whatsoever is there in the world—and the world only has limited things. Whatsoever is limited will only give you sadness. Why? Because you expected happiness from it, you expected perfection from it—that it cannot give.

You see what happens with a friend or with a lover when the relationship is nascent, young? Don't we expect and also find perfection in the heydays of a love affair? Does the partner not look almost like Mr. Right or Miss Perfection? And it seems that this one will deliver the goods; this one is the right one; this one has all that it would take keep me happy. You have loaded that man or woman with unrealistic expectations. He or she belongs to the world, and everything in the world is limited, so that man or woman is also going to be limited. Your expectations will not be fulfilled, and then your happiness will immediately turn into sadness.

Whatever you do for the sake of happiness ultimately makes you sad. That is how we keep inviting sadness. Hence, to stop sadness, stop wanting happiness. Whatever you think will make you happy will just end up making you sad.

Drop this quest for happiness. You already have something more important and more precious than happiness. Each one of us here is so rich that she does not need petty things like pleasure and happiness.

It is in fact a disgrace, an insult if we asked for happiness. It would be like a billionaire asking for a hundred rupees. You are already a multibillionaire. Now, why do you want some petty stuff? Why are you wasting yourself, begging for small-ticket items like happiness? You are so big. You must ask for something equally big. Why are you asking for little things? Not only are you asking for little things, when you do not get those things, you also behave as if you have lost something great. Imagine a billionaire crying because he has lost ten rupees.

That is what the condition of humankind is. The fellow is yelping loudly, tears and wails, and you ask him, 'What has happened?'

'I lost ten rupees!'

'How much do you have?'

'Two thousand billion!'

And he feels he has lost a fortune. That is our condition. So many multibillionaires sitting here and asking, 'Sir, how do we earn ten rupees?' You really want that? None of us wants that!

We all are one.

> **" DROP THIS QUEST FOR HAPPINESS. YOU ALREADY HAVE SOMETHING MORE IMPORTANT AND MORE PRECIOUS THAN HAPPINESS. EACH ONE OF US HERE IS SO RICH THAT SHE DOES NOT NEED PETTY THINGS LIKE PLEASURE AND HAPPINESS. "**

(France, 2016)

Part II

— ◆ —

Peace Is the Desire Behind All Desires

13

Exactly Who Is Happy Here?

> IF ONE IS REALLY HAPPY, IT IS AN INTERNAL CONFIRMATION.
> YOU DON'T HAVE TO SEEK VALIDITY FROM EVERYBODY. YOU
> DON'T HAVE TO GO AROUND TOM-TOMMING YOUR HAPPINESS.

Listener: Is renunciation of worldly pleasures necessary for spiritual growth?

Acharya Prashant: But where are the pleasures? I do not see any pleasures! I do not see anybody being pleased. You are talking of renunciation of pleasures as if pleasures do exist. Where are the pleasures? Go to a weekend party and show me who is happy. And if people were indeed happy, why would they drink? They drink so that they can forget their miserable state. Who is being pleased in all this? Please, tell me.

But you know, we like to pamper ourselves. We flatter ourselves when we say, 'Oh, I am living a life of pleasures and spirituality will snatch away my pleasures, so should I consider spirituality or not?' What kind of bluster is this?

Nobody is happy here, please. Just scratch the surface and you will find. What do you think, those Facebook faces are real? Why do you think people have to display their teeth so much? If one is really happy, it is an internal confirmation. You don't have to seek validity from everybody. You don't have to go around tom-tomming your happiness.

So, please drop the illusion that people are indeed happy. This thing about being happy, truly happy, is called Joy. We don't have it, and that is why we run after flimsy pleasures.

Spirituality is not about dropping the real thing, please. It is about dropping false pleasures so that you can have real Joy. False pleasures are the same as suffering. So, spirituality is about dropping suffering so that you can have Joy.

All these things that we do to get pleased are just a confirmation of our internal state of wails and tears. Look at the faces of the people on any busy road, stand at a crossing and watch. People are rushing to their offices, it is 9 a.m.; just look at their faces. Are they really in pleasure? Where is pleasure?

Spirituality wants you to have true pleasure. To be spiritual is to go hunting madly, wildly for real pleasure. And to differentiate the real thing from the fake one, a very different name is given— Ananda. Not prasannatā (gladness), not khuśi (delight), not sukha (pleasure)—Ananda. That is real, and that is not dependent on an intoxicant; that is not dependent on when Amazon would put up its next discount fest; that is not dependent on how soon your neighbour loses his job so that you can be happy; that is not dependent on how quickly you can dupe your girlfriend into going to bed with you.

Unconditional pleasure. Unconditional, continuous, uncaused pleasure—that is Joy. Irrespective of the circumstances, there is a subtle thing within that refuses to be miserable—that is Joy.

Vedanta says, do not settle for anything less than Joy. You deserve that. Otherwise, you are just wasting your life running hither-thither, trying for this and that.

Be adamant. Don't surrender. Don't prostrate to temptations or threats. Say, 'I want something that time cannot take away. I want something that situations and conditions cannot take away. I want something that I can be utterly secure of. I want something that I can wholeheartedly trust. I don't want to live in the flow of time where everything just comes and goes and nothing is ever reliable. I don't want relationships that need to be fortified. I don't want money that I need to be anxious about. All these are all right—one has to have money, one will definitely have relationships—but I want something higher and deeper than that. Only then will I say that I have succeeded as an individual.'

So, Vedanta impels you, encourages you to go for real success. Real success is Joy. Doesn't matter what one is doing externally; as we said, internally there is something that is always jovial. Even in the greatest of miseries there sits someone within who has a joke to offer. That is Joy.

'You are coming to behead me? Even in this situation I find a PJ (poor joke) coming to my mind! What do I do? I know I will be gone the next moment in the physical sense, but still, before I go, can I share a little joke with you?' Joy!

> " Spirituality wants you to have true pleasure. To be spiritual is to go hunting madly, wildly for real pleasure. And to differentiate the real thing from the fake one, a very different name is given—Ananda. "

(IIT Bombay, 2021)

14

Are Earthly Pleasures a Hindrance to Spiritual Growth?

> **SPIRITUAL JOY DOES NOT COME AT THE COST OF EARTHLY JOY. ALL JOY IS EARTHLY BECAUSE ALL JOY IS TO THE ONE WHO IS THE PRODUCT OF THE EARTH. NO MAN, NO JOY.**

Listener (L): I want to have spiritual growth, but I also want to experience earthly freedom and experiences, like travelling to unfamiliar places etc. Are earthly pleasures a hindrance to spiritual growth?

Acharya Prashant (AP): There is no dissonance between spiritual Joy and earthly living. The one who is not spiritually developed may travel to all corners of the Earth but would still remain joyless. So, what is the point in travelling?

There is the wandering monk; look at his Joy. The fakir (monk) also travels from place to place, village to village, sometimes from country to country. Traditionally in India, sadhus (monks) would forbid themselves from staying too long at one place; they would keep travelling.

Buddha and Mahavira, the great ascetics, travelled all their lives. Even Guru Nanak made voyages, long-distance travels to the east, to the south and the west. This is one kind of travelling, in which you are already full of Joy and you are travelling to disseminate that Joy. You are travelling so that even others may have that Joy.

And then there is the travelling tourist, the average traveller. What does travel give him? Some consolation, some very feeble support to enable him to carry on with his otherwise wretched life. He saves money to travel once or twice a year, and not much good comes out of that travel because he is not internally complete.

Even the Earth discloses its real treasures only to the spiritually accomplished. The earthly living itself is heavenly for them. And that would also tell you what hell is: To the one who is not spiritually accomplished, to him the Earth itself is hell.

So, it is not as if there are two different worlds offering two different kinds of Joy. That is the mental model you are coming from. You are telling me, 'There is the earthly joy, which is an inferior kind of joy, but still quite alluring. Then there is a metaphysical, transcendental Joy, spiritual Joy. And the spiritual Joy is quite attractive, but it seems to come at the cost of earthly joy.' No, wrong! That's where you are mistaken.

Spiritual Joy does not come at the cost of earthly joy. In fact, there is nothing called 'spiritual Joy'. All Joy is earthly because all Joy is to the one who is the product of the Earth. No Man, no Joy. If you do not exist, who is there to be Joyful? And who are you? Someone who has arisen from the earth. Who are you? You are the soil, you are the water, you are the air, you are the sunlight. Without these, would there be any human beings?

So, the one who is Joyful is always an earthly one. Therefore, there is no distance or distinction between these two kinds of Joy. In fact, if you create two dimensions of Joys, then you do not know either of these dimensions. It is a very common misconception and we all need to get rid of it. We feel that we have to give up earthly pleasures to have spiritual Joy, and such stories have come to us from various sources. They continue to keep coming to us. No, not at all true!

Spirituality is wisdom. Spirituality is deep intelligence. Spirituality is to give up the inferior in favour of the superior.

That which you call 'earthly pleasure' definitely has something which is worth rejecting, worth dropping. Therefore, spirituality is to drop incomplete, costly and ephemeral pleasures in favour of an unending pleasure called Joy. You could even say that spirituality is the art of absolute hedonism.

The common man satisfies himself with bits and pieces—some crumbs here and there—of a little bit of happiness and a little bit of pleasure. The monk, the spiritual seeker says, 'Nothing doing. Not only do I want happiness, I want absolute happiness!' He is ambitious. He is very greedy. Because he is very greedy, he tells you to shun normal greed. Because he is absolutely greedy, he tells you, 'Do not be just a little bit greedy.' You think that he is against greed. He is not against greed; he is against everything that is incomplete. So he says, 'If you have to be greedy, you must not be incompletely greedy, but absolutely greedy.'

Spirituality is absolute greed. Spirituality says, 'I do not want anything small. I want only the Infinite, the Ultimate.' See what dimension of greed it is.

Similarly, happiness and pleasure. The common man says, 'Give me happiness, at least an hour a day, please.' What does the spiritual one say? 'I want the total, unending, undiminishing, eternal happiness.' And where does he want it? In some other world, some other planet, some other galaxy? Where exactly does the spiritual seeker want it?

L: On this Earth.

AP: When does he want it? After seven hundred years, after death, in the seventh or eighteenth life? When exactly does he want it?

L: Now.

AP: After fifty years, when he turns seventy-five and enters the last ashram of his life? Is that when he wants it?

L: No. Now.

AP: If Joy is absolute, would you want to postpone it? It would be so alluring that you won't be able to postpone it. You would want it right now.

That is spirituality—to have the highest happiness and have it right now, here. The Highest, right now, right here.

Now, do you want the earthly things? Are they still attractive? If the earthly things are attractive, then that should tell you that you have a faculty for attraction. If even a little attracts you, it means that you know how to get attracted. And if you know how to get attracted, then how would you feel in front of the Immense?

I repeat: If just the little attracts you so much, what would your condition be in front of the Immense? You would go bonkers.

That is how the spiritual mind wants to live—in absolute craziness.

> ❝ THAT WHICH YOU CALL 'EARTHLY PLEASURE' DEFINITELY HAS
> SOMETHING WHICH IS WORTH REJECTING, WORTH DROPPING.
> THEREFORE, SPIRITUALITY IS TO DROP INCOMPLETE, COSTLY
> AND EPHEMERAL PLEASURES IN FAVOUR OF AN UNENDING
> PLEASURE CALLED JOY. ❞

(Advait BodhSthal, 2019)

15

How to Get Peace of Mind?

> " LOOK AT EVERYTHING THAT DISAPPOINTS YOU. LOOK AT
> EVERYTHING THAT ADDS TO YOUR RESTLESSNESS. LOOK
> AT EVERYTHING THAT YOU ARE DOING JUST TO FULFIL A
> RESPONSIBILITY AND KNOW THAT IT IS NOT YOUR DESTINY.
> KNOW THAT YOU MUST NOT REMAIN CONFINED. "

Listener: If I compare my today with yesterday, I find there is a growth in everything, be it family responsibility, accountability, professional growth, money, status, knowledge, etc. Eight years ago, I probably just had a dream of these things, but at that time I was happy from within. Whatever I was doing, there was a reason and for that I was happy. I used to pursue many hobbies and activities, such as playing guitar and visiting orphanages, and praying to God. Even though I was introverted, I was happy from within. Eventually my dreams started to come true.

But even seeing all that I achieved today, at times I feel very low, as if nothing is touching me. I feel that all the stress that I took for all this is worthless and really unnecessary. I have lost my peace of mind, my calmness. Please guide me.

Acharya Prashant: So, your dreams have been realized. That is what you wanted, didn't you?

Now, what you can see is that you do not feel, in your own words, 'happy from within', and this feeling is made stronger by the contrast you see between your lukewarm state today and your happy state of a few years back. The more you compare your state today with that of the past, the more you find a difference, the more you are able to see that things today are not what they used to be probably ten years back or fifteen years back.

The conclusion that you have drawn is that the past was a happy time, and after that happy time you have slid into a relatively unhappy time. That is why when you are talking of the situation that you are in today, you are parallelly mentioning your situation of the past. You find that you must mention your situation of the past because it is only in relation to the past that you are finding today's situation bad.

Now, do not make a mistake. It is sufficient to see that you do not feel well today. Enough! It is enough to see that you are restless today, that you lack in immersion, that peace eludes you, that an inner joy is found wanting. Do not call your past a period of satisfaction. Do not look up to it. If you do that, you will also start looking forward to it.

Is it not obvious that what you were in the past has led to the current situation? And if your current situation is not one of contentment, then how can you be full of praise for the life that you were living in the past and the decisions that you made then? Are the decisions you made in the past not responsible for how you are living in the present?

You have written almost a fairy tale—'I used to dance, I used to play guitar, I used to serve the destitute. I was the ideal girl with the ideal life.' Why did this ideal girl then land into the situation she today finds herself in? An ideal life cannot have non-ideal results. Don't you see the obvious contradiction? You talk of the dreams of your youth. You also say that the same dreams have now been realized. What are the things that you have mentioned as having?

You have begun by saying, 'If I compare my today with yesterday, I find there is a growth in everything.' So, first of all, this today that you are lamenting is only a growth over yesterday. If yesterday was great, then today should be extra great. You will have to firstly confess that your misery of today is an accumulation of not today's problems but problems of a lifetime. That which today shows up as having gone bad has been going bad constantly and consistently over your entire lifetime. It is just that then it was not evident, and now it is open and obvious.

All that which you had in a little measure in the past has grown and become substantial. So, what then is the misery? The misery is, you still go back to the past and say, 'You know what, I was happier in the past!'

You were happier in the past exactly because you had very little of these things, but at that time you wanted these exact same things. Why then do you dream about the past? Why then do you mention your past as a golden period?

You are saying that you used to play every day and you used to pray to God. What were your songs about? What were your prayers about? Your songs have borne results. Your prayers have been answered. All that you prayed for you have in ample measures today—you have family, you have responsibility, you have money, you have status.

Look at your songs of that time. Were you not asking for the very same things? You have them now. You were just sowing the seeds then. Today you are harvesting and tomorrow you will have to consume what you are harvesting today. Look forward to your tomorrow now!

Chilli seeds were sown, and now that you are harvesting them, some of the chilli is hurting your eyes. You are feeling bad. Tomorrow, you would be consuming what you are harvesting today. How will you feel tomorrow?

Forgive me if what I am saying hurts, but I am not here to console you. Eight years back, if I could have said the same things to you, maybe today you would not have needed to send this question to me. And if today I do not say what I am saying right now, can you imagine the question you would be sending to me eight years later? Do you know how that question would read? I cannot allow you to write that question. So, I must say what I am saying right now.

It is simple. The matter is not new at all. It is the same old rut, the same old cycle. In the youth, there is freedom. Freedom from what? Freedom from the bondages of childhood; freedom from the limitations of a child's body. So, there is freedom. But what does one use that freedom for? One uses that freedom to gather more bondages. Now that you are free from the dictates of mommy and daddy, you use your freedom to start running after girls or boys. Now, the girl or the boy would soon be your new mommy or daddy and would ask you to become a mommy or a daddy. Having gotten rid of one mommy or daddy, now you have gathered two mommies or daddies. That is what you use your freedom for.

Yes, with adolescence, with youth, you start writing colourful poems. Youth is when the poet in you opens up. But what are all your poems about? Your poems are all about inviting bondages, aren't they? Now that the bondages have indeed come upon you, why do you cry?

Kabir says, 'What do I do with this mind? Why can't I cast it away? Why can't I just grind it in some mortar? Why can't I just break it? It did what it did, firstly, and having done what it did, now it is repenting. What do I do with such a fool? Such an obstinate fool.'

You asked for a family, you got it. That's the story of so many young girls. She is dreaming of her nest, she is dreaming of feathers and featherbeds, she is dreaming of cosy and warm home, love songs sung over a guitar. Yes, the guitar! And that is why the guitar is so popular among the youth: the guitar adds romance to your flappy dreams.

Now, what music do you hear? Where is the guitar now? Where are the poems? Today, we see a bigger flow of tears. Remember how the wind used to caress your hair when you were a young girl? Where is the hair now? They are all falling and you are busy trying hair ointments. Back then, before sleeping, you would be busy writing a love poem; now you are busy counting how many hair have fallen today. And the prince charming of your great dreams, he is bald!

But you have a lot; you have rightly begun by saying that. All that you dreamt of eight years back has today grown—family responsibility, accountability, money, status. That is what you wanted—some growth in life. That is what your great teachers told you: you must have growth. Now, you do have growth! Why are you complaining?

Life was wrong then and life is wrong today. Do not think that some accidental crisis has hit you. What you are passing through is the justified sum-total of your actions, thoughts and intentions, of the way you have been and the way you are.

Now, if you continue to live the same way, please think of your future. For sure, you will have a lot of growth. You know what these growths are called? Tumours! What is the definition of a tumour?

An unhealthy growth in the system. That is what cancer is—a growth.

You will have to drop the notion that you need to go back to the past. You will have to disown the totality of what you are. The law of duality is straightforward—in the past you dream of the future, and when the future arrives, the past appears glorious. The future is both a continuation of the past and a contrast to the past. It is not a special happening; it is the story of every man and every woman.

You must see it through and through. You must look at the beginning of it, you are right in the middle of it, and you must also know that it does not ever end. You will have to end it for it to end. Are you prepared to end it? And by ending, I again do not mean that you must hark back to the past. It will have to be a new beginning altogether.

Look at everything that disappoints you. Look at everything that adds to your restlessness. Look at everything that you are doing just to fulfil a responsibility and know that it is not your destiny. Know that you must not remain confined.

If you want to change the tepid state you are in, you will have to change almost everything about you. If your clothes remain the same, if your thoughts remain the same, if your food remains the same, if your surroundings remain the same, your boredom too would remain the same. Do you want to continue with it?

You have been put on a rail track; it is well laid out, it offers no scope for deviation. The script is unforgiving; the script makes no allowance for anything of the beyond. The more you live within the script, the more the script dictates that you live within the script.

Your life story so far is a typical example of a scripted life, and I know the next chapter of that script, and I also know the chapter after that. Do you want to live by the script?

By the way, this encounter today—this meeting, this question that you asked, and the response that I gave—is not in the script. Either you can conveniently forget this encounter as an accidental deviation, or you can use it as an opportunity to break away and break free.

You will not find the answer that I gave in any script of the world.

> " THE LAW OF DUALITY IS STRAIGHTFORWARD—IN THE
> PAST YOU DREAM OF THE FUTURE, AND WHEN THE FUTURE
> ARRIVES, THE PAST APPEARS GLORIOUS. THE FUTURE IS BOTH
> A CONTINUATION OF THE PAST AND A CONTRAST TO THE PAST.
> IT IS NOT A SPECIAL HAPPENING; IT IS THE STORY OF EVERY
> MAN AND EVERY WOMAN. "

(Uttarakhand, 2017)

16

Why Is there Inner Chaos? How to Find Inner Order?

> *ONLY TRUTH MEETS TRUTH. IF YOU ARE CARRYING ANYTHING FALSE, YOU WILL BE DENIED. WHAT IS THE PRICE YOU HAVE TO PAY? THE PRICE IS TO DROP EVERYTHING THAT IS FALSE ABOUT YOU. THE MORE YOU DROP THE BAGGAGE, THE CLOSER YOU FIND YOURSELF TO THE TRUTH. THAT IS THE PRICE TO BE PAID.*

Listener (L): When there is chaos in our life, we feel challenged and we struggle to overcome it, but when everything is going on in an orderly manner, we feel that nothing is happening, that life is at a standstill. Please explain.

Acharya Prashant (AP): Chaos and order are very relative; they are not objective. It depends on who you are. If you take yourself as a socially conditioned or biologically ordered being, then even spiritual progress will look like chaos to you. A Rumi, or a Kabir, or a Krishna is a messenger of anarchy and great disorder. A socially or biologically ordered person will say that Rumi just brings about chaos and Krishna is deviating from all the accepted principles, so he too is disorderly.

Who are you? You always define chaos and order from your own vantage point. Sometimes it is better to be chaotic than to be socially ordered. Kids appear chaotic; later on they become ordered. Mostly, their order is not something to be really celebrated. The chaos was powered by freedom; this order is powered by bondage. You decide which one is better.

Divine order often appears like chaos. But you should also remember that transcending the social/biological order does not mean you are entering a disorder. If you are transcending the order imposed upon you by society, then you are entering a divine order, a mystical order. That order will not be comprehensible to everybody, so they might say you are very disorderly now.

But that, again, does not mean that what appears disorderly is actually divine order. Do not get into that. You turn your room totally chaotic, and when somebody asks why your room is in such a shabby condition, you say it is like this because it is divine order. No, not everything shabby is divine order.

If you are spiritual, it is your responsibility to present a good example, but that example is never a manufactured or a fabricated one. You naturally become a good example to the ones who are seeking goodness or Truth, not to the others.

The fundamental responsibility of the spiritual man is towards himself. At the centre of the responsibility lies the question, 'Who am I?'—and who am I? We have talked of this before. 'Who am I? I am the restless one. And I am not speculating, I am not merely quoting from scriptures; I am coming from my own experiences. I am restless day in and day out. I am the confused one. I am the tired one. I am the one who feels incomplete. If that is the one I am, what is my responsibility?' What is the responsibility of the thirsty one? To find water, full stop. That is your responsibility: find water.

And if you are seen finding water, you naturally, obviously, and effortlessly become a good example for everybody else who is seeking water. The very fact that you could obtain water for yourself becomes a great motivation to others. 'If he could get it, surely it is possible. If Krishna could have it, if Ashtavakra could have it, if Jesus could have it, there surely would be some glimmer of hope for me as well.'

L: How do we develop the faith to pursue the Truth?

AP: You are already pursuing the Truth, though in a very distorted way. Nobody ever pursues anything else. Falseness is a myth. Each of us is already a lover of the Truth, but we are pursuing the Truth in our personal ways, with an eye on self-preservation. We want to get the Truth but also remain intact, preserved.

So, it is not as if you need to develop a zeal to find the Truth; you already are eager for the Truth. Every single man on the street, just anywhere, born, unborn, to be born, is a seeker of Truth. I dare say even plants and animals are looking for the Truth; even they are in search of liberation, and that is why they respond to love. Anybody who responds to love is just a seeker of Truth, because that is what love is—to be pulled towards the Truth.

To be attracted towards Truth is love. To be attracted towards peace is love.

Don't ask me how to have a zeal for the Truth. A better question, a more useful question would be, 'I am already pursuing the Truth in my personal ways. Are my ways right?' Question your ways. Don't ask for the Truth.

He is pursuing Truth. She is pursuing Truth. You are pursuing Truth. I am pursuing Truth. Everybody is a pursuer of Truth. But we all are pursuing Truth in our own crooked ways because we don't want to lose ourselves in the pursuit of Truth. We don't want to pay the price. We want to get the Truth at a discount.

L: What is the price we have to pay?

AP: Only Truth meets Truth. If you are carrying anything false, you will be denied. What is the price you have to pay? The price is to drop everything that is false about you. The more you drop the baggage, the closer you find yourself to the Truth. That is the price to be paid. It is a good price to be paid—it is not even a price. If you are being unburdened of unnecessary baggage, is it a price you are paying or a gift you are getting?

But we are so attached to this baggage that we don't want to drop it. If we are asked to drop it, we feel as if some great injustice is happening. Then we say, 'Spirituality is for the selected few; they are the ones who could keep it away. Actually, they are irresponsible also. I am the responsible one, I will keep carrying my cancer!'

The baggage is a cancerous lump, a tumour. Why are you carrying it on your head, rather in your head?

L: You said that we prioritize ourselves and try to keep ourselves intact. How can we stop prioritizing ourselves and start being passionate or interested about the Truth?

AP: Thirst! You are already thirsty. You need not look for Truth as a passion, as an interest. You have to look for Truth as a thirsty person looks for water. Will the thirsty one say that 'looking for water is my hobby'? No, it is not a hobby. It is a life-saving thing. If he does not get water, he will die.

Spirituality is not a pastime or a co-curricular affair. It is not something that you do all the weekends or in your spare time. It is about saving your one dear precious life. Please don't waste it.

L: If I put myself fully into spirituality, am I not being selfish? Should I not care for others' needs also?

AP: You have to figure out your real need. Your real need would always be something that would raise others as well. This too is an important question that bugs most of us. The question is, 'If I look after my spiritual needs, am I not becoming selfish? Am I not stopping from caring for others?' No, not quite.

The one who really knows himself, and therefore his real needs, is a blessing to everybody. The scripture says that a man never gets liberated alone; he and his tribe get liberated together. He has such an effect on everybody, and that effect, I say, is not deliberate. The effect that a liberated man has on the entire ecosystem is instantaneous, unplanned and effortless. The word 'tribe' here means your surroundings, your ecosystem, family, community, country, and everybody. Just by your presence you liberate.

That does not mean that you sit and liberate; it means now you are somebody who will live in a way that would awaken and arouse liberation in others as well. Now that you have it, you will distribute it. And you will not need to distribute with a plan or with deliberation. You will distribute just because you breathe. Your every breath would mean a fragrance to the world.

L: So, a spiritual person cannot cause distress in others?

AP: If it appears that he is causing distress to others, it is useful distress. It would many a times appear like that he is causing distress to others, but that distress is worth welcoming. The others would definitely feel that he is doing something very evil, but let the others feel that. Others may even declare that this spiritual person is evil because he is catering to his own self-interest, his own self-liberation. But that is their problem. They are not liberated. They can claim anything.

L: So, I am not obliged to stop my spiritual journey because others think it is selfish?

AP: You are not obliged to stop for them, but you may have the compassion to stop for them. Please understand, these are two different things.

Suppose A curses B. B may feel like going up to A and telling him that he is wrong, he is misunderstood. Why does B feel the need to explain and justify? Because B is hurt and that hurt is personal. The same B curses a Buddha, and the Buddha too stops and says, 'No sir, you are wrong.' Why does the Buddha come up to him and tell him that? Not because the Buddha is hurt personally, but because the Buddha is full of compassion towards this person. When B came to A, she came because she had a personal grudge.

L: Can the other person differentiate between a Buddha and someone operating from a centre of hurt?

AP: It depends upon the other person, how hungry he is for the Truth. If the other person is anyway looking for some kind of Buddha-presence in life, he will realize the Buddha. On the other hand, if the person is deeply mired in his own tendencies and unconscious self, he may not realize the Buddha or recognize the Buddha.

L: So, it is determined by the attitude of the recipient?

AP: Obviously. But right now, it is not about A; we are discussing about B. When B goes to A, she goes because she feels personally offended. When B goes and protests, 'Why are you calling me evil?' then B is defending herself. When Buddha goes to A, then Buddha is not seeking respect or approval; Buddha is not personally lowered or offended.

It is not about A. Why must we be so bothered about A? Are we A? We must forget about A. If our mind is full of A, we will remain a slave of A.

The Buddha, too, engages with the world. He, too, wants to correct the world. But he says, 'You must be in deep suffering, otherwise how could you have abused a Buddha so much? You must be in deep ignorance; otherwise, how could you have not recognized the Buddha? And therefore I am coming to you because I empathize with you, because I am full of compassion towards you. The abuses are proof that you are the strongest claimant to my compassion.'

If there are six patients, to whom does the doctor rush first? The one who is in the worst shape and the worst situation. The one who can abuse and hit even a Buddha is surely the patient in the worst condition. So, the Buddha would never leave him.

And when the Buddha goes to him, this fellow will get another opportunity to slap the Buddha. The Buddha will bear the slap because he is a Buddha. He may not always bear the slaps; sometimes it might be best to slap the fellow back. It depends. We will better leave it to the Buddha.

> **❝** FALSENESS IS A MYTH. EACH OF US IS ALREADY A LOVER OF
> THE TRUTH, BUT WE ARE PURSUING THE TRUTH IN OUR
> PERSONAL WAYS, WITH AN EYE ON SELF-PRESERVATION.
> WE WANT TO GET THE TRUTH BUT ALSO REMAIN INTACT,
> PRESERVED. **❞**

(Bengaluru, 2018)

17

What Does it Mean to Live in the Present?

> **WHEN YOU DO NOT EXPECT FROM TIME WHAT TIME CANNOT GIVE YOU, YOU ARE ALREADY TIMELESS. WHEN YOU DO NOT EXPECT FROM LIFE WHAT LIFE CANNOT GIVE YOU, YOU ARE ALREADY IMMORTAL.**

Listener (L): 'Living in the present' is an oft used and abused term. All our actions are directed towards the future, towards achieving something. And then this question of 'living in the present' comes up. Suppose I have a train at 10 o'clock and I am doing some work at 7. Can I be in the present without thinking that I have a train to catch?

Acharya Prashant (AP): 'Living in the present' is one of the most abused terms currently. We conflate these two—present and now. We must wisely draw a distinction. When it comes to the present, we tend to imply the present moment. We immediately link the present to time. Now, that is a very gross error. What does the present have to do with time?

What does 'present' mean? That which is present. That which is always. Because your perception is limited to this moment, you want to add the caveat 'currently'. Because beyond currently it is difficult for you to really, directly see anything, so you say 'currently'.

The present is that which is. Not that which is and would not be, or that which was not and now is. It is that which *is*. In this, there is no involvement of time. And if you take away time from the equation, what does 'that which is' imply? That which is independent of time. That which *is*, independent of time. That which is *independent* of time. That which is, that which was, and that which will remain; hence that which is unchangeable, that which is not subject to the vagaries of time—the Truth. That is the present. What does that have to do with 'now' or any such things?

The present means nothing except the Truth. The one, immutable, unchangeable Truth; the one all-pervasive, incomprehensible present.

Now, in this unchanging sky, all kinds of changes are free to happen. In fact, nothing except changes can happen in the present. Understand this carefully. That which will not change is bound to be one, it cannot be many. Hence, whatever is happening is bound to be subject to change. There cannot be many presents. There cannot be many Truths.

But within the present a lot happens, and all of that is subject to time—it arises in time and then it falls in time. The sky is there. Birds climb up and then they climb down. Clouds come and then clouds dissolve. Smoke arises and then smoke dissipates. Suns, moon, stars—even they are a matter of time; they were not always there.

So, in the present there is constant coming and going; there is a flow of time. There are as many flows, streams of time as there are divisions of mind, as there are persons, as there are fragments of persons. Infinite streams of time keep flowing in the present. The present is a vast sky that encompasses these streams from their beginning till their end.

Now, what will this stream of time, from its beginning till the end, comprise? The past, the future, and that which is in between, the now. So, the present envelopes past, future, now—everything.

The present has no special relationship with the now. It may sound new to many of us, so I repeat—the present has no special relationship with the now. Remaining in the present, seated in the present, surrendered to the present, the now is no more significant than past or future. You are well entitled to dwell in the future. There is no problem with that. It is not at all a spiritual crime to think about the future.

Even if you say that you are in the now, is your 'now' really independent of past and future? The now anyway contains all the past. So, even if you say you are in the now, you are anyway living in the past. It is just that the past has been sanitized. When you say past, it appears filthy; when you say present, it appears hygienic. But it is just a verbal deception.

Now, past, and future are all one. It is just that same stream of time. Timelessness does not mean that you are located in the now. It means that you are somewhere beyond the stream, not at some special point in the stream.

Contemporary self-help books and so-called contemporary wisdom literature make us feel as if there is something special about the now. This is ignorance. This is total ignorance. I repeat, the now as a point in time is no more special than any other point in time. The speciality, the magic lies not in the now, but in freedom from the entire stream that contains the past, the future and the now.

If I ask you what is the time right now, you will tell me of a particular time. That is our definition of now. Is there time without the past? If the clock strikes 5 right now, is it not obviously coming from 4, and won't it obviously proceed to 6? So, is there any wisdom in saying that 'I am living in the now and it is 5 p.m. right now'?

You are in the present when it does not matter to you whether you are in the future, in the past, or in the now. That is when you are really in the present. And if you conflate the present with now, then such absurdities as you mentioned—live in the now—would necessarily arise.

You have a flight to catch at 10 p.m. and it is already 8 p.m. Some great teacher has advised us, 'But you must live only in the now. Any thought of future is sacrilege!' Then my question is, will that teacher pay for your flight? Because you are definitely going to miss it.

That is the whole fun of presence. Do not confuse presence with physicality, because physically you can be only at one point in space, at one point in time. Presence does not mean that you are here. Here and now have nothing to do with presence. Presence means it doesn't matter where you are and what time it is, because it is all the same, because I have a solid, rock-like support beneath me that doesn't vary with the situation—either in space or in time.

But you know what, out of ignorance, or out of deliberate mischief, confusing the present with now serves a great purpose for the ego. That purpose is consumption. However, there is something of the wise within us that does not want to provide energy to the false. When your latent tendencies start showing up and start compelling you, then your wise core does not want to fuel them. It says, 'No!'

If you insist that life is right now, you make that synonymous with fulfilling all your desires right now, and these two very quickly and conveniently become synonymous. If there is no future and if the future doesn't matter, then when am I to fulfil myself? Right now. So we consume, because all desires are about consumption. Show me one desire in which consumption is not involved. It is always consumption of some kind.

So, now you do not need to pay heed to the wisdom that arises out of the heart. Now you will say, 'No, I have only this moment to live, and I must totally fulfil myself in this moment.' And what is this fulfilment? Consumption. This is not a fulfilment that is pre-set, pre-achieved, preordained. This is a fulfilment that you have to get through achievement, desire and consumption.

It is another matter that those who advocate this do not see that even to consume you require the future. One morsel of bread being brought from hand to mouth spans an infinity of time; even that cannot happen in the now. Universes rise and fall in the time you bring the cup to the lip; even that cannot happen in the now.

But they say, 'No, the now is everything.' Corporations would certainly love it. Your industrial masters would certainly love this philosophy. A power-hungry mind would certainly love this philosophy. Now is so powerful! And the ego is always famished, always feeling deprived of power. You know what power is? An ability to bring changes outside. If I can make the world move according to my wish, I would call it power.

L: Would it be right to say that fear is the real cause of all problems?

AP: Fear *is* the problem. After that do you need more problems to arise? When is something a problem? Show me one problem that does not involve fear. And if it does not involve fear, if it does not excite fear in you, is it a problem? So, fear need not *cause* problems, fear already *is* the problem. That is the very characteristic of all the problems. They excite fear in you.

If you can go through any situation fearlessly, would you still call it a problem? That is the difference between situations and problems. Situations *are,* problems *threaten.* So, there is always fear involved in a problem. And if the threat is not there, it is just a situation, not a problem.

L: Whenever I feel troubled by my past or future, I try to focus on my breath. That works for me, it brings me back to the present for a while. But now you are saying there is nothing like the present. It is confusing.

AP: No, you are not looking at the fact. The mind never wanders to the past and the future. The mind always remains in the now. In the now, the mind thinks about the past and the future. So, your now is always coloured by the past and the future. The mind has no capacity to go to the past or to the future; the mind invites the past and the future to the now. In fact, that is why the now is nothing except an aggregation of the past and the future. The past and the future by themselves are toothless, they cannot come to harm you. They come to harm you only in the now.

When does the future appear as terrible? Now! Does the future appear terrible in the future? Similarly, the past haunts you. Does the past haunt you in the past? When does the past haunt you? Now! So, when the past has to haunt you, it comes to the now. When the future has to trouble you, it comes to the now. So where does the trouble lie? In the now.

All your thoughts are in the now. All your trouble is in the now.

L: So, isn't this whole theory of 'living in the present' escapism?

AP: Of course it is escapism. Not only can it not help you, but it is also just a promotion of consumerism of all kinds.

The past cannot trouble you and the future cannot trouble you. All your troubles are experienced in the now. All your thoughts are in the now. All your speculations are in the now. All your pains are in the now. You anticipate that you will get hurt in the future. When are you suffering? Right now. You are anticipating an injury two years hence, but when are you suffering? Now!

That is why the only method is an honest observation of life as it is right now. If you can observe the now, you can observe the entire stream of time. When you observe yourself as you are right now, you will find yourself in the past, in the future, everywhere—all of them present to you in the now.

The now is where the misery lies. The now is the point of solution. Hence, freedom from now is the only spiritual goal. Can I totally forget what time it is now? Can I totally forget where I am right now? Of those sitting here, the ones aware of the time right now are not listening. And those who are conscious of who is sitting to their left and right are also not listening to me.

Freedom from the now means presence. Now you are outside the stream. To you, the stream means only the now, because the ego is always situated at one particular point. Except for that one particular point, the ego does not know anything. Oh, it can fantasize, but it cannot really be there. You might have played a hundred roles in your life, but what matters to you? The role that you are playing now. It is another thing that the role is determined by the hundred roles you have played before. But, to you, what is it that matters?

Do you see how this whole thing is working? There is this entire flow of time. And in this flow, the ego gets identified and attached to one point. That point is called here-and-now. The here-and-now is your misery. You are imagining that you are a limited body sitting on a chair at 10.15 p.m. on the night of 16 October 2016. That is your misery. That is not your reality.

What does freedom from the now mean? It means that all this doesn't matter too much to me. How does it matter whether it is 16th or 18th October? It matters in the sense that I might not have paid for the session on 18th October, so I will have to leave. But beyond that, it does not matter. Or it matters if the doctor has given me only two more days to live, so on 20th October, I might not be physically around. Beyond that, it does not matter. Death does not deserve more than that.

L: Does 'living in the now' come from the conscious mind?

AP: No, not at all, because all consciousness has here-and-now as its centre. You are always conscious of things *as* somebody. And who are you? You are somebody here and now. That somebody changes with time and situations.

Consciousness is not absolute. Do you know the relative nature of consciousness? Whenever you look at something, don't you look *as* somebody? And who is this somebody? This somebody is a product of time and situations. This somebody changes the moment the situation changes, time changes. And when this somebody changes, the world totally changes.

L: How do I live in the present?

AP: By not taking this question too seriously, because even this question is a matter of now. Let there be something more tempting than this question and you will forget this question. Even this question is a product of situations. And whatever is a product of situations, why bother too much about it?

The day this question becomes an integral part of your being, the day it becomes impossible for you to cast it away, we will answer it. Right now, it is situational. There comes a point when the question starts resonating in the heart. Then the question and the solution are no longer different.

Whatever is a product of situations has to be taken as situational, and hence it can be looked at in a jolly way. 'Ah, it is all right. You came to me in the flow of time, you will go away in the flow of time, it is all right. Coincidences gave you to me, coincidences will take you away from me. It is all right.'

L: But I believe that this is a genuine problem that I am facing.

AP: Will this problem remain with you ten days later? Were you with this problem even two hours before this session? Were other things not occupying your mind? Don't you see that so much of these questions is just thoughts that rise and fall with situations? You are asking this question only because we have right now cultivated a situation in which spiritual or intellectual inquiry can be done. A question is a real question when it is no more separable from the breath. Now you are a moving question. We are all so curious in curious environments, and the curiosity fades away the moment dinner is served.

Time! Time! Time! Flow! Flow! Flow! Let the flow. Flow! In the flow, do not look for stuff that is permanent. Your questions are all about that which does not change. But the questions keep changing. By using a question that is so prone to changing, you want to reach the unchangeable. How is that going to happen? Do not search for the stuff in wrong places.

When you do not expect things from time that time cannot give you, you are already timeless.

When you do not expect from life what life cannot give you, you are already immortal.

L: What about patience? We have lots of questions, but it seems as if we have this desire to fix something right now very quickly.

AP: You see, patience is of two types. One—'the real will happen sometime in the future and I am waiting for it'. This patience involves deprivation. 'I don't have the real and I am waiting for it.' Usually when you talk of patience, this is the kind of patience you refer to. 'Something great is going to happen in the future. The flow of time, the stream will give me the unchangeable. All these changes will bring me to the unchangeable.' That is your first type of patience.

There is another kind of patience. That patience is patience towards the foolishness of mind. What is real is already there, but the foolish mind is unable to come to terms with it. Wait for a while and the mind will fall in place. Now you are not deprived. You are only saying, 'It is there, already there. It is just the sense of "I" which is unable to acknowledge it. I have it in my house and I am unable to find it.'

And these are two very different things. One, 'I don't have it in my house, I have lost it somewhere. Let me go and launch a frantic search or file an FIR. Let me look for it out somewhere in the universe.' That is the first kind of patience.

The second kind of patience is: 'It is there in my house; I am just unable to locate it. I have deep faith that I already have it, but my senses and my mind are so limited and so foolish that they keep forgetting. They just cannot locate, they cannot identify it. The problem is not of achievement but of identification.' So, have patience. The mind lives in time. In time, it will be able to identify. Remember, the mind here is not being told to search; it is only being told to identify. This is the second kind of patience.

Both involve a factor of time, but they are dimensionally different. In the first, you operate from the centre of deprivation. In the second, you operate from the centre of fullness: 'It is there, but what to do with this foolish mind?'

L: So, is the second kind of patience maintained by the same impatience of the mind?

AP: No, the second kind of patience is just surrender. The second kind of patience is when the mind is wise enough to accept that it is foolish. Accepting foolishness is great wisdom. When the mind is humble enough to acknowledge from its own day-to-day experiences that its power to know, power to ascertain are utterly limited, it says, 'Oh, I need to be more considerate towards myself.' It is that patience.

You go to the gym. You can't lift anything more than ten pounds. Now you know about the power of the mind and the body—limited, right? So now you have patience. Patience—not that the Truth will descend on you one day, but with your physical and mental capacities. 'The Truth is there, but what do I do if my hands are so weak? The Truth is there, but what do I do if my eyes cannot see beyond a point?' This is humility arising out of honest day-to-day observation.

L: Is the entity that sees the limitation the same entity which is limited?

AP: No. The limited entity comes upon its limitation due to the blessings of the unlimited. Otherwise, the limited entity has fantasies about being unlimited. You can keep wandering outside the gym and assume that you are a macho man. It is only when you are powered by something beyond yourself that you say, 'I want to go in and I want to verify what my actual strengths are. Not only will I verify, but I will also humbly acknowledge that this is the factual strength of my mind-body mechanism.' Left to itself, the ego would never want to do that.

Assumptions are wonderful, as they help you maintain your dreams. They help you maintain your self-cultivated fanciful image. The ego by itself would not want to come in touch with the facts. To come in touch with the facts, you require a touch of the Truth. And that is available, so you don't really have to explore.

L: You mentioned that the ego can operate from either of the two centres—fullness or deprivation. Does the ego get tired of feeling deprived?

AP: Oh, the ego can fill itself up with deprivation. 'I am full of hollowness! I am stuffed with hunger!' That's how smart the ego is.

> " THE SPECIALITY, THE MAGIC LIES NOT IN THE NOW, BUT IN FREEDOM FROM THE ENTIRE STREAM THAT CONTAINS THE PAST, THE FUTURE AND THE NOW. YOU ARE IN THE PRESENT WHEN IT DOES NOT MATTER TO YOU WHETHER YOU ARE IN THE FUTURE, IN THE PAST, OR IN THE NOW. "

(Uttrakhand, 2016)

18

What Is Meant by Living Totally?

> *LET THOSE WHO FEEL THAT THEY HAVE BEEN RENDERED HOMELESS, SEARCH FOR THE HOME. YOU HAVE FUN. LET THOSE WHO FEEL THAT THEY ARE GODLESS, SEARCH FOR GOD. YOU HAVE FUN.*

Listener (L): Sir, you have said, 'Whatever you do, do it totally.' But you have also said, 'Whatever you do, you must remain unaffected by the doing.' How to put these two together? Is there a contradiction? If yes, how can it be reconciled? What is meant by doing something totally?

Acharya Prashant (AP): Usually, when we say that something is to be done totally, we equate that with a stretch in time, a stretch in energy. 'Instead of investing five units of resources in it, I invested fifty units of resources because I wanted to do it totally. Instead of going one mile, I went all the way for ten miles because I wanted to do it totally.' So we equate this totalness with a stretch, with an expanse. In other words, what we call as 'doing something totally' means going as far as our desire, our motivation wants us to go.

'I have not yet had enough of it, I want to have it totally. So let me have a little extra, a little more.' This is what is commonly meant by doing something totally. It is equated with a stretch in desire fulfilment, in the expending of energy, in the investment of time, in the application of concentration. I want to submit that this is not what is meant by doing something totally.

What, then, is meant by doing something totally? Doing something totally means doing it from a point of totality. It does not mean how far you go in doing that thing. It means being sensitive of the point from where you are doing this thing. And these are two very different things.

The conventional interpretation of doing something totally would lay emphasis on how far you go: do it totally, so go far. But the real meaning is: 'It does not matter how far I go. What matters is from where I start, from where am I coming.'

The conventional ones would say that if a full plate of meals was served to you and you did not finish off each of the delicacies, then you have not had the meal totally. They would say, 'Something is still left, something is left undone, something still needs to be covered because the plate is not yet empty. You have not gone into it totally.' That is not the correct meaning of going into it totally. Going into it totally means that even if you take just one bite, just one morsel, you take it from the point of totality. So, even if you have left the rest of the plate untouched, even if you have left the entire plate untouched, it is still possible that you have totally eaten because you are eating from a point which is contented, which is total. 'Total' means complete, undivided, not fractured, not desirous.

So, going into something totally does not mean that you have to keep diving into it till your desire is quenched. That is a very misleading interpretation. But often it is convenient to circulate this interpretation since it promotes consumption. You say, 'I want to live totally', and what does that mean? That means you must consume everything that is available for consumption—you must travel to as many countries as possible, you must have as many items as possible to eat, to display, to benefit from. No, that is not what is meant by living totally. Living totally means: even if you do not travel outside of your little village, yet you live totally in that village.

It does not matter what you are doing. What matters is from where you are doing it. These are two very different things.

It is not the action that matters. It is the point of origin of action that matters. Actions would always be dictated by situations, but your centre cannot be dictated by situations.

So, you cannot be particular about action. If you really have eyes, you will not want to look at the action and judge the actor based on the action. But that is what we commonly do. We judge the actor based on the action. We judge the doer based on the deed. But deeds can vary. What is right in one situation will not be right in another.

You may remain thoroughly and consistently compassionate in situation A and situation B. But your action in situation A coming out of compassion can be diametrically opposite to your action in situation B, coming again out of compassion. In both these places, you are the same compassionate one, yet your actions will be seemingly opposites. So, if you are being judged only on your actions, the judgment would go haywire.

Living totally, I repeat, does not mean that you need to have a flamboyant lifestyle, that you need to be lavishly spending or lavishly consuming. Living totally means, 'I operate from a point within me that is not hungry, that is not thirsty, that lives and abides in its own internal satisfaction. Which means that even as I eat, as the body is given food, a point within me does not need any food.' Even to say that it does not need any food is not correct; it is beyond hunger and satisfaction. Neither can we say that it is desirous of food, nor can we say that its desire for food has been satisfied, because it is something dimensionally different from all material, all food, all desire and all fulfilment of desire.

You may go and eat at the most expensive five-star property or you may eat at a roadside dhaba—there is something within you which is not a function of the place where you are eating. You might be talking to an old man or you may have an infant in your arms—there is something within you that does not change even as your behaviour towards these two entities is different. So, all that which is external keeps changing according to the situations, but something within you remains still.

Living totally means that you remain the same in the moment of your deepest fulfilment and in the moment of your deepest frustration.

You are very fulfilled; your mind, your body, all are feeling the vibration of that fulfilment. It is an ecstasy, a rise, the whole organism is excited. Yet something within you feels not excitement. Not that it is feeling bored or dull; it is just that it is not feeling excited. And we are saying 'not excited' only to emphasize that it does not have the same quality as the mind. Otherwise, to even say that it is not excited is to stretch language beyond its limits.

And then there is the moment in which you are depressed, irritated and heavy, and the mind is feeling the burden, the body is feeling the pain; the whole system appears to be overloaded with grief with all kinds of neurotic energies. Yet there is something within you that is not at all frustrated, not at all feeling low. That does not mean that it is feeling high. I repeat, the phrase 'feeling low' is relevant only in the context of the mind that is feeling low. That 'something' within us, that point, is feeling neither high nor low. It simply remains untouched. That is the point of totality.

You see, parts can mutate, change, increase, decrease, transform, change shape, size, colour, properties, or they can rise, fall, dissolve. The total has no way to change. The total is helpless in this regard. Were the total to change, it wouldn't be the total.

So, to act totally means to have that unchangeability. Actually, it is better to say that let that unchangeability have total control and possession of you. Now do you see that there is no need to reconcile the two statements? Being total is the same as being untouched.

But you will find this contradiction, and hence the need for reconciliation, if you take the conventional definition of 'doing it totally'. The conventional definition, being incorrect, is going to inevitably lead to that contradiction. According to this conventional definition, when you do something totally, you must be coloured more and more with the experience which pertains to the fulfilment of desire. And if you identify so much with the fulfilment of desire, then you tend to become dry as the desires increase and get wet as the desires keep on getting fulfilled. So, there is nothing unchangeable about you—dry and wet, dry and wet, black and white, black and white.

It doesn't matter what you do. It doesn't matter where you are. What matters really is that what you do and where you are do not become important enough to define you.

Let your situations, your circumstances, your possessions, your particular destination in life not become important enough or significant enough to define you. Let your self-worth not be dictated by things that are external. But since everything is external, let your self-worth not be dictated by anything at all, which means you should not have any concept of self-worth at all. If you have a concept of self-worth, it would necessarily be a concept dependent on something because a concept by definition depends on another concept.

So, if you have any concept of self-definition, and even if in your own assessment you have chosen a concept that appears insulated from dependencies, in reality every concept would *always* be dependent on something. When that 'something' will change, your concept of self-worth will change, so you will become a victim to the vicissitudes of life. Life will throw you up, you will feel up. Life will put you down, you will feel down. And that is no fun. That is no fun at all.

Living fully, in that sense, means being insulated from life. That is why the one who lives fully has also been classically called as the one who does not live any more, and these are the same thing. To live fully is to have gone beyond life. To live fully is much the same as death. In what sense it is the same as death? We have to understand this.

There is a dead body lying on the floor. You slap it, the fellow does not react. This is the kind of death that we usually know of. This is a death where helplessness takes over; you lose the power to react. And then there is the death in which you have vaporized, you have sublimated, you have gone beyond. It is not as if you cannot react; it is that you cannot even be slapped. You are no more. Who will slap you now? Who is going to be slapped now? Life cannot touch you now because you have dissolved in life. It is not as if you have cut yourself off from life, which many spiritually-minded people do. They escape life.

This has to be understood. There is an apparent contradiction here. You have to put these together. If you just pick one part of it, you will be misled.

You have to live so totally that life stops affecting you. Totality by definition is that which remains unaffected. Can you add something to totality? Can you subtract something from totality? Can you divide totality? That is what is meant by living totally.

It is cloudy, it is shiny, it is day, it is night.

The shop is doing well, the market is down.

They welcomed me, they insulted me.

What fine weather, what sloppy weather!

I am feeling energetic, my whole body is in pain.

It is all right.

There is someone who is weeping. You go to him or her and you say, 'Don't weep, friend. It is all right.' And then there is somebody who is jubilant, dancing, excited, euphoric. You go to him or her and you say, 'It is all right, friend. It is all right.'

You are up, it is all right.

You are down, it is all right.

You are celebrating, it is all right.

You are mourning, it is all right.

It is all right. In all cases, it is all right. That is living totally. Living totally means living from the centre of totality. It is all right.

L: It lacks drama.

AP: All the drama is there, and you are a participant. Knowing that you are a participant is called witnessing.

Witnessing does not mean that you have to stay away from the drama; witnessing does not mean that you will be hiding somewhere behind the curtains and watching the play from there. 'The entire world is the stage on which a grand drama is being enacted. And who am I? The watcher, the witness who is watching from afar.' No! That is not what is meant by witnessing.

You will never be the watcher. You are very much a participant and will remain a participant. If you say that you are the witness, you have brought another character to the stage and this character is called the witness, and this is just self-deception. Can you imagine this? There are already ten characters on the stage, and then you say, 'No, I am the witness!' All that you have done is to increase the characters to eleven.

There is nothing called the witness. Witnessing just lies in knowing that you are a player, a participant. Know that you are participating, and know that it is a drama in which you are participating. Know that the play requires you to cry out, and then cry out; let the stream flow. Know that the play requires you to laugh; let there be an eruption of laughter. Remaining untouched or being a witness does not mean that you will be lukewarm in your tears and in your laughter.

Do what is required of you in the play. Be a good actor. Do justice to your role. As you do justice to your role, you know that you are role-playing. When you know you are role-playing, you will be a good actor. A poor actor is the one who totally forgets that he is an actor. And an equally poor actor is the one who remembers that he is an actor. If you remember that you are an actor, you also remember that you are something beyond the actor, something besides the actor. Then that which you remember will interfere with your acting: 'No! I am not merely an actor—I am also a witness!' Now this witness will interfere with the actor and the acting.

Actually, this witness that you take yourself to be is just another role. You could not be playing two roles in the same moment. But that is what happens to the victims of conventional spirituality. They start saying, 'You know what, I am not merely the actor. I am the witness.' Now this witness will not allow you to act fully because this witness is not a witness at all. Now you are playing two roles in the same moment without even knowing that you are in a double role. It is a strange situation!

You must not say that it is just a role nor that there is something beyond the role. Remembering that you are just an actor would be to remember that you are a witness also. And anything you remember is just a function of memory. Forgetting that you are an actor would mean that the possibility of memory again taking over is very much alive.

Don't remember. Don't forget. Whatever has been forgotten can again be brought back to the memory. Do not trust your mind in matters of Truth. It is the mind that remembers; it is the mind that forgets. You must not remember the Truth, nor must you forget the Truth. The Truth can neither be remembered nor forgotten.

There are those who say that they keep remembering the Truth; they are misled. The Truth cannot be remembered. Then there are those who say that they have forgotten the Truth and need to be reminded; they, too, are lying. The Truth cannot be forgotten either. The Truth can neither be remembered nor be forgotten. It is beyond the mind.

So, do not try to have anything to do with the Truth. Let Truth do whatever it wants to do with you. You do not lay your hands on the Truth—because you cannot.

You see, words are dangerous. When I say 'operate from a point of totality', it is often misconstrued. How?

A person keeps on feeling hollow internally. What is this hollowness? It is a feeling, and all feeling originates from the mind. Now, the person sits here and then there is this question on living totally. And he says, 'You know what, earlier I was feeling hollow. Now I am feeling full.' There has been no real change.

Please see, I am not advising you to feel total. I am not advising you to feel full. When you feel hollow, you place your trust in the feeling. And when you say that you feel full or total, you again place your trust in your feeling.

Living totally does not mean believing that you are total. Living totally does not mean feeling full. It means having faith in something that feeling cannot touch.

You will ask me, 'Sir, if our feelings cannot touch it, thoughts cannot know it, how do we have faith in it?'

After a few hours, we will be approaching dawn. It will still be dark. The stars will still be visible. Not even the first ray of the sun would have arrived, yet a little bird starts singing. It has no visual, or sensual or mental proof of the approaching day. Have her eyes seen something? No, because sunlight is still not there. Is she relying on memory? Maybe, but then we have to see that even a little baby bird starts singing, so it couldn't be a memory which is acquired from this particular life's experiences that it could be relying on.

Faith is to know that the sun is near even when there is no proof of the sun. You just know.

There is no proof, yet I know. Not only do I know, but I am also so certain of it that I will sing about it. I am singing and my singing has such great certainty in it that by listening to my songs, people come to know that the sun is near. My song itself is the proof of the sun. There is such certainty in faith.

If the bird is singing, it is certain that the sun is near. That is faith.

If I am saying that 'it is', it must be because I am saying it. What bigger or better proof can there be? All other proofs will be external; all other proofs will just be arguments. The only final proof is the certainty in my heart that no document can verify, no logic can validate. There is something in my heart that says, 'Yes!' That is the final proof and that is faith. That is living totally.

Now it doesn't matter whether my song is acclaimed as the best song. It doesn't matter whether I sing the sweetest or the loudest. One day I may sing for five minutes; the other day I may sing for an hour. It doesn't matter for how long I sing. But whether I sing for a minute or an hour, my song is total because it is coming from totality.

That totality is not something that you can grasp. That totality is something that you can only surrender to. If you say you know it, you are bragging. If you say you do not know it, you are deliberately acting stupid. It is not possible to know it, and it is also not possible to not know it.

Fullness is not the opposite of hollowness. Fullness is freedom from the need to feel either hollow or full.

And this is something subtle. We keep on feeling small and hollow, and then we go to a teacher or a master and they convince us to feel full. No, such fullness is in the same dimension as hollowness.

I repeat, fullness is not the opposite of hollowness. Real fullness is the freedom from the need to feel hollow or full.

'How am I feeling? Neither hollow nor full. Both hollow and full.'

That is non-duality. That is Advaita.

Do you see how all of this converges into one? Do you see how all divisions are unnecessary? Do you see that there is nothing called non-duality without faith? Do you see how Advaita and śraddhā (faith) are one? Do you see how all of these are just one but because of the mind's limited capabilities, different names, different viewpoints are ascribed to them? Do you see how all of this is so simple, so simple that you need not bother about it?

So, you can just have fun. Leave Truth for those who feel that they have been deserted by the Truth. Let those who feel that they have been rendered homeless search for the home. You have fun. Let those who feel that they are godless search for God. You have fun.

L: Sir, in spite of knowing that this is a play, why do we get embroiled in it?

AP: It is because of your concept that this is a play. When you know that something is just a play, and when you say that something is just a play, you mean it is something superficial and artificial, right? When you have already declared something to be superficial and artificial, will you allow yourself to go fully into it?

So, whenever the moment of immersion comes, you are reminded by that inner voice, 'Oh! It is just a play', so you resist. You forcibly prevent yourself from immersing into it. You will not want to go deep into it. You will keep telling yourself that it is just a play. 'My teacher told me that it is just a play. All this spiritual literature is telling me that it is just a play. And if it is just a play, how do I participate fully in it?'

If you hold a concept that it is just a play, you will not be able to live fully. You will also not be able to do that if you hold a concept that it is not a play but it is real. Why? Because then if you have to play the dying man on the stage, you will feel that you are dying, and then you will be overtaken by fear.

So, if you think it is a play, you will not be able to live. And if you think it is not a play, you will not be able to die. Either way, you are stuck.

The best part is, do not think about what it is. Please spare yourself from thinking about the Truth. It is neither a play nor is it something different from a play. It is neither real nor unreal. You will never be able to put in words what it really is.

You meet people of both kinds. There are those who say, 'Oh, it is just a play!' You will find them shallow. They will never be able to weep fully. 'If it is just a play, how can I let my mind be broken fully? How can I let myself suffer fully? It is just a play. For the sake of an artificial thing like a play, would I allow myself to suffer? It is just a play; it is a limited thing. It deserves limited investment. How can I weep so much that my head starts spinning and aching? For the sake of the play, I will not do so much'—which means that there will be no depth in your living. Whatever you do would be just mediocre, half-hearted, not having any warmth in it.

And if you say that what you are doing is real, you will be buffeted by all the ups and downs of life, like a plank upon mighty waves which is being thrown up and then being mercilessly brought down. And you do not know what is happening. You are anchorless, you are listless.

So, do not go by these things that life is a play. Watch the play and remain a witness. And by that I do not mean that life is not a play. I am saying, stop thinking about life and start living. You don't have to make sense of life because life has no sense at all. You do not have to derive any meaning or purpose out of life because it has no meaning or purpose at all.

If you say that life is a play, you have claimed that you have been able to conclude something about your life. Such conclusions are always meaningless, frivolous and painful. Be there, and being there is sufficient.

L: So, if we are sad, we should remain in that state?

AP: Yes, of course.

L: We should not think about it?

AP: No, not at all. All suffering arises from concepts. To use another concept in order to ameliorate suffering is to use poison to kill poison. It may give you some temporary apparition of relief, but it would be destroying your entire system. Somebody is suffering, 'Oh, I am so small, I am so small!' The Guru comes and tells him, 'No, child. You are not small. You are wide. You are infinite. You are Brahm!'

The child was weeping because he was feeling little. Now he is bloated because he is feeling that he is Brahm. What do you think is going to happen next?

L: He is going to be beaten up.

AP: So, don't think about your size at all. You are neither big nor small. If you think you are small, you are in for suffering. If you think you are large, you are in for an even bigger suffering. Those who think that they are not Brahm definitely suffer, and those who think that they are Brahm suffer even more.

That's what the Upanishads very classically say. They say, 'Those who do not know fall in a deep well. And those who know fall in a well, yet deeper.'

Spirituality often proves to be a well that is even deeper than ignorance. Knowledge is a well deeper and more deceptive than ignorance. Be neither ignorant nor knowledgeable.

L: What stops us from being fully immersed?

AP: Time. How do I belong fully if I know that time will take this away? I don't want to get hurt. I am carrying the burden of all the hurt from the past already. Now, I cannot open up. Opening up would mean becoming vulnerable to more hurt. Now, I cannot be immersed. Immersion would mean that I have again brought my armour. Now, again someone can come and assault.

Something may happen next and in anticipation of that which may happen next, you do not allow that which may happen right now.

L: But how do I then convince myself that being hurt the next time is okay?

AP: Because you are already not hurt. It is not about it being okay when you are hurt the next time. The fact is, all these times when you convinced yourself that you are hurt, were you actually hurt? It is just that you had been taught that it is proper to act hurt in such situations. Look at the facts, look at the evidence.

In Indian culture, if a woman hugs somebody—a stranger, another man—in front of the husband, it is possible that the husband may get hurt. In other cultures, it is possible that in front of the man, the wife actually kisses someone else and the man feels no hurt. Is hurt something innate or is it something you have absorbed? You have taught yourself to get hurt. But you actually were never hurt. You are just wearing hurt upon yourself.

Hurt is a cultivated quality. Your essence can never be hurt. How can you hurt the Total? Only the unreal part of you gets hurt and it is anyway quite eager to get hurt. Hurt gives it a chance to act as if it is real. 'You see? I am real! That is why I am in pain.' That is why pain is such a coveted thing. That is why pain is one of the sought-after commodities.

If there is one thing that is a hot seller in the market of human aspirations, it is pain. Look how pained we all are—full of pain. I don't know whether we live fully, but there is one thing that we are always full of—pain. This is the one thing that is never in short supply. Go to anybody and ask them, 'What are your joys?' and they may stare blankly at you. But if you ask them, 'What are your pains?' they will say, 'Now, you sit. It is a long story. Let's first have a cup of tea. Please ensure that you don't run away. It is an epic! How can it finish so fast?'

We need pain in order to justify being what we are, what we have taught ourselves to be, don't we?

L: So, both pain and pleasure are unreal. But why is pain more sought-after than pleasure?

AP: Because pain gives the hope of pleasure, because pleasure is always a hope, and that hope is called pain.

You see, can you feel pain except in comparison with an imagined pleasure? You say that you are deficient in something. How do you know that you are deficient? How do you know that you are deficient except with an imagined fullness?

You have two units of a resource. You say, 'It is so less!' How do you know it is less? Only by comparison with an imagined state in which you have ten units. You define those ten units as pleasure, and these two units are defined as pain. Both of these have been put as quantities by the mind. To go to ten units is to prepare to feel bad when you come down to two. To be at two is to keep crying till you have ten.

When you are at ten, you are shivering in apprehension that you may now fall to two. Look at the conditions of those who have the riches. They are so eager to protect them. The fear that this may go away keeps assaulting them. So, their hope lies in securing what they already have.

And look at those who have two units. Their desperation lies in having only two and then they live in the ambition of one day reaching up to ten. Ten does not give them security. Ten only gives them the additional responsibility of securing the ten that they have now got. They know very well that time can take away the ten units. The ten units do not belong to them; they are just accidental. Something may snatch it away.

So, even if you have ten, you still cannot have pleasure. Whereas, when you were at two, you said that ten will give you pleasure. Having come to ten, you find that ten cannot give you pleasure because the ten is temporary. Now, what do you want to do? You want to secure the ten, and no security is ever permanent. You know that all your attempts to secure something will fail. You cannot secure even your own body—how will you secure your riches? You do not even know whether the next breath would happen, so how do you know whether all your stuff in the bank will still be there the next moment? That is why you keep shivering.

Both pain and pleasure are pain. Both pain and pleasure are suffering. It is not as if spirituality is about moving away from pain. Spirituality is about moving away from both pain and pleasure. And having returned to your innate fullness is the point of Joy. That point where pain and pleasure are just visitors—they come, they go. I live in my house. The house is named Joy.

L: So, pleasure is actually a concept.

AP: Of course!

L: It is a forced concept.

AP: Of course! Pleasure is a forced concept. You know what? One of the biggest instruments of pleasure—you will be surprised to know this—even sex, is also just a concept.

All those things that you associate with pleasure, with pain, with hurt are all concepts that we have been indoctrinated into. Remove those concepts and then show me where is pleasure and where is pain. Then there is just life. Just life—simple, total and joyful.

> " I AM SAYING, STOP THINKING ABOUT LIFE AND START LIVING. YOU DON'T HAVE TO MAKE SENSE OF LIFE BECAUSE LIFE HAS NO SENSE AT ALL. YOU DO NOT HAVE TO DERIVE ANY MEANING OR PURPOSE OUT OF LIFE BECAUSE IT HAS NO MEANING OR PURPOSE AT ALL. "

(Advait BodhSthal, 2016)

19

Guard Your Peace

❝ IF REST IS TRULY DEAR TO YOU, YOU WILL HAVE TO DISCARD
EVERYTHING WHICH IS A SOURCE OF DISQUIET IN YOUR LIFE.
YOU WILL NEED TO LIVE IN PURE LOVE FOR RESTFULNESS. ❞

Listener (L): Truth, Love and Joy is our nature. The scriptures declare that it can be easily realized, we just need to rest and relax. But the mind does not rest. Why is it so difficult to rest? How have we completely forgotten who we are and where our home is?

Acharya Prashant (AP): You want to rest. And the scriptures say you must rest, and they also say rest is facile. And you are asking, 'Why am I unable to rest? Where is my home? Why have I forgotten my address?'

You cannot rest where you are. That would be an impossibility and a tragedy, if at all it happens. Imagine that a person who should have been walking on his legs is being trained to walk on his head, and now the entire body is aching and the head is spinning. And in that same position, the person reads and consults the scriptures, which say, 'Be as you are and relax.' And the fellow says, 'Yes, let me be as I am, and I will relax.' What does the person then decide to do? He decides to remain with his legs in the air and wonder why he is unable to relax.

Rest is easy when you are located in ease. Rest is easy when you are at the right place.

But how difficult is it to invert your geometrical position when you are walking as in a śīrṣāsana (headstand)? How difficult is it? It is easy. But that inversion must take place. If it does not happen, you are seeking rest in a wrong and impossible position. It won't come.

'Be as you are' means, *unbecome*. Unless you unbecome, there is no possibility of touching base with your being. When you talk of being, please see that your becoming has taken you far away from your being. Forget about being the True Self—right now you are not even the child that you were born as. Not even the child is pure, simple and innocent. Even the child is biologically conditioned. And now, you are not even as innocent as the child. Can you see how far you have come? And you want to rest and relax in this very same state? It won't happen, it cannot happen.

If rest is truly dear to you, you will have to discard everything which is a source of disquiet in your life. You will need to live in pure love for restfulness.

You will need to live as someone with a fractured arm. If your arm is fractured and not yet plastered, and if somebody wants to move or dislocate it a little, what do you do? You cry out, you scream, you resist. You are ultra-sensitive, aren't you? You will have to be that sensitive about rest. If that arm is lying somewhere, you want it to remain lying there, don't you? You don't want people to come and fiddle with it. Similar must be your attitude towards peace and rest.

You are extremely touchy, you are extremely sensitive about your arm. You won't tolerate nonsense, would you? You won't tolerate inattention, would you? Somebody just walks past you and casually brushes against your arm. Is that all right?

L: No.

AP: No. They will have to be careful. You say, 'Be careful with me. Don't mess with me, don't disturb, don't touch, stay away. And if you are to deal with me, deal in a way that does not disturb my arm.'

You will have to protect it as the mother protects her womb. If you are a woman, you would understand that. When you are carrying the child within, do you allow the world to mess with you? And if somebody does try to play the fool, you respond ferociously. You are protecting something precious.

That must be your attitude towards rest. That must be your approach towards peace and Truth. They must always be at the centre of your consciousness and at the centre of your mind, your very first priority.

It is with deliberation that I have taken the example of a fractured arm. I could have said, 'See how you protect a flower'; I didn't say that because ours is a pitiable condition. Remember, we said that we have come very far away from our natural innocence. We said that even the child is not very innocent, and we are not even a child.

So, an example steeped in pain and tragedy has to be taken. The example of the fractured arm is apt. It must pain you a lot. Don't try to rest with the fractured arm. Don't try to be casual with it—you are otherwise asking for the impossible. Instead, when the arm is fractured, be vigilant and then slowly, gradually you will come to a point when you don't have to be so guarded anymore.

Right now, be very, very guarded. Guard peace like a lioness guards her cubs. Would you want to mess with a lioness who is with her little cubs? All her cubs are with her, playing and suckling—would you want to indulge in the play? Would you want to go anywhere close and fiddle with them? Would you? The lioness could easily show you that she can be more ferocious than a lion. And the cubs would have a treat.

If you have indeed realized that the precious is possible—I am not even saying near, I am not even saying here or immediate, I am just saying possible. You have just a glimpse of the precious one. And if you are indeed sincere in living with the precious one, then be vigilant. Respect your peace and know that it can be snatched away any time. Know that impossible has become possible for you.

The saints might have told you that rest is your natural state, but come on, look at yourself and look at the world. You really think that a human's natural state is that of peace and rest and Truth and simplicity? Have you seen how little kids fight and feel jealous and lie and steal? Don't they cheat when they are playing with each other? Doesn't that seem to be more natural? That is fate.

We are not born to be Buddhas; we are born to live and die in a rut. It might be your destiny to be liberated, but your fate is to remain mired in muck. It is a strange thing that a human's destiny is to be liberated, but fate doesn't allow that. And that is why humans are forever in conflict. The heart yearns for liberation, and the entire mind-body complex wants to stay in confinement.

So, like millions and billions of others, your fate, too, is to be born a mere mortal, live the ordinary life of a conditioned social mortal, eat, laugh, cry, marry, procreate, get old, get sick and die. That is one's fate. Nobody is above that fate.

The impossible seems to be happening with you. Our fate is to remain engaged and involved with trivia; you seem to be getting a glimpse of the immense. Something unnatural is happening with you, something abnormal is happening with you. If you respect what is happening with you, guard it like a lioness. If you are indeed getting inclined towards inner rest, you are one in a million.

Humans are not born to remain restful. Look at your eyes. Have you ever watched your eyeballs? What are they continuously doing? Are they ever restful? Like your thoughts, they are wandering. Is the mortal one designed to stay restful?

L: No.

AP: But here you are talking about rest. Do you know what a rarity it is to ask for rest? An invaluable rarity. Please treat it as invaluable. Please give it the respect it deserves. Please do not allow it to become the world's toy.

I don't know whether to call you lucky or unlucky. Most people never ever realize that they are in deep, deep trouble. They are so much in trouble that they have lost all sensitivity towards trouble, like a person relaxing in a burning house. It is not as if he or she is not feeling the flames, but they have just gone numb.

Only the chosen ones, the rare ones, only they start sensing that they are losing out on something. Only they sense that they were not born to eat, breathe, shop and die.

Now that this seems to be happening with you, a glimpse of the realization seems to be dawning upon you, you probably are quite unlucky, because now you have an onerous responsibility on your shoulders. And the responsibility is to guard the womb.

Now that the ray of light has probably chosen to enter you, you will have to guard it, nourish it. Let it become your very being. Or you can choose to just let it all slip away. That is easy. Depends on you.

It is not going to be easy. It takes a lot of effort to remain restful. It takes a lot of doing to remain a non-doer.

It is a mischievous paradox. One of God's jokes.

" GUARD PEACE LIKE A LIONESS GUARDS HER CUBS. "

(Nainital, 2018)

20

Peace Is the Desire behind All Desires

❝ BE ACCOUNTABLE TO THE REAL ONE, NOT TO SOCIAL
MORALITY. BE ACCOUNTABLE TO GOD. BE ACCOUNTABLE TO
TRUTH. THERE, IF YOU COMMIT MISTAKES, SEEK FORGIVENESS.
ONLY IN THE EYES OF TRUTH MUST YOU UPHOLD YOURSELF.
YOU HAVE NO OBLIGATION TO BE PROVEN RIGHT IN THE
EYES OF SOCIETY. ❞

Listener (L): How can I be less identified with my body?

Acharya Prashant (AP): You will always be identified. To be identified is to seek completion. The ego sense says 'I exist' and it wants to say, 'I exist as something—X, Y, Z'.

So, the ego will always be identified and attached with something. It will say, 'I am A, I am B, I am C', but it would always need something to call its own.

Now, what is it that you want to call your own? What is it that you want to be closely associated with?

Find the Right One.

When you have found the Right One, you will not feel the need to be associated with the inferior ones, the false ones. Find the Right One to call your own; find the One who will never betray you; find the One that never passes away; find the One you can completely rely upon; find the One that is not an in-between but the Ultimate.

Ultimately, what is it that you want? Ultimately, what is the desire behind all desires? Call that your own; be identified with that. What is it that, which if obtained, would make all further attainments unnecessary? What is it?

L: Completeness, fulfilment, peace.

AP: Identify with that. Instead of asking for disidentification, identify yourselves fully, be dedicated fully, be owned fully, be committed and attached fully. In other words, surrender totally to peace, to completeness. This would mean that not for a moment would you entertain thoughts that talk of incompleteness, not for a moment would you promote within yourself that which calls you limited, petty, afraid, insecure.

The ego needs the right partner; it needs the right bed to sleep on. Give it the right partner, give it a nice resting place. When you have given the ego a nice resting place, it sleeps there like a child and relaxes.

Love peace so much that you would not bear being separated from it even for a moment. Love peace more than your life. Say, 'I am prepared to lay down my life, but I am not prepared to live without peace.' Pay the highest price possible. Be totally identified with peace.

L: It seems very attractive, but isn't it a way to run away?

AP: No, it is not a way to run away. It demands intense action at all times. In fact, it is impossible to escape away in peace. The world is such that it would challenge you, attack you, invite you. You cannot escape. The world is everywhere. You have to stand your ground and really fight. You have to fight for peace.

And you think that if you quit a place, it is some sort of cowardice. Most people are unable to break away from their situations, their workplaces, their home or from their relationships not because they are responsible or committed but because they are afraid. So, quitting or going away is an act of great courage.

In fact, most people who stay put are the ones who lack courage. They keep dying every day but are unable to break away. It requires a Buddha to break away from his kingdom, his wife, his so-called responsibilities, his sons. It requires a Buddha to really go away.

Would you call the Buddha an escapist? Would you call him a coward? No. He was committed to peace, and he said that if the royal palace, the beautiful wife, the kingdom, the respectability, if none of it is giving him peace, he won't take the kingdom. He paid the highest price—that is why he is the Buddha.

Don't you see the people around you, how they are stuck and how they still return to their personal hells every night and go back to the same places every morning? It requires one real courageous person to reject that cycle.

L: It is not so much the fear of not having a place to sleep or food to eat. It is the fear of the society. What will the society say?

AP: That is psychological dependence. We all know that we will not starve, we all know that we will get a shelter. It is just psychological dependence because of which we are identified with people, institutions and relationships. Instead, be identified with peace, be identified with Truth, and then you don't have to be dependent on anybody else. Then you can continue with everybody in peace or break away in peace. Breaking away is not a big deal anymore then.

L: If I am continuing with everybody in a peaceful state, can I also be angry at someone while being in a peaceful state? Can the peaceful state continue while I am also being angry?

AP: The peaceful state is always there. Had that peaceful state not been there, anger will not appear as anger.

L: It appears as anger to others, so they may interpret it as anger. But maybe it is not really anger.

AP: Others will know anger only as a behavioural pattern. They will see the red face or shouting. They will call it anger. Let's keep others aside for a while. Let's look at our own perception of anger.

How do you know that you are angry? How do you know that it is a special state? How do you know that it is not routine? Why do you pick up the topic of anger to discuss here? It is because you very well know that anger is not natural and peace is natural. Otherwise, why would you discuss anger as a problem?

There is something within you which knows that anger is alien and artificial, and that something is peace. Even in the moment of deepest anger you are never really satisfied with being angry, you are never comfortable with anger. Don't you see how your body rebels against anger? If you are angry for too long, your body will crumble, you may get a heart attack. If you are angry for too long your mind will crumble. So, even the body-mind complex knows that anger is not your natural state, which means that even the body-mind complex knows that peace is the natural state.

So, you are already at peace even in anger. It is peace that calls anger as anger.

L: Exactly. Because sometimes the anger is only on the surface, like a wave, but when seen from deep inside, it does not seem as anger.

AP: Seen by?

L: By myself.

AP: Yes, that's all right. Wonderful!

L: Sometimes other people express some anger towards you, but there is no judgment because there is nobody to receive this anger, really. But at the same time, you feel that you have to protect yourself in a certain way because someone can be aggressive and physically violent.

AP: You can even be judgemental. There is nothing wrong with being judgemental. If being judgemental means knowing the false as false, then being judgemental is quite important.

L: I call it discernment.

AP: Yes, you can call it discernment. Often in the name of not being judgemental, even discernment is quelled. Judge, but judge with discernment. Judge, but judge in peace. Judge, but judge rightly.

Existence does not offer any obligations to behave in particular ways. All that existence says is, live in your essential nature; it does not say behave in particular ways. An elephant behaves in a way elephants do, tigers behave differently, and fish behave differently. You, too, can behave differently, but that difference is not a particular pattern. The mind has its various colours, various swings and moods that keep varying, so the kind of behaviour you exhibit is not an object to be ratified as right or wrong.

You have all the right to shout at someone. You have all the right to even hit them. You have as much right to hit someone as you have the right to embrace someone. But whatever you do, do it honestly.

Do it rightly. Do not perform from a point of ambition, or from a point of fear or greed.

L: So, we should be authentic. Even in anger, be authentic. So, I should say, 'I am angry because of your comportment, not because of fear. And I want to let you know that this is the limit that you should not cross. I have to protect myself.'

AP: And having done that there is no need of guilt at all. Not at all!

Be accountable to the Real One, not to social morality. Be accountable to God. Be accountable to Truth. There, if you commit mistakes, seek forgiveness. Only in the eyes of Truth must you uphold yourself. You have no obligation to be proven right in the eyes of the society.

> " LOVE PEACE SO MUCH THAT YOU WOULD NOT BEAR BEING SEPARATED FROM IT EVEN FOR A MOMENT. LOVE PEACE MORE THAN YOUR LIFE. "

(Rishikesh, 2016)

21

Consuming Happiness versus Cultivating Happiness

> " ALL GOOD THINGS CAN BE UTILIZED BY YOU IN TWO
> WAYS: BECAUSE THEY ARE GOOD, THEY CAN BE INSTANTLY
> CONSUMED; OR BECAUSE THEY ARE GOOD, THEY CAN BE
> FURTHER CULTIVATED. "

Listener: Sir, what does it mean to enjoy happiness in full freedom? Is it the conditioned mind of the common man that stops him from cultivating and preserving happiness? How can the common man grow from being a consumer of happiness to a cultivator?

Acharya Prashant: Happiness is a glimpse, a glimpse of the absence of suffering. That is why we like happiness. That is why everybody says, 'I want to be happy.'

Why do we say we want to be happy? Because our default state is of suffering. And humans suffer much more than any other being in the world. No being is capable of suffering as much as humans are. A human is a suffering animal. Other creatures have pain but not so much suffering. To suffer you require a consciousness with depth. Humans have it; other beings have it only in a limited manner.

You could say that every person is born suffering and every person is born to suffer. The physical apparatus has been arranged so as to ensure that a person suffers. Trapped in this body, you want great things to happen to you, so you suffer. Confined to a little stretch of time, a little expanse of space, you want everything to be limitless, hence you suffer. Your consciousness wants to militate against everything that your body has arranged for you. It is a very peculiar situation. You could call it tragic.

That which your consciousness wants is not at all what your body is configured to give you. The body gives you one thing, and what consciousness wants is not merely different but dimensionally different, so humans suffer. Because we suffer, we are always hungry for happiness. That is why in the world of Homo sapiens, happiness is such a precious commodity. Everybody wants it without exception.

What do you want?

'Happiness! I want to be happy!'

Happiness sells. It doesn't matter what is being sold and where. If you just probe a little, you will find that it is happiness which is being sold. Happiness is valuable for human beings because they are suffering. So far so good—but now there is a glitch.

The normal, common happiness, as we get it, is just a by-product of suffering. Those who have known have said that our so-called happiness is just another name for sadness or suffering. It cannot come without sadness; it either comes along with sadness or as a product of sadness. And it is not merely preceded by sadness, it is also succeeded by sadness. And when sadness reaches some kind of a crest, the curve takes an inflection and there is a little happiness, and just as you are consuming your happiness, what is being cooked for you? Sadness again.

So, the happiness that we get is just a glimpse. It is a valuable glimpse even if it lasts for a limited time; it still tells us that freedom from suffering is possible. It is a thirty-second trailer to a three-hour movie. The thing is that trailers do not last long and trailers are free—for a movie you have to pay your way in.

Happiness comes to you so that you become interested, you become inquisitive, your longing gains depth and you start seeking permanent happiness. You say, 'Oh! What was given to me was so ephemeral—thirty seconds, that is all. It was good, but I want the real thing, I want something which will last. And thank you for giving this little happiness to me, it whetted my appetite. Now I want deeper happiness.' That is called cultivation of happiness.

What is consumption of happiness? Thirty seconds were given to you and you ate them up. 'The seeds were given to me, and what did I do with them? I consumed them.' This is consumption of happiness. That is what most people do. Seeds were given to you, there was some potential, but you consumed the seeds.

And then there is another one who starts loving the taste. That person says, 'I just had a few seeds, and if these seeds are so delicious, I want them to become my life. I do not just want to gobble them up; I will sow them, I will let them strike roots deep into the earth, my inner earth. I will let them become full-fledged trees for myself.'

This cultivation of happiness is called, in classic parlance, the pursuit of Joy or Ananda. The consumption of happiness is called bhoga or consumption of sukha. When sukha and bhoga go together, happiness is consumed. However, Ananda is cultivated. You could call this cultivation sadhana (spiritual practice). With sukha, no sadhana is needed. For Ananda, sadhana is definitely needed.

To make things clearer, you could say that our normal happiness is ephemeral and dualistic—dualistic because it is preceded and succeeded by sadness—and great happiness is permanent and non-dual, non-dual because it is total freedom from suffering. It is freedom not merely from sadness but also from superficial happiness.

Real happiness, which is Joy or Ananda, is not merely freedom from sadness but also from superficial happiness. Ananda means that now you are free from both sukha and dukha. And that is called cultivation of happiness.

If you are the common man, what will you do with the seeds that are given to you? You will consume them for instant gratification. But if you have something large, a bit expansive within you, you will be patient. You will say that you are prepared to work your way through to deeper happiness and you will use the seeds; you will use the trailer to reach a place far deeper.

So, there is this three-day camp (referring to the conversation sessions). What is this? These are just seeds. You may, as most people do, just consume these seeds, let out a loud burp and go home. 'The teacher came and served us some delicious seeds. We put some sauce on them, some pepper, some seasoning and consumed them. The teacher is so wonderful, he comes every six months with his bag full of seeds, and what do we do? Seeds are delectable. Who can refuse them?'

And there will be the one odd person who will say, 'If the seeds are great, I don't want the matter to end here. I will sow them and I will raise an entire crop. Thank you to the visitor for introducing me to the taste and showing me the possibility, but now the onus is on me. I will take things ahead from here.'

All good things can be utilized by you in two ways: because they are good, they can be instantly consumed; or, because they are good, they can be further cultivated.

It all depends on how much you love yourself.

“ REAL HAPPINESS, WHICH IS JOY OR ANANDA, IS NOT MERELY
FREEDOM FROM SADNESS BUT ALSO FROM SUPERFICIAL
HAPPINESS. ANANDA MEANS THAT NOW YOU ARE FREE FROM
BOTH SUKHA AND DUKHA. AND THAT IS CALLED CULTIVATION
OF HAPPINESS. ”

(Bengaluru, 2019)

135

22

The Great Joy of Choicelessness

> " A THOUSAND THINGS ARE IMPORTANT TO US BECAUSE WE
> ARE A THOUSAND PEOPLE INSIDE. WE ARE NOT ONE. AND
> BEING A HOUSAND INSIDE, HAVING A CROWD WITHIN IS SUCH
> A PAIN, IS IT NOT? "

Listener: When I was studying J. Krishnamurti I saw a statement of his which implied that when one has options, choices, then one is not free. But earlier, I used to think that when I have choices I am free. Now as I am listening to Vedanta from you, it is signalling the same thing: when we are choiceless then we have freedom. Can you please explain the relationship between choicelessness and freedom?

Acharya Prashant: Isn't there great joy in being choiceless? You don't have to struggle. You don't have to be torn. You don't have to keep brooding over this and that. Life becomes so easy.

'There might be a thousand things I do not see; I see only the one thing which is the Truth, which is related to my identity of being Truthful. I see just that.' It makes life so easy. Once you do not have the pull of a thousand choices acting upon you, think of the liberation you would get. Else everything in the world is an opportunity, and nothing in the world suffices.

Where does that put you? Everything is an opportunity and no choice is good enough to be the final one—where does that put you? A rolling stone wandering from here to there, and wandering in frustration, wandering in angst because whatever you have done has not been good enough. Why is it not good enough? Not because the choice was wrong but because the choice *existed*.

If you want to be sure of something being good for you, being right for you, just see whether there are competing choices. One mark of the real thing is that it affords no competition; you would have nothing else in mind. People may come and threaten you, somebody may come and lure you; you will say, 'No, but this is the one way I know. I know not in the sense of habit but in the sense of realization. You are offering me a thousand diverse roads to travel; I don't even see them. They exist only for the ones who are tempted by them. I don't even see them.'

Remember, even knowledge is not objective. If you have knowledge of something, it is because that thing first of all meant something to you; otherwise you won't even have knowledge. And knowledge can be such a burden; you know so many things and they are all going around in the head.

'I don't even know. Why don't I know? Because I don't need to know! The deal is done. Why do you need to have so many options? It is not that I am the proverbial frog in the well; it is just that I know very, very clearly.' The frog in the well has no choices out of ignorance, and spiritual choicelessness is out of total realization. 'I have known and I have reached a finality. Therefore, I am not considering options at all.'

And that is the summit of life. That is where you want to reach. That is freedom from experiences. Otherwise, one will remain a sucker for experiences all his life. 'I want to do this, next I want to do that, next I want to do that, and that, and that, and that!'

Does the liberated man not do diverse and various things? He does, but he does not do them to satiate himself. He does everything being satiated, not wanting to be satiated. Do you get the difference? 'I already have contentment. Now, with my contentment I want to go there, reach there, attain this, discover that.'

What is the difference, then? The difference is, if you are going to a place to attain contentment, then success and failure will weigh too heavily on you because just too much is at stake. You need to succeed. Contentment is at stake. So much is at stake. Contentment is everything. 'I need to succeed, I need to succeed!' And if you need to succeed you cannot play the game in freedom. When you are desperate for success, you are frozen.

Whereas, when you are already content and you want to achieve something, then you are actually taking it just like a game. And when you are taking it just like a game there is so much joy, so much agility, so much manoeuvrability. There are just so many degrees of freedom that you get—why? Because now you are not afraid of failure. 'I am not afraid of failure because I have already succeeded. I am entering the game and I am already a winner. I am a winner even before the game starts. Now I will play with abandon.' Now there would be a certain freedom from botheration. 'I will be carefree.'

And those who are too careful in life will know the importance of the word 'carefree'. How many of you are bogged down by care in your life? A lot of us, right? We will give our right hand to be carefree. Care is thought, care is concern, care is just too much weight on the top floor. What happens to any structure that is top-heavy? Would you want to ride a top-heavy car?

We live very top-heavy lives. Centre of gravity is almost here (*pointing at the head*). When you are already content then the centre of gravity is where it should be, not here *(pointing at the head)* but here *(pointing to the chest)*.

Many young people here and the youth especially relish choices. If you are being forced into doing something, then it is an improvement to have choices. You are being forced into marriage, your parents have seen a man for you, and they are saying, 'Go wed this one. No choice, this one is final!' In such a situation it is all right to ask for a choice. But how about a situation where you have some forty-one boyfriends all at once? Are you related to even one of them? Is there any love anywhere? Now you know what choicelessness means.

Choices are good to have only when you are being forced into one loveless channel. When somebody is exercising his tyranny upon you, your will, your opinion doesn't matter. In such a situation it is a better thing, an improvement to have choices. But then, you, the youth of today, are hardly subjected to such behaviour by circumstances or your family. I don't suppose today's parents chase their kids with an ultimatum of one final choice. Parents don't do that. They hardly make decisions for their kids today, at least not in urban areas.

Instead the malice has appended itself. We have started believing that diversity in choices is a symbol or metric of our empowerment. We feel that the more choices we have, the more empowered we are. The truth is just the opposite.

Let choices exist externally. When they exist just outside of you they are not even choices, they are just things. Internally there should be not choices but clarity, and where there is clarity you do not see too many things; you see just one thing. Therefore, a measure of your mental health is: Do you keep weighing options? Do too many things keep going around in your head? Are you frequently indecisive about what to pick?

One mark of a realized man is that his decisions come in a flash, once he has all the data that is. If decisions require data, he will take time to gather data. Once the facts are in front of him the decision does not take time. He does not need to appoint an inner committee to ponder. He will ask for data and when the data is there, he says, 'Now, this is it, done!' because he is not being internally ruled by competing desires. If he is desirous, he is desirous of just the Truth. He does not have multiple desires in ten different directions.

Remember that each of the choices that appeal to you correspond to a particular desire within you. I like him, I also like him, and I also like him, and all three of them are saying something. One is saying, 'It is my birthday today, let's spend the evening together'; the other is saying, 'I am down today, come and console me'; and yet another is saying, 'Well, I have got some fantastic things: there is this special bundle of books. Come, let's read together!' They are all related to me through competing desires. There is the desire within me to be a big brother to someone; there is a desire within me to be knowledgeable; there is a desire within me to have fun. And none of these three desires is the desire for Truth.

Now, what happens? The desire for fun says, 'There is the birthday party, go there', so this choice becomes appealing. Do you see why this choice matters to me? Because I have a particular desire that corresponds to this choice. I am fragmented within and the thousand parts within me become the thousand choices outside of me. As there is a desire for fun, so there is a desire to gain knowledge. So, this fellow who says 'come, let's read together' becomes significant to me. And I also have the desire to be moralistic, to be big brotherly, to have the upper hand in the emotional sense, so the third option becomes meaningful to me. He is saying, 'Oh, I am down, please come. Your company will lift my mood!' It is a great opportunity to prove that I can be a good counsellor, that I know emotional management better than this chap.

A thousand things are important to us because we are a thousand people inside. We are not one. And being a thousand inside, having a crowd within is such a pain, is it not? You are nowhere. None of those thousand is you actually, and each of those thousand has a certain inclination. One of them wants dosa, the other one wants to travel to Mars. Now, how do these two become compatible? One is always crying, 'Dosa, dosa with spicy sambar!'; the next one is thinking of cryogenic engines. Now, how does the cryogenic engine find any relationship with sambar? One within you is a political animal deeply interested in politics; one within you is a gardener; one loves verses and bhajans from saints. Now, is it possible to cultivate all of these at the same time? Political cunningness and saintly innocence?

But we manage to do that, don't we? So many of us are sitting here, and it is the fifth day today, and in between a lot of us would have found time to exercise our political imagination. So many things are happening in politics every day. And having read the Upanishads, we go back and see what the prime minister is doing and how he is being encircled by the opposition and such things. How do we manage to have these two concurrently?

I am not saying one of them has to be dropped. I am saying all the relationships that we have with the world must come from a single centre. Your political opinion has to have a consonance with your Upanishadic knowledge. Else you are making them sit in two different rooms in your psyche, and this fragmentation will not let you breathe. Externally you may diversify your portfolio, but in the inner world it has to be just the opposite. There should be one and *only* one, and the one you have you have to be absolutely invested in it. Hundred percent investment in just the One. If you diversify your portfolio inside, you are ruined.

Put all your inner capital in Truth incorporated. Externally you will then have all the freedom to invest at whatever place you like. And then you will always also have the guts to invest in outrageous ventures. Miracles can happen. You may also lose whatever you have invested, but then you are not afraid of losing. You are not even dying to get miracles. You can play. Think of it. Winning and losing come much later.

The tragedy is that most of us cannot even play. Our problem is not that we lose so much; our problem is that we do not even play. What is worse, losing or not even playing? When you prepare too much to play, you cannot play. When you have the apparatus which is put meticulously in preparation of the play to secure the play, then you cannot play. Then all that you are doing is the arrangement.

'I am arranging, and I am arranging with such precision that all my energy has gone into the arrangement. The real thing never happens. I have the security agencies in place. I have brought forty thousand fire extinguishers here. I have done everything to prepare for the party. I have informed the police. There is all the security and the bandobast. Five different agencies are video graphing the event. I went around and commissioned twenty different caterers'—so much choice, right? 'Twenty different caterers I commissioned! I spent a lot of time on it. I spent my entire life commissioning the security agencies, the photographer, the videographer, the caterer, the event manager. But I forgot one little thing—the party itself.

'Everything has been neatly arranged for the party. I wanted to have backups. You know, if plan A fails, plan B has to be there, then C; then after Z, there is ZA, ZB, ZC and so on.' All those backups and choices and options, they all have to be in place.

When you care for these things so much, then care is the only thing that you care for. Then care is what you live for; the party is gone. Everything is in place except the party. Forty thousand fire extinguishers and no fire. One thousand security guards but with nothing precious enough to secure. Hurts, doesn't it?

You built a mansion and it is fiercely guarded. The only little problem is that there is nothing worthy of being secured or guarded there. But the guards are all top-class, you can call them commandos. It is an elite arrangement—but it is a void inside. What are you securing?

'No, no I have made all the arrangements, you see! Even if an intruder breaches the first ring of security, then there is a second ring, and then there is this, then there is that, and then there is an automated alarm that goes off and para commandos from Jupiter land straight away!' Layers, buffers, backups, options, all defending nothing, nothing at all. Like a jewellery case being used to deliver trash, it had layers of packaging.

That is the thing with choices. You have so many choices but the chooser is in such a bad state. What do you want to care more for, the choices or the chooser? Care for the chooser and the choices will fall in place.

Who is the chooser? We are the chooser. Care for who you are within. All choices are *to* you, all choices are *for* you. You change and the choices that are visible to you will change. So many things that used to present themselves will no longer present themselves. You will just forget that choice. If something does not appeal to you, would you still call it a choice? It is not even an option, it is just a thing now because it doesn't appeal. Why does it not appeal anymore? Because you are no longer the person you were.

Care for the chooser. With the chooser remaining the same, having a plethora of choices is just self-deception. If you remain the same, none of your choices are going to help you. And we cultivate so many choices in the hope that at least one of them will be of some help. None of those choices will help you because you are looking in the wrong direction, you are looking at things. You have to look at the chooser, at yourself.

> **❝ IF YOU WANT TO BE SURE OF SOMETHING BEING GOOD FOR YOU, BEING RIGHT FOR YOU, JUST SEE WHETHER THERE ARE COMPETING CHOICES. ONE MARK OF THE REAL THING IS THAT IT AFFORDS NO COMPETITION. ❞**

(Advait BodhSthal, 2021)

23

The Joy of Being Drenched in Love

> **Love is when you start seeing the deep desire beneath all your superficial desires. Love is when you start seeing what you are really thirsty for.**

कबीर बादल प्रेम का, हम परि बरसा आइ ।
अंतरि भीगी आतमा, हरी भई बनराइ ॥

Love clouds have gathered, they are raining down on me,
My entire soul is soaked in it, all around there is greenery.

~Saint Kabir

Listener (L): Could you elaborate on what Saint Kabir implies by being drenched in love?

Acharya Prashant (AP): Just sing what Kabir Sahib is saying. Just sing. I may keep trying for two hours, but I will just not be able to go beyond Kabir Sahib. I won't be able to say in two hours what he has said in these two lines. So, do not try to understand him through me; understand him through him. Just sing. It is anyway so lucid and self-explanatory, is it not?

Without love there is merely dryness.

Without love there is merely logic.

Machines work on logic, especially computing machines. And the thing with humans is that at least half of their brain works on logic. Without love there is just logic, and it is extremely dry. Humans cannot live by logic alone; humans cannot live by arguments alone. In fact, not only are both logic and love important, but if one of the two has to be chosen, it would be the one that is more fundamental of the two—love.

Why is love more fundamental? Because when you say that there is yearning of the mind for the Truth called love, and then there is the bodily resistance to it called vṛtti (tendencies) and Prakriti (physical nature), you have to remember that not only the yearning of the mind towards love is love but the resistance of Prakriti to love is also love.

Now, that sounds paradoxical. We say we are easily split into two: one part that unreasonably wants to merge into something greater, relax into sleep, and then there is another logical part which wants continuation and security. What I am saying is, the unreasonable part is surely pulsating with love, but even the reasonable part, even the logical part is driven by nothing but love, though indirectly. Even when you resist love, it is because of love; it is just that the resisting of love is misguided.

Love is more fundamental.

You rush towards dissolution. There are moments in your life, there are special incidents when you just want to sacrifice everything for something holy, something very lovely, something very precious. And then there is the usual instinct of self-preservation. This instinct towards self -preservation says, 'Hold on, don't die, don't dissolve, don't surrender, just continue!'

You must ask, why does even the instinct for self-preservation exist? You want to continue in time so that at the end of time you might meet your beloved. Something in you says, 'I want to jump out of the stream of time right now. I want the inner clock to stop right now.' And the logical part of you says, 'Be a little considerate. Use the intellect. Create a better future. Tomorrow, you will get what you so desperately want.'

So, even the logical part is looking for the same thing that the so-called illogical part wants. Both want the same thing; one wants it right now, the other wants it in the future. So, obviously, both are driven by love. One is driven by crazy love, the other is driven by love tempered with and modified by logic.

Our life is nothing but an interplay of these two instincts. These two instincts are sometimes called as Yin and Yang, sometimes Purusha and Prakriti, sometimes Apollonian and Dionysian. But these two—thesis and anti-thesis—keep shaping our life.

There was just dryness, and now sap is running through the veins of the trees. There is greenery. Something within has just been showered with ambrosia. I see a juicy fruit appearing. I see blood running through the veins.

Kabir Sahib is first and foremost a poet of love. But that is such a stupid thing to say because you cannot be a poet of understanding. All poetry is just love, and therefore all great saints have been poets, irrespective of whether they wrote in prose or verse. You don't make it happen; it rains upon you. You cannot compel or guide or instruct a cloud to bless you with showers, or can you? All you can do is to not run indoors when it rains.

'Kabir badal Prem ka, ham par barsa aaye' (Love clouds have gathered, they are raining down on me).

Do here what Kabir Sahib is lovingly singing about. When the cloud comes, he remains available to be drenched in rain. Otherwise, we all have umbrellas to avoid getting wet. And as technology evolves, we will have even better means to avoid getting wet.

'I didn't allow the clouds to come, it just happened with me. Who is the One who does this to me? What does the One want? Does the One want anything? Maybe the One is just responding to my want. It rained upon me, and the entire world appears green now!'

What is going on? Did Kabir Sahib say the cloud of love rained upon the entire world? 'Kabir badal Prem ka, ham par barsa aaye'— or did he say 'jag par barsa aaye' (raining down on the world)? Where did it rain? It rained upon him. And what has turned green? The world has turned green. That is strange. It is raining here, and greenery is sprouting there. What nonsense!

Oh, it is just love. Nonsense is too long a word, eight characters. Cut that by half. Instead of saying 'nonsense', say 'love'. Four units are sufficient. And in Kabir's language, it is not even four, it is dhaai (two-and-a-half)!

Something has happened to you and the world has changed. Now that you are in love, you cannot look at the world the same way you used to look at it. This again contains a lot of revelations in its own simple, understated way.

Usually, our love is about one special thing or person. So even if you say that you see greenery somewhere, that greenery commonly refers to just a man or a woman. So, you are in love, she is your hariyaali (greenery). That is how you colloquially put it in Hindi, don't you?

But Kabir Sahib is saying, 'Hari bhayi banraaye. The entire jungle has turned green. I see greenery not merely in one tree but in the entire jungle.' That is the difference between common love and Kabir's love. In your love, there is just one green tree. In Kabir's love, the entire world has turned green, there is nothing dry anywhere anymore. What does it mean?

Love is a great, great pain. It is not without reason that Kabir Sahib is saying, 'Kabir badal Prem ka, ham par barsa aaye.' Do you know why he uses the troupe of clouds and water and rain? Because love burns, love hurts. Love is nothing but the realization of separation.

In Kabir's love, because you become very, very sensitive to your own yearning for the Truth, you also start seeing how everything in the universe desperately wants just that same Beloved as you. You hardly see a difference between yourself and others. What is the difference between you and you *(pointing at different persons)*? How do you say we are different? If the two of you have exactly identical desires, would you still say we two are different?

Difference implies difference in desires. And the difference in desires is so easily visible; it is right there for everyone to see. You want something he does not want, and he wants something only he wants. He wants to go back to a particular house that is only his, you will get up and look for a pair of slippers that belong only to you. When you want to drink water, you want to drink it for yourself, don't you? You are thirsty, water is your particular, personal desire.

Love is when you start seeing the deep desire beneath all your superficial desires. Love is when you start seeing what you are really, really thirsty for. Superficially, the desires of different people are different. Deeply, we all share one desire.

So, what happens in love? In love, two things are happening simultaneously: One, you have come in contact with your deep self that wants union with the Beloved; two, you have seen that this is what all people want. There is nobody who does not want deeply the same thing as you do. Superficially, one wants black and the other one wants white; deeply, both of them want only satisfaction.

Now the world is not full of strangers. When there are just strangers, there is dryness. If you are with a group of strangers, is it a very juicy situation? Not really. However, when you are with people you call as your own, the juice flows freely. A college reunion, and beer flows freely. 'I am with people who are my own.'

The true lover starts seeing that everybody is exactly like himself or herself. 'So not only are all these people my own—they *are* me. They are not strangers; they are not even my own—they are identical to me. And if they are identical to me, how can there be dryness? You are not only my brother; you are me. Forget about being a stranger; you are not even my sibling, you are not even my mirror image—you are me. Those eyes are searching for just the same thing as these eyes.'

There is nothing else that anybody's eyes are looking for. It doesn't matter what the object of our perception is; we are searching for the same thing. Now, are you with aliens, are you with foreigners? You are not even with family. You are with yourself. That is love.

So, I said love means two things. Love, firstly, means total dedication towards the Beloved, and secondly, total disidentification with the world. But first of all, you need total disidentification with the world because unless you are totally disidentified with the world, how will you identify with God?

And that is why saints have so much compassion for the world. Now, can you relate these two things? Saints have great love for God; but, at the same time, we have seen saints lay down their life for the sake of the world. If Jesus is the son of God and Jesus loves God much more than anything or anybody else, what is Jesus doing among men and women of this world? What is the primary concern of Jesus?

L: God.

AP: The love of God. That is what he principally wants, right? Does Jesus say, 'I am the son of this world'? He says, 'No, even my mortal mother is a virgin. How can I be the son of this world? I belong to my Father.' And if Jesus belongs to his Father, why is he so laboriously, so painstakingly working for the people of this world?

That is the thing about love. These are the twin features of love. Because you love God so much, you also see that all others love God equally; it is just that they are a bit deluded. In spite of loving God so much, they do not know how deeply they love. It is the stream which must be flowing towards the ocean and instead it starts getting lost in some lands and quagmires and various places.

And therefore, the saints work tirelessly for the world because they know that 'You are me. Therefore, by working for you, I am actually working for myself. Antar bheegi Aatma, hari bhayi banraaye. Me, me everywhere. I am with my own people. It feels great. And therefore, it also implies that I cannot go to God alone. Because if you are me, how can I go there alone? I will have to take you along.'

Now, that explains why saints keep singing for the world all their life. They know fully well that they cannot go there alone.

'He is me, she is me. He is me, she is me. How can I take the flight alone?'

> **IN LOVE, TWO THINGS ARE HAPPENING SIMULTANEOUSLY: ONE, YOU HAVE COME IN CONTACT WITH YOUR DEEP SELF THAT WANTS UNION WITH THE BELOVED; TWO, YOU HAVE SEEN THAT THIS IS WHAT ALL PEOPLE WANT.**

(Jaipur, 2018)

24

In the Middle of Your Wounds, Celebrate

> **❝** WHEN YOU ARE IN A MIDDLE OF A VERY, VERY SERIOUS BATTLE, IT IS THE RIGHT TIME NOT TO TAKE YOUR CONDITION TOO SERIOUSLY. **❞**

Listener (L): Sir, I read some couplets by Saint Kabir. He wants to become one with God or Truth so much, but he is pained that he is unable to do that. At times, I believe this is the only thing left for me to do. But other times I feel I need to pause, just for an hour or so. How can I be so strongly devoted at one moment and not wanting it at all the next?

Acharya Prashant (AP): One lives in a house which is disorderly and filthy, and the lover, the beloved is expected and he might knock any moment. One is busy cleaning up, but there is just too much to clean. At the same time, one recognizes that only a very clean house befits the beloved. If the house is filthy, it becomes useless, not worthy of entertaining the guest. So, one is trying his best to clean the house. All else is done, only the cleaning up remains, so one is hurrying up. But wherever one goes, only filth and garbage can be found.

At this time, two opposing forces act on the mind. One says, 'Hurry up, display more energy! The date is all set, what you have wanted for ages is at the doorstep. He is coming! He is coming!' You can almost hear the footsteps, and there is this trivial and yet significant task still remaining. It is such a trivial thing and yet such a great hindrance. What if the beloved comes and goes back? What if he says the house doesn't deserve his presence?

So one hurries up. And in hurrying up, in doing the best, in tirelessly striving to clean up, she gets tired and annoyed. Is the annoyance against the beloved or against the filth?

L: The filth.

AP: Ha! You are annoyed not against God, not against Truth, but against your own filth. You desperately want the Beloved in the house, but the house is in such a mess.

And God cannot be called somewhere else; you cannot meet Him in a restaurant. You have to call Him to your very house. He won't accept foreign, alien, artificial places. He says, 'Show me where you live, and if that place befits me, I will be seated there. And if it doesn't, you have lost me.'

You will have to keep hurrying. You will have to keep washing. You might meet Him any time now, and you must meet Him pristinely clean, not even one stain. You must look somewhat like Him for Him to embrace you.

And if you are annoyed, irritated or tired, please know that God is not responsible for your tiredness. It is the huge amount of dirt accumulated since centuries that is tiring you. It is quite a challenge, this cleaning up. The house is large, and it has not been cleaned since a long time. Heaps of rubbish are emerging from unexpected places.

You didn't even know that such garbage existed. You are surprised: 'I was living with this for so long, and now that I have a mop in my hand and a scrubber, mountains of nonsense are showing up!'

It is all right to be irritated. Be more irritated and be quickly irritated. Be done with this—the irritation, the annoyance, the mopping, the drying.

L: Use the annoyance to speed things up?

AP: Yes! Who wants to live in an annoyed state? Get over it, go past it. And remember, the annoyance is good news; in some ways it is auspicious. It shows that the dirt is being uncovered—the dirt which had been safely hidden lying, rotting beneath the carpet is now shown the light of the day. The air has become heavy, there is dirt all over, but that means the cleaning process is effective. That is good news. Look a little deeper—you will find reasons for celebration.

In the middle of annoyance, celebrate. So the moment of celebration comes early. If you are cheerful while preparing the house for the Beloved, chances are the meeting will happen earlier than expected, and the meeting will be more successful.

What if the Beloved comes and finds you with a broom in your hand, cursing and abusing all and sundry? You open the door covered in dirt, with a broom in one hand and mop in the other. You curse the Beloved as well. The house, too, has not yet been prepared. He looks at the house and says, 'Lady, are we to meet here? Better luck and better house next time!'

Sing a little, dance a little in the middle of cleaning up, like the proverbial washerwoman who hums a sweet little tune. What is she dealing with? Filth, and yet she is humming. It is a meaningless song, nothing of great depth, yet the act of singing itself is a vindication.

When you are fighting for the Truth, you have to keep singing in the middle of the fight. Fighting is heavy, full of wounds. It is very important to keep humming and singing, joking a little about your blood-stained condition.

When you are in a middle of a very, very serious battle, it is the right time not to take your condition too seriously.

L: Sir, the cricketer Virender Sehwag used to hum in the middle of the games.

AP: It has to be done anyway. Why do it crying when it could be done singing? You know very well that you have come just too far to go back. You cannot take a U-turn and go back. You have left all too far behind, so you are in it for good. So, why be irritated, why be depressed? If one has to go through it, why not go through it cheerfully?

This struggle will give you enough reasons to feel depressed, defeated, dejected. In those moments, sing, hum, throw a joke at yourself. I assure you that if you are just a fighter and not a singer, you cannot keep fighting for too long. The fighter must be a singer as well.

That is why most of the great saints were also poets. It is not a coincidence that they talked in verse. Why did Kabir sing? Why did Bulleh Shah sing? Why did the Upanishads sing? Why did the Gita sing? Why did the Quran sing? These are all songs.

The warrior is the one most qualified to sing. In fact, if you are not a warrior, your songs will be hollow. The greatest of songs have arisen from the depths of suffering. If you have not known suffering, there will be no beauty in your song.

A poet has said:

'Viyogi hoga pehla kavi, aah se upja hoga gyaan' (The first poet must have been someone estranged from the beloved, and the first songs must have emerged from the poet's sighs).

'Nikal ke aankhon se chup chaap, bahi hogi kavita anjaan' (And the first poem must have silently flowed down from the poet's eyes).

> **If you are just a fighter and not a singer, you cannot keep fighting for too long. The fighter must be a singer as well. The warrior is the one most qualified to sing. In fact, if you are not a warrior, your songs will be hollow.**

(Rishikesh, 2016)

25

Go Naked, and Dance

> **BE COMFORTABLE WITH NOT KNOWING AND WITH CHANGES OF ALL KINDS. DON'T LIVE BY IDEAS, DON'T LIVE BY ANYTHING; JUST LIVE.**

The soul, like the moon,
Is now, and always new again.
And I have seen the ocean
Continuously creating.
Since I scoured my mind
And my body, I too, Lalla,
Am new, each moment new.
My teacher told me one thing,
Live in the soul.
When that was so,
I began to go naked,
And dance.

~Saint Lalleshwari

Listener: Sir, please explain the meaning of this verse by Saint Lalleshwari.

Acharya Prashant: The truth is that the soul is not something that can be grasped. And when it exhibits itself and manifests itself, you can grasp it. But whatever you grasp will change the next moment, so you are beaten again.

For instance, you look at the moon and it is beautiful. What do you like about the moon? The moonlight. Does the moon hold any attraction without the moonlight? The moon and the moonlight are one, but do you know the source of the moonlight?

When there is moonlight, its source is rarely present. Rarely do you see them together. But you may say that although we do not see them together, we do see the sun at other times, so we know the source of the moonlight and we are able to perceive it.

We are able to perceive the sun, but do you really know the source of sunlight? To know the source of sunlight you will have to know the source of the light in your own eyes. Is there any sunlight without your eyes? Is there any sunlight without a perceiving eye? Finally, to know the source of the light in your own eyes, you will have to know the source of consciousness.

Now, consciousness cannot go into its own source because when you say that you want to know the source of consciousness, it is your consciousness that is saying that it wants to know its own source. Consciousness is always directed outwards; it is not designed to travel within. So, it will never know where it is sprouting from.

So, first of all, as far as the moon is concerned, you will never really know where that charming moonlight is coming from. For that, you will need to know your own source, you will need to know your own soul.

But we may still say, 'Why does it matter where the moonlight is really coming from? Is the moon not sufficient? Why do we need to dig deep?' The moon is there, and one loves the moon. One is not interested in philosophical or metaphysical questions like the source of the moonlight. One says, 'I just want to live in the present. I just want to live in that which is obvious, that is, which is manifest. I do not want to go deeper. I love the moon.' Then the argument is all right.

But then Lalla (Saint Lalleshwari) would smile and ask: Which moon do you love? The moon on the first of the month, the fifth of the month, the tenth of the month, or the fifteenth of the month? Which moon do you love?

That is the thing with Truth. When it exhibits itself, it does so in ever-changing ways.

So, it beats us both ways. When it does not exhibit itself, you have no way of knowing it because knowing the Truth would require knowing your own essence. One is caught. It is an impossible task. And when one says that 'I will confine myself to the manifested Truth', the problem that one faces is that the manifestation is continuously changing. Which manifestation do you like? Nothing in the universe stays still even for a microsecond. Everything is continuously changing.

That is why in Lalla's poem, the opening lines talk of the moon and the ocean. What you call as the ocean is an abstraction, a mere idea. Is there a thing called an ocean? The ocean is forever changing. Which ocean do you love—the ocean at noon, the ocean at 1:00 p.m., or at high tide, or at low tide? Which ocean are you talking of?

Loving the Truth or knowing the Truth presents us with great difficulties. We want to love a thing, and the Truth is never a thing. It is never a thing when it is not manifested. And even when it is manifested, it is in a flux, continuously changing, never a definite unchanging thing.

In the universe, nothing called a thing exists. Everything is in movement. So, you can love the universe only if you want to love the movement; only then you can love the universe. If you want to love the universe, you will have to love the universe with all its movements because there is nothing called a stalled or stationary universe.

And that is the trouble with loving. When you love an idea, you love a frozen idea, an idea with a boundary. The reality is always in motion and that is why our love falls flat. You love pictures, and reality is like a video. Your love cannot cope with videos. You can, at most, love pictures. They are easier to love because pictures can be co-opted. You look at somebody's smiling face and you say 'this is the one that I love'. The one whose face you see smiling in the frame actually started frowning right after the click, but that won't be visible in the picture. You are stuck at the smile. The smile, however, came and went away; the frown went away as well.

If you really want to love a person, you will have to love the flow that the person is. But that flow is not really controllable or definable. If the person is real, the flow will be wild and unpredictable. How do you love them, then? And that is why we do not want to love the wild. We are far more comfortable loving somebody who is very defined, predictable, within norms, within bounds. If someone who is totally on their own—in other words, random, patternless—comes in front of us, this person will be very difficult to love.

We can love only what we firstly know. We have a great urge to know because unless we know, unless we have knowledge, we cannot control it. The ego is so afraid all the time that it cannot live without knowledge of the other. You want to have knowledge about the other so that you do not feel afraid, so that you can have some security and some control and defence with respect to the other.

Lalla is saying the moon is indeed lovely, but how do you love the moon? The moon is really so fickle, the moon keeps no promises. You might be a poet and you might be writing a beautiful rhyme for the moon tonight. And what does the moon do tomorrow? It changes! You are betrayed. You may keep complaining, but the moon will keep changing. The moon is changing even as you are writing the rhyme, the moon is changing even as you are offering the words, so is the ocean—both are always in movement.

To love, to know, you will have to either settle in the fact of unknowability, or if you are too eager about loving the manifest, the material, the obvious, then you will have to learn the art of loving a new thing, a new person every day. That obviously defeats our purpose—we want to resist change; we want to have the same person who we met one fine day ten years back. In fact, if that person shows even the faintest intention of changing, we charge them with disloyalty. We say that 'you are changing'. But the person is indeed changing, and he will keep changing in spite of your utmost intentions and efforts.

Spirituality is the art of loving nothing and loving something that will not remain, and knowing that both are one. To love nothing is to love God, the formless, and to love something that will continuously change is to love God in form, in time and space.

But we are not all right with both of these or either of these. We want a third possibility. We want a form that won't change. Sorry, that wish cannot be granted. If you want something that does not change, then settle for the formless. If you want something that would never change, then settle for nothing because only that never changes. And if you want something, then settle for change, because whatever is something is always going to change. But what do you want? You want something that should not change. Now, that is an impossibility.

Do you see how we are unable to know or love anything? We are just like the moon. Inside of us is an endless abyss, a total vacuum. We are not very comfortable with that. We like stuff; we do not like empty rooms, we like filled rooms. And inside of us is a great, clean, unoccupied space. We do not like clean spaces, do we? And on the periphery, on the outside, we are a flow that cares for nobody, a flow that must breach all promises except the promise it made to its source and the promise it made to time.

The promise that it has made to its source is that 'I will start from you and end in you'. The promise that it has made to time is, 'I will not stop as long as there is time, I will flow'. That is what you are. Look at your mind. Does it ever stop? But we hate it when it doesn't stop. We try a thousand methods to control the mind. Look at your body. Does it ever stop and look at the efforts that you put in to take control of your entire system? See what all you do just to be on top of yourself.

Humans are comfortable neither with their soul nor with their body-mind. They are not comfortable with the soul because the soul is unknowable, and they are not comfortable with the body-mind because they do not listen to human diktats. Whatever you tell your mind is a diktat towards stillness; you want the mind to be arrested somewhere. The mind won't listen to you, so you do not like it. Now, that is a terrible situation. You do not like your soul either, because for you to like something you first of all need to know it.

A spiritual person, a realized one, someone like Lalla, is comfortable with both—the great nothingness from where the flow arises and the unpredictability of the flow. She is all right if she does not know. And if you are all right with not knowing, then you will also, in parallel, be all right with the flow.

Remember that you are not all right with the flow because the flow does not offer you the luxury of knowledge. When something is flowing, knowledge fails in front of it. It is going to a direction where knowledge does not hold, stand or provide relief.

Be comfortable with not knowing and with changes of all kinds. Don't live by ideas, don't live by anything; just live.

Do you think that the crescent moon that you saw this evening is any less beautiful than the full moon? When things are changing, they are beautiful in every form *as a result* of the change, provided you do not have fixations. If you have fixations, obviously you cannot see the beauty in the various phases of the moon. The moon does not only have fifteen phases, the moon actually has an infinite number of phases. But if you have certain standards of beauty, if you have certain ideas of beauty, you will not be able to see and appreciate beauty. And if you do not appreciate beauty, the moon is not lessened; your own moment goes wasted. You will miss the moment if you cannot appreciate the moon with all its phases.

So, do not be stuck with ideas about propriety, Truth, love and beauty. You will miss everything that you have an idea about. If you have an idea about a thing, you are sure to miss that thing.

'Since I scoured my mind and my body, I too Lalla, am new, each moment new.'

She has not done something special. Everybody *is* new. There is nothing except newness. The soul is new because it cannot be old. To be old, one requires time and the soul is timeless. How can you be old if the clock is not ticking? And inside of you no clock ticks, so there is no question of you ever being old. Inside you are anyway always new. No oldness exists there. And on the periphery, you are always changing. That which was old is always being left behind, so there is only newness. But we do not experience that, we do not live in that.

Lalla says she also had to do something or undo something in order to remain forever new. What was that? She scoured her body and her mind, she left them behind, she burned them away, she stopped taking them seriously. She came into a different kind of association with herself, which was not identity-based, and then there is only newness.

Do you know what that newness means? It means that now you cannot live a bored life, you cannot live as you are sleeping, that now you cannot even be short of energy. Life presents you with so much, but to get it, to enjoy it, to live it, you require energy. Don't you see how bad our relationship with energy is? Either we don't have energy, or we have energies that have gone bad.

Lalla is saying that her flow is natural now. She has removed all that could have vitiated the flow, disturb it, contain it. She has basically removed herself. So when she is dancing, it is only the dance. She will not say 'I am dancing'; it is just the dance. She has removed herself from the equation. If she is swimming or reading or playing or singing, there would just be the swimming, the reading, the playing or the song.

The doer that we are, the fearful doer, the control freak vanishes. Things happen on their own. When things happen on their own, then things are new. When *you* do things, then you only do that which you are secure and comfortable with, and that is the old. It is old because you can be secure only with that which you already know. If you want to get a taste of the new, remove yourself and then everything is new.

'My teacher told me one thing, Live in the soul.'

We must get this. Living in the soul is exactly the same as living in the body-mind. Living in the undifferentiated, unqualified Truth is just the same as living in this world of qualifications, names, diversity, differences, colours and patterns. Both require one common quality, and that quality is: one need not be afraid of the unknown. To live in the soul you must not be afraid of unknowability because the soul is not in a dimension that consciousness can perceive. So, you have to be secure even without knowledge. The same quality of mind is also required to really love the world, love life, and live blissfully. What is that quality? To live without seeking security, to live without having the support of knowledge.

In the domain of the soul, knowledge simply does not apply because that is not the dimension of knowledge. And in the domain of the world, knowledge applies but fails, because if you apply knowledge all you will get is repetition of the old. Knowledge means that which you know of. So, if you have knowledge of something, what will you do? You will repeat that thing.

So, you require one common quality, whether you are a person who is deeply of the soul or a person who is deeply of the world. That common quality is a feeling of security, an unreasonable security. One is prepared to live without being certain through knowledge. One is still certain but not through knowledge. To have certainty without knowledge is called faith. When you do not really know something but you are still certain, it is called faith.

Spirituality is not about avoiding the world. Real spirituality promotes and strengthens that quality within you which will help you succeed in the world as well. If you can be devoted to the heart, then the mind, too, will remain healthy. If you can live peacefully with the vacuum of the soul, you will also be able to have peace even in the dizzying diversity of the mind.

Only the one who is all right with great nothingness will be all right with a maddening diversity. The mind is the world of infinity and an infinite number of things exist in the mind. The soul is the world of zero; nothing exists there. You would either be comfortable with both or with none of them. Make peace with zero so that you can be all right with infinity.

'When that was so, I began to go naked, and dance.'

Lalla's nakedness is not merely about giving up clothes. What are clothes? Clothes are what society would have you wear. If nobody taught you to, would you? Clothes are the body that society gives to you. Giving up of clothes means you have given up on society. 'I no more have the social body.' That, however, does not mean that Lalla was now living in the physical body. She had given up the physical body as well, and the proof of that is that she had given up the social body.

As long as you are identified strongly with the physical body, you will have to have a social body as well. If you are conscious about your body, about your face, about your organs, you will do things with them. You will want to either promote them or decorate them or hide them. Why do people hide their body? That is because they are identified with the body. In fact, the very reason humans create society is that they have biological identification. If you are not biologically identified, you will not want to create a society. That is why even animals in varying degrees create societies for themselves.

Body-identification leads to the creation of society. In fact, historically also, this is the reason why any society came into existence. Give up society and soon you will find that you are giving up on your body-identification as well. That is why a Mahavira has to go naked; that is why a Buddha has to go to the jungle. They are not going to the jungle; they are going away from society; they are giving up that which is unnecessary. They are almost like a snake giving up on an entire shell, an entire covering.

Lalla goes naked. Nakedness is when you are comfortable with yourself. When you are comfortable with your soul, only then are you comfortable with your body and your mind.

Most of us live in total discomfort of ourselves. What do I mean by total discomfort? We are uncomfortable with our heart, and we are also uncomfortable with our thoughts. We cannot do whatever the heart is always impelling us to do, and because we cannot do that, our thoughts are always crude and we keep on getting all kinds of ugly thoughts.

You know why you have all that stuff in your mind? Do you know why your thoughts are so ugly—because of which you keep spending your life in guilt—so ugly that you just don't like that mind which entertains these kinds of thoughts? Your thoughts are bad because you don't have a healthy relationship with your heart. Take a plant and keep clipping its roots or keep applying some kind of poison to its roots. What kind of branches and leaves would you find in that plant? Crippled.

It is the radiance of the heart that makes the eyes shine. It is the touch of the heart that brings sweetness and composure to your voice. It is the touch of the heart that brings rhythm to your songs. Otherwise, you can keep practising and become an accomplished artist, but your art will still not have that quality which makes life worth living.

I was listening to a very accomplished singer singing songs of Mira and Kabir. I heard for a while and then I could not help smiling. The singer had all the nuances of voice, all the control over her craft, and yet there was nothing Mira-like in the song. The singer was a master of the art, yet it was so obvious that it was not Mira who was singing. Somebody had just borrowed Mira's words and was trying to present them in the most decorated way possible, and that was not helping.

You might be a singer of experience and repute, yet you need to have Mira's heart before you sing Mira, and that heart cannot come by way of practice. When you love your internal nakedness, the physical body exudes beauty, and then even if you wear a social body, that too is beautiful.

Similarly, Kabir's language is social, or is it not? Did Kabir invent a new language? No. So there is the social body, there is the common language, but that language is arising from an internal silence and that is why it is beautiful. Kabir singing his own songs—that is what is meant by nakedness. Now the outside is in great balance and in a great tandem with the inside.

What comes first, Kabir's voice, Kabir's words or Kabir's heart? That is what Lalla's guru had told her. He told her, 'Be on the outside as you are on the inside.' That was the only instruction he ever gave her. 'Be on the outside as you are on the inside.' That means that your words should arise from your naked heart and then they can take any shape. Of course, the shape will be determined by the body and the mind and society, but their source must be pure within. That source is very important.

Lalla is naked, so is Kabir, so is Buddha. They are all naked. We are not naked even if we have given up all our clothes, and Kabir is naked even if he is wearing a lot.

Even if we give up clothes, we do it as per the social standards, don't we? When you are in the swimming pool, you are with very few clothes, but that swimming pool is actually a social institution. If you enter the swimming pool wearing your usual shorts, you would be censored. Society wants you to wear a particular kind of clothing while entering the pool.

So, even if you have to go naked, you go naked as per the benchmarks. Even our nakedness follows an imported direction. That is no nakedness.

How can we improve the relationship with energy? By improving the relationship with the source of energy, the master of energy. There are these two dogs, Koham and Soham, who turn strangely vicious after midnight. They just attack everybody randomly, blindly. After midnight and till dawn they keep patrolling in front of the BodhSthal (location of the session) and anybody who passes that area is barked at—not just barked at, also chased. But if you are having a walk with me, they don't do anything to you. They are my pets. If you are walking with me in front of BodhSthal, Koham and Soham will walk by your side as if they are your best buddies.

To have a great relationship with Koham and Soham, show that you have a great relationship with their master. Then, even without knowing you, they become respectful towards you. It is the same with energy. All energy arises from nowhere. In its most subtle form, energy is consciousness, and consciousness in its subtlest form is an imperceptible awareness. In its crudest form, energy becomes matter. That is the link between the source and the world. Matter is energy, energy is consciousness, consciousness is nothing.

If you can be all right with nothing, you will be all right with consciousness, with energy and with matter, and that sums up everything. Your entire world is nothing but this consciousness, energy and matter. To be all right with the world, just be all right with the master of these three. And who is the master? Well, you cannot know that master. That is why I am repeatedly calling that master as nobody, as nothing.

Be comfortable without knowing, that is the key. Be comfortable without knowing and you will have lots of energy. Be comfortable without guarantees of security and you will have lots of energy. A little bit of energy can be invoked even by thinking, even by motivating yourself, but only a little bit. It won't suffice; you will remain hungry. There is great fun in just living—living without assurances, living without guarantees, living without promises.

When you look around, what do you seek? You seek meaning. Just change this habit. Instead of seeking meaning, seek nothing.

Look around as if you are looking at nothing, look around as if you are staring at a vacuum. But to do that you will need to have vacuum inside, not desires. If you have desires inside, you cannot look at the world as if you are looking at a vacuum.

Look at things and see nothing. Try that. Look at things and see nothing.

> THE MIND IS THE WORLD OF INFINITY AND AN INFINITE NUMBER OF THINGS EXIST IN THE MIND. THE SOUL IS THE WORLD OF ZERO; NOTHING EXISTS THERE. YOU WOULD EITHER BE COMFORTABLE WITH BOTH OR WITH NONE OF THEM. MAKE PEACE WITH ZERO SO THAT YOU CAN BE ALL RIGHT WITH INFINITY.

(Uttarakhand, 2017)

170

Part III

———◆———

What do the Scriptures Say?

26

Mind Is Suffering

〜・〜

" BE READY FOR TAPASYA, PENANCE OR ASKESIS, KNOW
VEDANTA DEEPLY, AND BE A RUTHLESS RENOUNCER. DO NOT
HESITATE FOR A MOMENT IN GIVING UP. LET GO LIKE A KING.
THE KING KNOWS HE HAS SO MUCH, SO HE CAN DROP AT WILL.
DROP WITHOUT A SECOND THOUGHT. GIVE AWAY AS IF YOU
HAVE AN INFINITE TREASURE WITHIN YOU. "

वेदान्तविज्ञानसुनिश्चितार्थाः सन्यासयोगाद्यतयः शुद्धसत्त्वाः ।
ते ब्रह्मलोकेषु परान्तकाले परामृताः परिमुच्यन्ति सर्वे ॥

*Doers of askesis who have made sure of the aim of the whole knowledge
of Vedanta, the inner being purified by the yoga of renunciation, all
the hour of their last and passing beyond death are released into the
worlds of the Brahm.*

~Mundaka Upanishad, Verse 3.2.6

Listener: Who are the doers of askesis? What is meant by passing
beyond death?

Acharya Prashant: The verse must be understood clearly and as per the fundamental principles of Vedanta, else there is scope for misinterpretation.

'Doers of askesis'—those who have gone through great penance, those who have known Vedanta completely—'whose inner being'—meaning the mind—'has been purified by renunciation, they come to their end passing beyond death and are released into Brahm'— they come to their end and pass beyond death.

We are obviously not talking about one particular moment of physical death here. What happens to the body is not too much a concern with Vedanta. Vedanta is not the science of the body. Vedanta is not very concerned with our anatomy. Vedanta is concerned with our suffering, and it is not the body that suffers. The body might get hurt, wounded, diseased or aged, but it never suffers.

The mind can suffer when the body is in pain. The body can become an object in the field of suffering, but the body itself is never the experiencer of suffering. The sufferer is always the mind. The mind is the subject, the sufferer, and it is possible that the subject— the mind—is suffering because the object—the body—is in pain. But that is not a compulsion upon the mind. The mind always has a choice whether it wants to suffer or realize. Vedanta is concerned with suffering; therefore, Vedanta is concerned with the mind.

Let's please remember the body never suffers. A particular condition of the body can potentially cause suffering in the mind, but not necessarily. The body is in one configuration; the mind says, 'The body is healthy, therefore I am satisfied.' The body shifts to another configuration; the mind says, 'The body is not all right, the body is diseased, paining, and therefore I am suffering.' That is a decision made by the mind. And as it is with every decision, here again, the discretion or indiscretion of the decision-maker is involved.

So, the aim of Vedanta is to bring discretion to the mind. Having known that the subject matter of Vedanta is the mind and its suffering, and that Vedanta wants to put an end to the suffering of the mind, we read the verse in the right light.

When the mind comes to an end, it goes beyond death because as long as the mind is alive, it is alive in the realm of beginning and ending. The life of mind is the tick-tock of time. Time denotes an initiation and a closure, a rise and a fall. Therefore, the mind lives in perpetual death. Equally, you could say that the mind lives in perpetual beginnings. But then, you see, the beginnings are not so much of a nightmare because they are associated with hope. Therefore, though beginnings are synonymous with endings, it is not the beginnings that haunt the mind so much.

The mind is buffeted by endings, death. Death matters a lot to the mind. And the mind continues to live in a domain where the spectre of death keeps looming large. Therefore, the life of the mind is always in the shadow of death. Therefore, when the mind comes to an end, death comes to an end. You will have to pay attention.

As long as the mind is alive, it is alive in the cycle of birth and death, rise and fall, entries and exits, beginnings and ends. That is the life of the mind. In this life of the mind, there is suffering. Therefore, this life of the mind must come to an end. When this life comes to an end, death comes to an end.

The death of mind is actually the death of the death of mind. Because the mind lives in death, hence, when the mind meets death, it is death to death. Is it getting too complex?

The matter is simple: it is not your nature to suffer. Nobody likes to suffer. It is an obvious thing. We are not dealing with the

175

stars here; we are dealing with ourselves here, and there is nobody who finds joy in sorrow. Human beings, across times, cultures, continents, ethnicities, ideologies, genders, all crave Joy. When they can't have Joy, they settle for its cheap substitute called happiness. That is what we all want, without exception. Not only human beings, even animals and other conscious beings do not like to suffer. If you observe the behaviour of any conscious being, you will find that it acts in a way which avoids suffering. Wherever it finds suffering, it turns away from there.

These are fundamentals you must keep in mind. Vedanta does not operate in a vacuum. Vedanta doesn't vaguely utter something for the sake of it. The purpose is very clear—to rid man of his needless suffering. That is the purpose of Vedanta.

To that end, Vedanta explores: What is it that suffers? Who is it that suffers? That is the reason why the question of identity is so central to Vedanta. That is why Vedanta keeps asking: Who are you? Who is the doer? Who is the sufferer? Who is the speaker? Who is the experiencer? This question is intimately linked to the situation of suffering. Because if you want to remove your suffering, you will have to, first of all, know who the suffering entity is. If you do not know who is suffering, how will you get rid of the suffering?

Having known who is suffering—the mind—you want to see what it is in the mind that suffers, what the process of its suffering is. And when you investigate the mind, you find that the mind does not have to do anything special to suffer. The way the mind is, a product of imperfect and conditioned consciousness, its very existence is suffering.

It is not that the mind has to get into something outrageously bad or be subject to vices or evil to suffer. The way the mind is, it is designed to suffer. It does not have to do anything extraordinary to suffer; it does not have to go out of its way to suffer. The very default situation of the mind is suffering. So, if you are suffering, there is nothing extraordinary about it. It is the most common thing to suffer.

The mind and suffering are just one thing—they cannot be separated. The mind and suffering are just one thing. It is not even proper to say that the mind suffers, it is more accurate to say that the mind is suffering, because when you say that the mind suffers, you entertain the hope that it is possible that the mind may not suffer. No, that is not possible. If the mind is, it will suffer. If the mind exists, it will suffer.

So, the mind is suffering. Therefore, if you want to bring an end to suffering, you will have to bring the mind to an end, and that is what this verse is referring to.

The mind, the common mind, the mind as we know it, the mind as we experience it and live it, has to be brought to an end. Life as we know it has to be brought to an end. Our existence as we have experienced it, the familiar kind of existence, the routine pattern-based life, has to end if suffering is to end. This ending of suffering can be called the mind's liberation into Brahm. The verse closes with these words:

'He puts an end to death and gets released into Brahm.'

So, there is nothing called Brahm-attainment. It is not that you will stay put, stay alive and be able to grab Brahm with your hands. No, it is not happening. When you are no more, Brahm is. Brahm denotes the absence of the one who was suffering due to his own presence.

How does that ending happen? Three things are mentioned in this verse: one, austerity, deep penance; second, knowledge of Vedanta; third, yoga of renunciation. If you want to bring the mind to its end, to its closure, which can also be called its summit or sublimation, peak or fulfilment, then be ready for these three. Be

177

ready for tapasya, penance or askesis, know Vedanta deeply, and be a ruthless renouncer. Do not hesitate for a moment in giving up. Let go like a king. The king knows he has so much, so he can drop at will. Drop without a second thought. Give away as if you have an infinite treasure within you.

Renunciation is not a thing of sorrow; renunciation is not something to be done with determination or sadness. Renunciation does not require determination; it requires celebration. You are throwing a party—isn't it a kind of renunciation? Think about it. 'I have so much that I am asking the world to feast on it, take it away. I have so much!'

Whereas renunciation as we know it requires so much willpower. That is because we do not really know renunciation. Therefore, we have to motivate ourselves a lot and think it over it a thousand times, and then we say, 'Fine, with a heavy heart I am parting ways with this precious diamond of mine.' That is not the way of celebration, is it?

So, renunciation has to be a celebration. 'Come, take it away. I am throwing a party!' Motivation is not needed. Determination is not required. Willpower is not needed. Festivity and celebration are required, and then you renounce with ease.

And that renunciation can come only with the knowledge of Vedanta because Vedanta reveals your true identity to you. Your true identity is that of the infinite true Self. Because it is infinite, nothing gets reduced from it even when you give up a lot; you may keep giving up and yet you lose nothing.

Without Vedanta, no renunciation is possible. And that is why you find people are so miserly: because they are not students of Vedanta, unfortunately. Nobody brought Vedanta to them, therefore they go about life like beggars—holding, clutching, gripping, snatching. 'I am so little, how can I afford to give? I am so small, how do I afford to part ways with whatever little I have?'

Unless your magnificence is revealed to you, you live in an imagined scarcity. You might have a lot, but you do not know that you have much, so you imagine a scarcity for yourself. And it does not matter how much you really have; what matters is how much you *know* you have. Therefore, knowledge is important. Therefore, Vedanta is indispensable. You must know what you have. Otherwise even the True Self, the Atma, is of no use. The Atma is complete, magnificent, unending, measureless—but useless. Limitless and useless because you do not know of it.

Once you know of your infinite nature, a certain royalty becomes available to you. Now you will live life in a regal way. Narrowness is no more. Now there is no more vulnerability to little things in life, no more identification with the small, the atomic and the trivial. There comes a great propensity to forget the routine, the usual, resulting in an unburdened mind. It is a mind not carrying the accumulated burden of tidbits, millions of tidbits of the past. Therefore, there is lightness. Therefore, there is a skyness.

So, renunciation becomes available to you through the knowledge of Vedanta, and the knowledge of Vedanta requires great penance. You have to put in effort. You have to go against yourself, because this knowledge is scary and this knowledge takes time; the fruits are not immediately visible. There will be a great temptation and a great inner argument to quit. You will forcefully ask, 'Why am I sacrificing so much when nothing comes of it? Why should I put in so much and deprive myself of all the little pleasures that the world is coolly enjoying?' These are the moments when you have to fight against yourself. And these moments will be aplenty.

Study of Vedanta requires you to be close to the scripture and sometimes close to a teacher. Neither is easy. But all becomes very easy once you are firmly grounded in Vedanta. It is just that you have to stay put till that moment. What separates the good student from the bad when it comes to knowledge? Just one thing: Did you quit or not? The bad student is the one who quits. Might sound strange, but this is the only thing that matters in the final tally.

You will arrive. Just don't quit. Obviously, you can make the process of arrival easier, smoother by doing a few more things nicely, decently, but the one fatal mistake is to quit. Nothing else is fatal. All other mistakes that you commit are irritants. They are like speed breakers. You will be punished in the sense that you will take more time to realize things, but ultimately realize you would.

That brings us to the definition of askesis or tapasya. The very definition is: *not giving up*. That is tapasya. Tapasya is to not give up even when your mind, your false self, gives you a thousand concrete arguments in favour of giving up.

Don't give up. Keep dragging yourself forward. If you can't run, if you can't walk, drag yourself ahead. In dragging yourself if you fall unconscious, so be it, but don't turn around to run away. Swoon, faint, fall, but don't retreat. The reward will be deliverance from death. The reward will be freedom from a mediocre run-of-the-mill life. The reward will be freedom from the unending and unmitigated punishment called life.

> **❝** IF THE MIND IS, IT WILL SUFFER. IF THE MIND EXISTS, IT WILL SUFFER. SO, THE MIND IS SUFFERING. THEREFORE, IF YOU WANT TO BRING AN END TO SUFFERING, YOU WILL HAVE TO BRING THE MIND TO AN END. **❞**

(Advait BodhSthal, 2021)

27

The Spontaneous Joy of the Mind

❝ YOGA IS THE DISAPPEARANCE OF THE FALSE, NOT A UNION OF
THE FALSE WITH THE TRUE. TRUE YOGA IS MERELY LOPA, NO
UNION IS NEEDED. **❞**

योगवियोगै रहितो योगी भोगविभोगै रहितो भोगी ।
एवं चरति हि मन्दं मन्दं मनसा कल्पितसहजानन्दम् ॥

*The enlightened one is a yogi, free of both yoga and the absence of
yoga; an enjoyer who is free of both enjoyment and the absence of
enjoyment. Thus, he wanders leisurely, filled with the spontaneous Joy
of his own mind.*

~Avadhuta Gita, Verse 7.9

Listener: Who is a yogi? What is yoga? What is meant by being free
of both enjoyment and the absence of enjoyment?

Acharya Prashant: The enlightened one is a yogi. Neither yoga
nor an absence of yoga are present in him. He is simply yogastha
(settled in Yoga). Why are these two absent? It is obvious. These

two are absent because there are no two. For yoga to happen, there must be two real entities getting united.

There is yoga but not the kind that proceeds from somewhere. There is yoga but not the kind that is a summation of two entities. This yoga is better described as lopa. There appeared to be two, one became lupt (vanished); there was then the lopa of one. 'Lopa' means disappearance.

So, it is not really the coming together of the two, because the two are not at the same level; that which you call the second one really does not exist in the dimension of the first one. Hence, in that sense, if the first one is true, then the second one can be called false.

Yoga is the disappearance of the false, not a union of the false with the true. True yoga is merely lopa; no union is needed. Who will meet whom? Only the Truth is there. Who will come and meet the Truth? So, the word 'yoga' is really a misnomer. It can even mislead.

You go to Rishikesh, and everybody is talking about union there. They do not talk of the meeting between the two, but three: mind, body and soul. In actuality, there are not even two, but they have dreamt up three and are running successful businesses. If there can be a fourth one to unite, then the business will prosper even more because now the task is bigger. 'You see, he unites only three of the neighbouring shops. I unite four, so my charges are thirty per cent higher!'

There are no two. How can there be three? You are asking, is there only one? There is not even one. No three, no two, and not even one. What yoga are you dreaming of? The dream has to go into vilopa. Two, three, four, five, six, all will then go down the Ganga.

Dattatreya is compassionate enough not to give you anything that you can hold because whatever you hold becomes you. If you are able to hold something, if your hands are clutching something, then that which you clutch becomes your hand. So, he is saying, only the yogi exists, only the one yogastha entity exists. He is calling that entity the yogi.

The verse says, there is neither yoga—why is there no yoga? Because there are no two. And it also says, nor is there an absence of yoga. Why is there no absence of yoga? Because when you look at the world around you, you see that, for most people, there indeed are two. So, for this one, this walking man that you are calling as yogi, surely the second one has gone, surely yoga has happened— but such yoga is not happening. I repeat, such yoga is merely lopa. Yoga has not happened. The Truth has not arrived. That which was not Truth, that which was anyway not at all, has lost its grip upon you.

Dattatreya has taken a liking for you. He says there is just an enjoyer, neither is there any enjoyment nor an absence of enjoyment. He doesn't want you to be left with anything. There is merely a self-sufficient enjoyment. The one having the self-sufficient enjoyment is called the enjoyer. And then he is saying that there is neither enjoyment nor an absence of it. Why not an absence of enjoyment? For the same reason as when we said that yoga exists because the yogi is there.

So, when the enjoyer is there, enjoyment is there, but this is not the enjoyment of the kind that you witness in the world. In the world, enjoyment is never self-sufficient, it always requires an external object. Here, enjoyment is there but it is contained in the enjoyer. It is not for a reason; it is not due to something or somebody; it does not begin and end. It is one with the enjoyer.

You are just Joy—just Joy, just Joy.

Call it Justness or call it Joy.

Call it Being or call it Joy.

Call it Me or call it Joy.

Call it Self or call it Joy.

Call it Truth or call it Joy.

No two: not Joy *because* of something, not Joy *in* something. *Just* Joy, self-contained, non-dual.

You can't have images of such Joy. You cannot *have* such Joy. Only such Joy can have itself. This is what Dattatreya is speaking about. If you are having Joy, there still are two.

What is happening?

It is Joy having Joy.

Call it Me or call it Joy.

> " IN THE WORLD, ENJOYMENT IS NEVER SELF-SUFFICIENT, IT
> ALWAYS REQUIRES AN EXTERNAL OBJECT. HERE, ENJOYMENT IS
> THERE BUT IT IS CONTAINED IN THE ENJOYER. IT IS NOT FOR
> A REASON; IT IS NOT DUE TO SOMETHING OR SOMEBODY; IT
> DOES NOT BEGIN AND END. IT IS ONE WITH THE ENJOYER. "

(Advait BodhSthal, 2018)

28

Pleasure, Happiness, and Freedom
from Misery

> WHENEVER YOU FEEL CURIOUS, ASK YOURSELF: WHY DO I
> WANT TO KNOW? WHO AM I TO KNOW? WHO IS IT WITHIN
> ME SO EAGER TO KNOW? WHAT WILL I DO WITH THIS
> KNOWLEDGE? IT IS A GREAT QUESTION TO ASK: WHAT WILL I
> DO WITH THIS KNOWLEDGE?

अन्धं तमः प्रविशन्ति येऽविद्यामुपासते ।
ततो भूय इव ते तमो य उ विद्यायां रताः ॥

Those who worship avidya enter blind darkness, and those who
delight in vidya enter darkness even deeper.
~Ishavasya Upanishad, Verse 9

Listener: What is the meaning of this verse? What is avidya? What
is vidya?

Acharya Prashant: If you worship avidya, you enter darkness; if you worship vidya, then you enter even deeper darkness. That is what the verse is saying. Intriguing and fascinating!

I am taken back many decades to the moment when this had first hit me. There was no way I could make sense of it as a child, but something within me knew that it was fabulous, much more fabulous than *Chacha Chaudhary* or *Nandan, Parag* and *Chandamama* (popular children's magazines). I mean, that was the stuff I used to read at that age. That is how I grew up, you know. So, there is *Chacha Chaudhary*, and then there are the Upanishads, and then there is something by Premchand, and then there is something by Tolstoy. This kind of a motley combination is there.

So, I was branching out in all kinds of possible dimensions in a very unplanned and erratic way. So, one moment I am enjoying Indrajal comics, the other moment I am reading *Cancer Ward,* which was a Nobel winning work, and these two are coming to me simultaneously—something very childish and something very intellectual, literature of the street kind and the university kind— and I didn't even differentiate much between the two. To me all these were things to be enjoyed, subjects to be studied. So, if I was fed up with *Lotpot* (a children's magazine), I would go to *Mundaka Upanishad*. You know *Lotpot*? Doctor Jhatka? And then there would be *Taar Saptak* (Hindi literature magazine) and Maxim Gorky. And then if it was getting too late in the night, my mother would shout, and I would go to my history books and textbooks.

I remember when the Upanishads first came to me. Earlier I was used to hearing that those who do not have knowledge live a life of dark blindness, but what the Upanishads said was extraordinary, and it toyed with the child's mind. Imagine an older sibling playing games with the little one and saying, 'If you are ignorant, mother will put you in the dark room. But if you become too knowledgeable, you will be thrown into the dark well!' This is what the Upanishads were saying.

'Huh? If I become too knowledgeable—what do you mean by that? I understand that if I get only eighty per cent, I will be scolded, but you are saying that if I get ninety-nine per cent, that too is a problem!'

And that mischievous smile on *his* lips! How do I forgive him? The father of the Upanishads would never reveal anything completely. He would incite you in a subtle way and leave you to find things out on your own. And how would I find my answers then? By dumping the Upanishad and then returning to Doctor Jhatka. I would say, 'To hell with you! This is too much.'

You know, the trend continued as I grew up and reached my teenage years. There were all kinds of unmentionable books as well—we didn't have the internet, we had to rely on books—but the Upanishads held their place. The Upanishads remained a permanent certainty, a fixture. Either the Upanishads, or some commentary on Upanishads, or some other Vedantic text or something. In some way or the other they remained. And that has kind of stayed with me, that strange mixture of everything.

Now, the verse says: Those who worship avidya enter darkness. What is avidya? It has to be understood very carefully. Avidya is neither ignorance nor false knowledge. Avidya is objective knowledge. Let this be very clear. It is that which takes you to facts. You can even stretch the thing a bit and say avidya leads you to objective truth. I know that sounds really bad, but don't you know people who keep talking of truth in a worldly way? They say, 'tell me the truth of this matter' or 'we want to know the truth', don't they?

So, avidya is that truth that they talk of—the objective truth. I never refer to it as the objective truth, I just refer to it as facts. But the world doesn't call it facts, the world calls it the truth. The world doesn't even say objective truth, the world says truth. 'Tell me the truth, how many marks did you get? Tell me the truth, where were you all this time?' Don't we say that?

So, that is in the domain of avidya. Knowing the world, knowing this objective expanse, that is avidya. The verse is saying that if you worship objective truth or objective knowledge or facts too much, you enter darkness because you are not really seeing anything. Of what use is seeing things if you cannot see the seer? You do not even know *why* you are interested in those things, or do you?

We are interested in so many things. A fellow who is addicted is interested in, let's say, weed or brown sugar, and he is inquiring with great energy, in fact desperation. If you just look at it in a particular way, you will see that there is as much force in his inquiry as there is in a scientist inquiring into matter. Can you visualize this fellow? He has not seen any action for three months, and he is approaching this one and that one and really inquiring: 'So, what's the deal? Where do I get things? Which shop? How's the market behaving?' There is inquiry involved here.

But it is certain to all of us that this inquiry has no value—in fact it is harmful—because the inquirer is driven by his *prakritik* tendencies, and it is a prakritik tendency to seek happiness. Don't forget this. What is it that motivates the addict to seek an intoxicant even when he intellectually knows that the thing is destroying him? His urge for happiness.

Everything in Prakriti (physical nature) is just seeking happiness. When it comes to mental stimulation, we call it happiness, and if the stimulation is a bit more physical in nature, then we call it pleasure. So, animals seek pleasure, human beings seek happiness, and these two are not very different. It is just that the gross physical body seeks pleasure, and the subtle mental body seeks pleasure called happiness.

So, these two are in the same dimension—pleasure and happiness. Pleasure lies in consuming the object of your desire; happiness lies in knowing that you control the object of your desire. You are happy because you know that the object you want to consume is fully under your control. That is happiness. And what is pleasure? Pleasure is that which you experience in the moment of consumption. You could also say that all happiness is the anticipation of pleasure, all happiness is a preparation for pleasure, all happiness is assumed pleasure. Finally, we want pleasure, nothing else. Because finally, we take ourselves to be physical beings, so ultimately we want pleasure, unfortunately.

This is the reason why avidya is so important to most people: because all pleasure comes from consumption, and all consumption requires objects. What else will you consume? Because you want to consume objects, that is why you investigate into them. This is avidya. That is the reason the seer is warning that those who worship avidya fall into a deep darkness.

When it comes to the addict, we dismiss him because it is obviously clear what his intentions are. He too is rushing after an object, is he not? He too wants to know the details of this and that, and so does a violent man or a terrorist. A terrorist might be full of knowledge, in full possession of a lot of information, a lot of details about the objects he wants to strike at, but there we do not patronize it because there we talk about intentions. We say, 'Well, yes. He is gathering a lot of knowledge, but his intentions are improper.'

Now, let's go to the scientist, and we are going to the scientists with due respect, but still consider this. All that science has discovered, what has it ultimately been used for? Has it not been used for your pleasure and happiness? Tell me, then, what is really the difference between the inquiry of the addict and the inquiry of the scientist? I don't want to demean science; I just want us to understand something very fundamental.

If you do not know yourself, then all your external quests will definitely be towards consumption and pleasure, nothing else. It doesn't matter whether you are an addict or a scientist.

Great science ultimately becomes technology for consumption. What else? You are in class eleven or twelve or pre-college, and then you move into college and university where you read about physics, then you move into modern physics, then to quantum physics, and then slowly you start seeing that what you are reading with such academic reverence is actually displaying itself in a very obscene way all around you. You are reading about, let's say, nuclear fission and the tremendous power that it releases, and then you find a fellow using heavy electrical equipment to pursue his obnoxious physical pleasure. His equipment consumes many kilowatts of power, it is heavy. And what is that equipment being used for? Consumption and pleasure. Where did those many kilowatts come from? They came from the same nuclear fusion that you were reading as science—science which has been pressed into the service of our animalistic ego.

That is what happens when you do not know *why* you want to know. Whether you want to study the structure of this or that, whether you want to study the structure of a cell within the human body, whether you want to study the structure of galaxies or the entire universe—have you ever meditated into what exactly within you prompts you to do all of this, or any of this? That we do not know. That is the reason the sage had warned us in advance: you will move into deep darkness if you do not know *why* you want to know.

Whenever you feel curious, ask yourself: Why do I want to know? Who am I to know? Who is it within me so eager to know? What will I do with this knowledge? It is a great question to ask: What will I do with this knowledge? And don't trust your intentions. It is far better to rely on your track record. Don't trust what your mind is telling you.

In the moment the mind tells you, 'I will use all this information to further the welfare of mankind', don't trust your mind, it is a cheat. See what you have done so far with all the knowledge or information that ever came to you. What did you use it for? You used it for consumption, for all kinds of silly things, didn't you? That is exactly what you are going to use this next piece of information for.

That classic metaphor of the monkey holding the sword is very topical, very relevant here, and should prove to be very discouraging when it comes to blind inquiry. Knowledge, objective knowledge is like a sword. Who is holding the sword? Why are you allowing the monkey to have so much knowledge? And if you must strive towards knowledge, if knowledge is so dear to you, then you better know what keeps the monkey a monkey. That kind of knowledge is needed, first of all. Before the monkey learns how to wield the sword, shouldn't the monkey learn why the monkey is a monkey in the first place?

Do you now understand the dangers of objective knowledge? That is the crisis this world is facing today—too many fools have too much knowledge. They know a lot. They have a lot of information. Just one thing they do not know of: *who* has that information? And if you do not know who has that information, obviously, you will never know what that information is going to be used for. You will not know, but *she* will know (referring to Maya). She uses everything for just one purpose—pleasure, procreation, furtheration.

Next, the verse says, 'Those who delight in *vidya* enter darkness as it were, yet deeper.'

Now, what is vidya, then? Vidya is subjective knowledge. Avidya, when it fructifies, takes you to the fact, and Vidya, when it reaches fruition, takes you to the Truth. Vidya is about knowing your own consciousness. Vidya is about knowing the one who knows everything. We are not referring to any esoteric god or something here; we are referring to this thing that we call as the self. Vidya goes into that.

So, vidya looks like something pretty good, pretty impressive. At least in the field of spirituality, vidya should be something very respectable and people should be aspiring for vidya. Instead, we are being warned here that 'those who delight in vidya enter darkness as it were, yet deeper'. Not only do you not get anything beneficial by pursuing vidya, not only are you harmed by pursuing vidya, but you are actually harmed much more by pursuing vidya alone than you are by pursuing avidya alone. It is a triple whammy. We expected that if we are pursuers of vidya, then we will be rewarded and respected. The rishi is saying, 'No, no, you will get nothing.' And to make things even worse for our notions, the rishi says, 'Knowing avidya alone harms you, but if you have vidya alone, it harms you even more.'

What happens to those who do not pay attention to the physical stuff and instead keep talking of consciousness? And remember that consciousness is the subject matter of vidya. Avidya talks of everything except consciousness. So, science, technology, everything comes in the domain of avidya. History, geography, the languages, mathematics, economics—all these are avidya. What does vidya comprise of? Consciousness.

Now, look at this fellow who is trying to get vidya. He worships it without knowing anything or much about the factual or objective world. Do you understand his situation? He is saying, 'I do not know anything about the world; I do not know anything about the material; I do not know anything about the body or sensual perception, but I am greatly interested in consciousness.' This man does not understand material things, but he is interested in consciousness.

Now, what is consciousness? Consciousness is that which remains sandwiched between the material and the transcendental. Without the material, man's consciousness is nothing. Remove your brain—where is your consciousness? Remove your brain—where are your grand thoughts? Remove your brain—can you even meditate? Have you ever found a headless man meditating? Even to meditate, you require this physical head, don't you? That is the nature of man's consciousness. Even though it aspires for the skies, yet it is factually rooted in the earth. It merely *aspires* for the skies, remember. Those skies remain unknown to it. But what is it factually rooted in? The earth.

Now, this pursuer of vidya, what is he saying? He is saying, 'I am a student of consciousness, all I care for is the skies. I have nothing to do with matters of the earth because they all come in the purview of avidya. Avidya I totally abhor. I don't want to know avidya; these are matters of the soil, the earth. I don't want to know any object. All objects are false. What does a spiritual man have to do with the world? Why do I need to know mathematics or geography or history or what is going around here? I am not interested at all. What am I interested in? God and transcendence!'

If you are studying consciousness, consciousness is these two (*points with index finger and thumb referring to sky and earth*). We said that consciousness has these two components, very loosely put. These are not components of consciousness, but for the sake of discussion I am putting it this way.

So, there are two components in consciousness—the physical component, which you could call as the brain or the body or the universe, and the metaphysical component. The metaphysical component is anyway unknowable. Who can know the Truth? Or can you? The metaphysical component is anyway, by definition, unknowable. Metaphysical is unknowable; the physical you do not want to know. What the hell are you left with? I will tell you what he is left with. He is left with a lot. We will come to it. This is the story of most spiritual beings, so be very alert. A trap waits for each of us; none of us are beyond it.

'Metaphysical is unknowable, physical I am no more interested in because I am a spiritual seeker, you see. Why are you telling me stories of the world? I do not know what is going on in politics; I do not know how to drive, how to cook, how to play; I cannot hold the racket in my hands properly. Everything that has to do with the physical universe, I am a dud at it! In matters of this world, who am I? A dud. So, factually, fundamentally, I am someone who is a dud in a double roll.' He is a dud with three D's—double D-U-D! But will he ever accept that he is a dud or a double dud? Will he? No. How will he compensate? How will he convince himself that he is okay?

You see, knowing the matters of this earth, knowing the matters of your mind, your body, your hormones, your emotions, your thoughts, or how the glaciers and the mountains are made and how you have explosions in the hills—all this requires work, effort. Even reading requires some work. Let's say you are not going physically to explore the African forests. Even if you have to read about them, it requires effort. Now, this fellow has convinced himself that 'I do not need any avidya'. He says, 'Forests? All that they have is physical trees! And avidya is nonsense, it is Maya, so I do not want any avidya.'

The fact of the matter is: acquiring avidya is tough. You have to struggle. You have to put in a lot of disciplined work. Knowledge just doesn't come easily on its own. You have to acquire it effortfully.

So, that option is closed because this fellow has both contempt for avidya and labour, for work. What will he do? He needs to have some knowledge. He needs to tell himself 'I know something'. If he says 'I know something about this world', then he will be exposed because some subject matter expert will come and question him, and he will not know anything.

Suppose he says that he knows something about a particular glacier. Then some professor in geography or geology will come and ask him a few questions, and he will be exposed. Suppose he says he knows something about the body. Then some expert in anatomy or some doctor or researcher will come and, again, expose him. He says 'I know something about history'—again, he will be exposed. So, what does he do now? There has to be something very, very evil, absolutely wicked that he does now. Otherwise, the rishi would not have said that those who delight in vidya alone enter a darkness even deeper. Something very sinister is brewing. What is it? Think.

This fellow needs to convince himself and others—in order to be respectable in his own eyes—that he knows something. Only two things are there to be known in the field of vidya: either this world or That, that which is unknowable. This world he neither knows nor can he claim to know because if he claims to know, his claims would be exposed. So, what does he do? And that which he does has been done by all the hypocrites and the priests and the charlatans throughout the course of history. What is it?

He will manufacture knowledge about the Beyond because he has to say that he has some knowledge. Worldly knowledge he has not, so what does he do? He concocts knowledge. He manufactures stories. He says, 'I have special knowledge of the beyond! I will tell you: God lives in a special palace!' Now, no scientist can dispute this. He can never be refuted decisively on this. Yes, you can argue with him, but you can never decisively disprove what he is saying because what he is saying is beyond any verification, it cannot be falsified. Or, he will say, 'Certain things are within the body, but no equipment or probe can detect them.' Now, what he is saying is, 'These things are there, but these cannot be detected.' How do you falsify him? You cannot falsify him. Or, 'Such an experience can be had; you can experience a great, exotic and uplifting bliss—but only if I bless you.'

This has been the method of the fraudster, the cheat who has labelled himself as a guru, and this has been happening since centuries and millennia. This bugger has no worldly knowledge; ask him about any academic discipline, and he is zero. He talks a lot; he tries to philosophize. But grill him on philosophy, and he will show up as ignorant. He has no knowledge at all, but he keeps talking about everything. And whatever he talks about, he talks about in a way that can neither be verified nor falsified. It is not open to experimentation at all.

So, he will say strange things. He will say, 'I know this special god who lives on this mountain. And I know him!' Or, he will say, 'In my past when I was there in that zone, on that hill, these special things happened to me.' Now, can you verify it? Can you falsify it? This is the way of the fraud. And that is the reason the Upanishad had warned us so much in advance.

Get the difference straight. The one who is pursuing objective knowledge alone is merely blind to his intentions. The one who is pursuing subjective knowledge alone is a hypocrite who is not blind to his intentions; instead, he is supporting his evil intentions. Who is a bigger fraudster and a bigger fool, then? Are you getting the difference?

The one who is pursuing objective knowledge is at most ignorant about what his real intentions are. He is working hard in the laboratory, let's say he wants to know something about plasma (the fourth state of matter). He is very interested in knowing that, but he does not know *why* he is interested. But this charlatan knows fully well what he is doing. What is he doing? He is making a fool of everybody. He is just fleecing everybody for the sake of his own carnal, material pleasure or popularity or prestige. So, who is the bigger evil? The second one.

Now you know why the seer here is saying that those who worship vidya alone enter darkness yet deeper. You will have no worldly knowledge, but you will start weaving stories—cock and bull stories, or snake and bull stories, stories and stories—and gullible and scared people will fall into your trap. And I didn't say uneducated people; sometimes even very educated people can act very foolishly. Because, you see, you are not talking of anything verifiable; you are talking of none other than God *(pointing upwards)*.

So, even if you are trained in science and technology, you can still start feeling, 'But, you see, this man is saying that he has directly met God on those hills. So, I mean, what if he is even five per cent right? Why should I run the risk of displeasing such a big man? It is far better to touch his feet and believe in whatever he says. After all, what do I lose? And his stories are big, seriously big. And his claims are so outrageous that I can't even dismiss them! He says that "if your nose has fallen off your face, then I can pick up your nose and just put it back"; he says that "if your hair has fallen, then you give me your hair and I will plant it back"; he says that "if your soul has left your body, you have died, then I can catch your soul like Jacques Kallis diving in the slips, and then I can put it back in your body".'

And you start feeling doubtful. You say, 'This man is surely talking a lot of horse shit—or snake shit, whatever—but what if there is even an iota of truth in what he is claiming? Let me play safe! I mean, all that he is demanding is rupees one lakh for five hundred millilitres of consecrated water. I can pay that to him. He says that if he touches a tumbler of water, then the water remembers his touch. Water has memory, he says, that too in front of technical people. And then he says, "Now this water has been consecrated. I will sell it for one lakh rupees!" I mean, it is just one lakh rupees. I can just pay and get some insurance cover, you know. Otherwise, who wants to incur his wrath?'

That is what the rishi is warning us against. Anybody who says that he has any knowledge of divinity is to be avoided like death. Anybody who says that he has had profound experiences in meditation is to be just smiled at. Anybody who says that he can see your aura is a fool. Anybody who says that he experiences energy rising from one point in the body to another point in the body is in self-delusion. These are the people the Upanishad is warning us against. Anybody who says that something physical starts happening to him when he visualizes God in this way or that way is just cheating himself.

Vidya is a very special field. It has to be understood. Now we will come to the real difference between avidya and vidya. It is usually never expressed this way; therefore you must now know what it is.

Avidya is objective knowledge with no consideration for the intention that seeks that knowledge. Vidya, too, is objective knowledge, but with consideration for the subject that seeks that knowledge.

So, it is not really that avidya is about objective knowledge and vidya is about subjective knowledge; both are about objective knowledge. Knowledge cannot be anything but objective. What else can you know? If you can know something, obviously it is an object. So, vidya, too, consists of objective knowledge, but in vidya you are not blind to your intentions. That is vidya.

You see, when you go to your colleges or universities, do you find your professor questioning you regularly as to why you want to become a doctor? Does that happen? It is almost like a shop. You want to buy a t-shirt; the seller will not ask you, 'Sir, why do you want to buy a t-shirt?' Similarly, your professors never ask you, 'Why do you want to become an engineer?' Maybe if the selection process includes a personal interview as well, for the sake of formality you are asked this question, 'Why do you want to do MBA?' and such things. But just once. Once you gain admission, then in the duration of the course nobody asks you why you are pursuing this course.

That is avidya. Your intentions are never questioned; your intentions are never explored. The professor will not walk in and begin the day with, 'So, what does philosophy mean to you? What is it in you that feels attracted to mathematics?' It would be a rare professor who would go into this question. As a professor of mathematics, he is not supposed to. And no student is ever evaluated on the purity or clarity of his intentions, or is he? If you have taken admission in a mathematics course, what percentage of your overall assessment depends on your intention? Zero. You are assessed purely on your objective knowledge. That is avidya. Nobody cares about who you are and why you are studying and gaining knowledge at all. That is avidya.

Vidya is just the same as avidya except that in vidya, the shikshak (teacher) is also a guru. He will keep asking you, 'Why are you studying this, son? Who are you in all this? Well, you know so much, but where are you in all this? Or are you just a hard disk, a data drive of some kind? Where is the self? Where is the "I"? What is the centre of all your knowledge? To whom is all this knowledge?' This is vidya. This is real vidya. And it is this vidya which is being talked of when it is said that that which liberates is vidya.

Here, the rishi is saying, 'Those who delight in vidya fall into a deep darkness'; at the same time, the scriptures say, 'Ya vimuktaye sa vidya'—that which liberates is called vidya. Now, how can there be this contradiction? Surely there is something called false vidya and true vidya. Here the seer is alerting you against false vidya, and in that other shloka the seer is telling you about real vidya, that which liberates. It liberates you from what? It liberates you from your blindness about yourself. That is called vidya.

So, do you need separate and special centres where spiritual training is to be given? Not necessarily. These same classrooms where the languages, sciences, humanities, arts and commerce and economics are being taught, these same institutions can act as centres of vidya as well, provided the ones there have the sagacity to act not merely as knowledge providers but wisdom enablers. Unfortunately, that is rarely the case.

But if you have to choose between a place that offers only vidya and a place that offers only avidya, if you have to, as they say, choose between the devil and the deep sea, which one must you choose? A place that offers only avidya. At least this place is honest to the extent that most of our colleges and universities are. A place that offers only vidya will be as corrupt as most of our ashrams and spiritual organisations are.

Ideally, both of these should be offered together under one roof in the same classroom. That would be the ideal institution. That is the kind of place, the kind of centre of learning that needs to be created. I do not know when that will come. That would be the real university and it would be indistinguishable from a temple. That would be the real university and the real temple. Today's universities are not universities at all because they offer only avidya, and today's temples are not temples at all because they offer only vidya. The seer is saying, you need both of them together.

So, it is not without reason that professors are respected, whereas godmen are vilified. There is a clear reason. And the rishi would agree, the rishi would say yes. It is not that a professor is a great human being, but a professor is certainly better than a godman. A professor at least offers you avidya, which is an honest, objective fact about the world or about the body or about the mind, whatever. But the godman is a fraudster who does not know the world; instead, he is offering you fantastic stories about the Beyond, and those stories will get you nowhere. It is just that instead of losing your ignorance, you will lose your bank balance. That is what the guru is anyway eyeing.

> **THE ONE WHO IS PURSUING OBJECTIVE KNOWLEDGE ALONE IS MERELY BLIND TO HIS INTENTIONS. THE ONE WHO IS PURSUING SUBJECTIVE KNOWLEDGE ALONE IS A HYPOCRITE WHO IS NOT BLIND TO HIS INTENTIONS; INSTEAD, HE IS SUPPORTING HIS EVIL INTENTIONS.**

(Advait BodhSthal, 2020)

29

Pleasure Is False Freedom from Suffering

> " SUFFERING IS NOT THE PROBLEM; SUFFERING IS THE
> SITUATION. THE PROBLEM IS THE FALSE HOPE OF AN IMAGINED
> STATE CALLED HAPPINESS. "

आविः संनिहितं गुहाचरन्नाम महत्पदमत्रैतत्समर्पितम् ।
एजत्प्राणन्निमिषच्च यदेतज्जानथ सदसद्वरेण्यं परं विज्ञानाद्यद्वरिष्ठं प्रजानाम् ॥

Manifested, it is here set close within, moving in the secret heart.
This is the mighty foundation and into it is consigned all that moves
and breathes and sees. This that is that great foundation here, know
it as the Is and Is not, the supremely desirable, greatest and the
Highest, beyond the knowledge of creatures.

~Mundaka Upanishad, Verse 2.2.1

Listener (L): Initially, taking on the spiritual path seems like a lot of suffering in itself. The process is arduous and takes a lot of time, while staying in the default state is easy. It is only at a much later stage where one begins to see that real relaxation can be had only through this arduous process. How to develop the right understanding at the initial level of the climb?

Acharya Prashant (AP): Suffering has to be an acceptable word. You have to train yourself to accept suffering as your default state. The problem is the illusion of pleasure; somewhere, you see the possibility of false freedom from suffering. Freedom from suffering is one thing; pleasure is false freedom from suffering. You have to discount that possibility.

There is going to be no pleasure, full stop. There is suffering and there will be suffering. The only thing I, as a person, have a handle on is the kind of suffering, the type of suffering that I endure. Do I want to suffer in a way that continues the suffering endlessly, or do I want to suffer in a way that dissolves the suffering progressively? That is the only thing I can choose. There is no third option.

Pleasure is a mirage; it does not exist. Discount it. Train yourself to suffer, suffer and suffer. And when you can suffer without admitting the possibility of pleasure, suffering is not insufferable, it is okay. Suffering appears unacceptable only because of the promise of pleasure. Once you convince yourself that there is no pleasure, then suffering is no more a problem; then suffering becomes the fact of your human condition.

Suffering is your very fact; it is the condition you are born into. There is no need to take it as something alien, as something unwanted. It is not a problem; it is our very situation, it is the core of our situation. If you call the core of your situation a problem, then you will force yourself to search for illusions. Don't be an illusion hunter. Know the reality of your existence and make peace with it, and the reality of your existence is suffering. Don't frown at suffering, don't crib; just suffer with dignity, wisdom and courage, and if possible, a smile. A little one? That much we can afford.

That is why the most detestable sight is the face of a happy person. If consciousness is to be valued, then happiness is the antithesis of consciousness. The more you can distance yourself from that illusion, the better it would be for you, and then you can choose the right kind of suffering.

When the choice is between the wrong kind of suffering and the right kind of suffering, it will be easy for you to choose the right kind of suffering. But when a third option sneaks in, then your choices get distorted. If there are only two choices, wrong suffering and right suffering, then you will go for the right suffering. But when the choice is wrong suffering, right suffering and happiness, now the choice is distorted. Now you go for happiness and that kills it all.

So, remove the third option altogether. It is either wrong suffering or right suffering. No happiness.

L: How does one develop the appetite to suffer?

AP: No, you don't have to develop an appetite to suffer. Suffering is like oxygen. Suffering is like the blood flowing in our veins. It is the grain of our reality. You don't have to have an appetite for it, it is there. You need an appetite only for stuff that is alien to you. You need an appetite for a brinjal or a cucumber because there you have a choice, a choice between brinjal and cucumber.

Suffering is your very essence. Suffering is your oxygen. Suffering is your blood. Suffering is your heartbeat. What do you mean by having an appetite for your heartbeat? It is there. You don't need to have an appetite for suffering. You need to have a loss of appetite towards happiness. Therein lies your problem. You are not placing your problem rightly.

Suffering, I repeat, is not the problem; suffering is the situation. The problem is the false hope of an imagined state called happiness.

L: If one lacks the ability to endure suffering or, as you said, bear it or pass through it with dignity, courage and a smile, does that indicate that one has too much appetite for pleasure?

AP: It indicates a lot of greed for happiness. There is some corner somewhere in one's life or mind that is calling and enchanting with the promise of happiness. And therefore, in comparison, in a foolish comparison, suffering becomes unpalatable. Otherwise, suffering would be very much acceptable. We said it is our core reality; why would it be unacceptable? But it becomes unacceptable when that chimaera comes calling.

Remove that illusion, remove that fancy hope, and then you will find that suffering is a purifier, suffering is an energizer, suffering is an elevator.

Suffering is love. Suffering is depth. Suffering is creativity. Suffering is great songs, verses, shlokas. But suffering will reveal its splendour, its beauty to you only when you first do away with happiness. As long as happiness remains an option in your mind, suffering will remain a problem, and if suffering remains a problem, then suffering will never disclose to you the bountiful beauties it contains in itself.

L: How to strike out that option completely?

AP: You have to see it as false. It does not exist. It is not as if happiness exists and you are discarding it. That option does not exist, so you don't have to strike it out—it anyway does not exist!

You are taking happiness as real; it is too much for you to totally discount it. You are believing too much in those who stand for happiness in your life. You are believing just too much in them. You are not able to strike them out.

I repeat, as long as happiness remains a hope, suffering will remain a problem.

> **❝** SUFFERING WILL REVEAL ITS SPLENDOUR, ITS BEAUTY TO YOU ONLY WHEN YOU FIRST DO AWAY WITH HAPPINESS. AS LONG AS HAPPINESS REMAINS AN OPTION IN YOUR MIND, SUFFERING WILL REMAIN A PROBLEM, AND IF SUFFERING REMAINS A PROBLEM, THEN SUFFERING WILL NEVER DISCLOSE TO YOU THE BOUNTIFUL BEAUTIES IT CONTAINS IN ITSELF. **❞**

(Advait BodhSthal, 2021)

30

Does Higher Pleasure Come with Higher Suffering?

> *You don't have to take up a very high kind of suffering. Do only as much as you can. The thing is, if you exercise even that level of suffering it will bring you a disproportionately higher pleasure.*

सत्येन लभ्यस्तपसा ह्येष आत्मा सम्यग्ज्ञानेन ब्रह्मचर्येण नित्यम् ।
अन्तःशरीरे ज्योतिर्मयो हि शुभ्रो यं पश्यन्ति यतयः क्षीणदोषाः ॥

The Self can always be won by Truth, by self-discipline, by integral knowledge, by life of purity. This Self that is in the inner body radiant, made all of light, whom by the perishing of their blemishes, the doers of askesis behold.

~Mundaka Upanishad, Verse 3.1.5

Listener (L): For the common mind there is the common suffering and then there is pleasure which is the lower pleasure. The common mind runs from suffering and desires pleasure. Now, come the Upanishads which say that there is higher pleasure, but for that you have to go through higher suffering, self-discipline. How does the common mind accept higher suffering?

Acharya Prashant (AP): There is a way out. In your current level of existence, which you might call a lower level, you have a certain capacity, certain appetite to take suffering; it is not beyond you. This is not a higher suffering but a lower suffering, suffering at your current level which you may call a lower level.

The thing is, if you exercise even that level of suffering, it will bring you a disproportionately higher pleasure. Once you taste that pleasure then you will realize that a formula has opened up, and then your willingness to take more discipline upon yourself increases because now you have tasted the results.

At your particular level you did the little you could, but the little you could do, the little you did do, was the maximum you could do at your particular level. The good news is that at any level the maximum you do is sufficient. You are not demanded to do something beyond yourself. Just do the maximum that is within your capacity. Good news is, you don't have to exceed your capacity. The challenge is, you have to do the maximum that is possible within your capacity.

Once you do the maximum that is within your capacity, you get results, and once you taste the results, your willingness to impose more discipline upon yourself increases. Now you know that a formula has opened up: 'The more I exert myself, the better the results will be.' Now you have been convinced with a proof, and what is the proof? The results. The results have arrived. 'Now, I know. Now, I am unstoppable. Now, I will go further and further, the complete distance.'

But the trick is, at your current level you have to do at least as much as is needed to show some results to you; otherwise you will be disappointed. The worst situation is of those people who work but do not work hard enough even to get the minimum kinds of results that are possible. So, you work, you have exerted yourself, you have taken some suffering upon yourself, and yet you have not done enough to get even some kind of preliminary results, so your score card stands at zero. Neither do you get anything, nor are you left with any motivation to do anything more.

So, if you are doing something, do at least as much as is needed to get the basic results, and those results will then egg you on.

I repeat: Each of us, irrespective of how weak we are, has within his capacity to work as much as is needed to get the basic results. And the basic results will bring some trust in you, some inspiration in you, they will help you experience something that is totally new to you, and its taste will be so convincing that you will be inspired now to move ahead with deeper vigour.

There is that initial period when you are working and there are no results; that is when you require faith and patience. Once the results start showing, the results will keep spurring you on and then it is so formulaic; now the ball has been set rolling and it will keep gaining momentum.

You don't have to take up a very high kind of suffering. Do only as much as you can—but please do as much as you can. On one hand, I am saying that do only as much as you can; in the same breath, I am also saying please do as much as you can. But in neither of these cases do I am saying please do more than you can. That is not needed, because that cannot happen. How can you do more than you can?

That is the reason nobody else is to be blamed if you fail: because you were not even required to go beyond your capacity. It was within your capacity to succeed. If you fail, it was only because you didn't exercise your capacity. Had you done your best, you would have obtained at least the basic results. If your score card always stands at zero, it is a clear proof that you are not even doing half of what you are capable of. That is why life punishes you.

L: Sometimes there are moments when the basic results are seen, but we become forgetful of them.

AP: No, if the thing has really shown results, it will captivate you. It won't allow you to regress. You cannot go back now. It is like gravity: you have started falling. You cannot say, 'I fell for a distance and then I stopped falling.' If you fall for a distance then you will not only keep falling, you will keep falling with increasing velocity. If you find that after a distance your movement stops then you were not falling, you were just rolling about in some horizontal plane. That is not called falling.

The algorithm is simple. Work hard, let the result come, let yourself be charmed by the results; let the result inspire you to work even harder, let a better result come, let it charm you even more; work even harder, let the charm become deeper, and so on and so forth.

L: You just said that if one is not falling with the force of gravity, then one is just rolling around in the horizontal plane. Can it happen that you rise up to a point and then get stuck? Or does that mean you never rose?

AP: You never rose, you just rolled. Now the trick for you is to keep rolling right till the edge of the cliff, and then you will fall. If you are told to fall you won't fall, so keep rolling.

In this real love there is nothing called a breakup; it just keeps getting deeper and deeper. You cannot say, 'I was spiritual for a while and then I dropped it.' That is the thing with the infinite: it inspires infinite love in you. Otherwise, why to needlessly flatter it by calling it infinite?

Infinite love, in infinite ways and infinite times. It is a love affair that renews itself, deepens itself; it is born, it is reborn; it grows upon you till it finishes you off. It is not a fleeting flirtation, it is not a momentary charm. It is not some kind of seasonal attraction. It has rained and the butterflies are out because the flowers have opened—not that kind of a thing. It is a one way thing—you are into it, then you are deeply into it, and then you are into it even deeper.

So it is said: Gatey, gatey, paragatey. Gone, and then gone even deeper, and then gone beyond (paragatey), and then swaha (finished). This is the name of this affair.

Gatey, gatey, paragatey. Gone, gone further, gone beyond, then finished, over. This is the nature of this love.

> " THE ALGORITHM IS SIMPLE: WORK HARD, LET THE RESULT COME, LET YOURSELF BE CHARMED BY THE RESULTS; LET THE RESULT INSPIRE YOU TO WORK EVEN HARDER, LET A BETTER RESULT COME, LET IT CHARM YOU EVEN MORE; WORK EVEN HARDER, LET THE CHARM BECOME DEEPER, AND SO ON AND SO FORTH. "

(Advait BodhSthal, 2021)

31

Is there Happiness in Spirituality?

❝ MAN IS A STRANGE MACHINE. MAN IS A STRANGE MACHINE
BECAUSE NO MACHINE, AS WE KNOW MACHINES, EVER
SUFFERS. NO MACHINE REALLY HAS CONSCIOUSNESS; NO
MACHINE EVER HAS AN 'I'. MAN IS A STRANGE MACHINE, A
MACHINE WITH AN 'I'. ❞

राजविद्या राजगुह्यं पवित्रमिदमुत्तमम् ।
प्रत्यक्षावगमं धर्म्यं सुसुखं कर्तुमव्ययम् ॥

*Of sciences, the highest; of profundities, the deepest; of purifiers,
the supreme, is this; realizable by direct perception, endowed with
(immense) merit, very easy to perform, and of an imperishable nature.*
~Bhagavad Gita, Verse 9.2

Listener: In the verse, Shri Krishna has used the word 'susukham',
which means very easy, and has called this raja-vidya the king
of sciences. In my experience, the ego seems to be like an
insurmountable mountain; going against oneself is extremely hard.
So, why is the term 'very easy' used here?

Acharya Prashant: Shri Krishna explains adhyātma (self-knowledge) or raja-vidya to Arjuna. That is the context. He says that raja-vidya or adhyātma or self-knowledge or Brahmajñāna is the highest, the deepest, the supreme purifier, realizable by direct perception, endowed with immense merit, very easy to perform and imperishable.

The path of adhyātma is accompanied by a relaxation of inner tension. Please pay attention to the whole process. Why does one venture into his interiors first of all? There is nothing in our system that is designed to take us within ourselves. The mind is configured to be stuffed with worldly objects carrying name, shape and form; the senses all look just outwards. In short, man is a creature designed to remain in the world. He dwells in the world, belongs to the world, arises from the world, and is consumed by the world.

Then why does the path of raja-vidya or adhyātma or self-knowledge appear as an attractive possibility to some people? This path is not at all intuitive. There is nothing in our tendencies, our pre-existing, biological design that encourages us or nudges us to look at the looker, to look at the mind itself. Yet we know that the path of Dharma or spirituality, raja-vidya or adhyātma, Atmajñāna or Brahmajñāna, not only exists but is actually the highest path if we go by the testimony of those who have ventured upon it.

So, why does a man go towards adhyātma, first of all? The reason is man's nature. No one likes to be miserable or to suffer. Given the way we are biologically designed and our default configuration and conditioning, we are pre-set to suffer. You could say man is a machine designed to suffer.

Man is a strange machine. Man is a strange machine because no machine, as we know machines, ever suffers. No machine really has consciousness; no machine ever has an 'I'. Man is a strange machine, a machine with an 'I'. The 'I' is enclosed in the machine, and the

'I' does not quite like that because the nature of 'I' is freedom; the nature of 'I' is Joy that accompanies freedom.

But the machine is a machine. The machine is designed to act just as per the design, and the design does not favour or even allow the machine to look within itself. However, the 'I' suffers. Irrespective of what the design of the machine dictates, the 'I' still clamours for freedom. The machine is designed to remain in bondage; it is designed to remain and function as per the design. The 'I' does not like any designs. The 'I' likes a designless sky, the 'I' loves a patternless sky in which there are no bondages, no restrictions, no algorithms, no blueprints.

So, we are creatures of suffering. We continue to live in a state of inner stress, an inexplicable restlessness. Now you will understand why Shri Krishna says that the path of raja-vidya is easy: it is easy because it arises from our un-ease. Because we stay queasy, therefore adhyātma is easy. Because we stay in a state of dis-ease, therefore adhyātma is the path of ease. The more you move along this path, the more you move on this path, the more you feel at ease.

That is the reason why Shri Krishna says that this path is easy in the same breath in which he says this path is the most mysterious, the most esoteric, the most hidden one. It is a kingly secret, he says. It is the deepest of all profound truths. It might be the deepest, it might even be the toughest, yet it is the only path that leads to ease. And is it too much to say that that which leads to ease must be rightfully called as easy? What would you call as easy—that which appears easy but leads to difficulties, or that which appears difficult in your calculations, in your assumptions, in your imaginations, but is actually a giver of ease if you adopt it?

Therefore, wise people always say that what they are choosing is actually the easiest. If you go to Lao Tzu, he will say that the Tao favours ease. He will say ease is right. Now, that can be misleading.

We might feel that that which appears easy is right. No, it has to be interpreted to mean that that which leads to inner ease is the right thing for you to do, and that which is right for you to do is called Dharma.

So, Dharma is that which leads you into ease, and that should be obvious. If we are stiff and rigid and tense and insecure and alarmed, then it should be great to be led into ease. Why would any man in his right senses call a movement into ease as something difficult? It would require a special kind of lack of self-love to deny oneself ease and relaxation by terming relaxation as full of tension, and ease as a thing of difficulty.

> We are creatures of suffering. We continue to live in a state of inner stress, an inexplicable restlessness. Now you will understand why Shri Krishna says that the path of raja-vidya is easy: it is easy because it arises from our un-ease. Because we stay queasy, therefore adhyātma is easy.

(Advait BodhSthal, 2020)

32

Choicelessness Is Only for Those Who Choose Rightly

> WHENEVER YOU SAY 'IT JUST HAPPENS', WHENEVER YOU SAY 'I
> GOT ANGRY', WHENEVER YOU SAY 'I AM DEPRESSED', IT IS A
> WRONG CHOICE BECAUSE YOU ARE NOT ADMITTING THAT
> YOU HAVE CHOSEN TO BE DEPRESSED. DISHONESTY AND
> WRONG CHOICES GO TOGETHER. YOU ARE NOT ADMITTING
> THAT IT IS NOT HAPPENING TO YOU; YOU ARE CHOOSING IT,
> ADMITTING IT.

समदुःखसुखः पूर्ण आशानैराश्ययोः समः ।
समजीवितमृत्युः सन्नेवमेव लयं व्रज ॥

*(Knowing yourself) equal in pain and pleasure, equal in hope and
disappointment, equal in life , in death and complete as you are, you
can go to your rest.*

~Ashtavakra Gita, Verse 5.4

Listener (L): How can we, in daily life, practice the equality that
is being talked of in this verse and go closer to the Truth? Does it
happen through sitting, walking, working, meditating, through
living mindfulness in the present moment?

Acharya Prashant (AP): Ah! You gave me a bad taste at the end of your question. All else was proceeding almost rightly. 'Living mindfully in the present moment'—bad words. Avoid them!

You are asking for a method. You are asking, 'How can we, in daily life, practice this and go closer to the Truth? Is it through sitting, walking, working, meditation?' The method is already there in the verse, in the quote. Please read carefully.

'Equal in pain and in pleasure, equal in hope and in disappointment, equal in life and in death and complete as you are, you can go to your rest.'

What is the method? Equality. This equality is the method. But you will have to understand. Here, equality does not mean deadness. To a cave—to the insides of a cave—day and night are equal. We are not talking of that dark, damp, dead situation. We are not talking of that kind of equality. To a dead man, beauty and ugliness are equal. We are not talking about that kind of equality. We are talking about remaining untouched. We are talking about remaining equally untouched by this and that. We are talking about remaining equally aloof. We are talking about remaining equally secure in this and that.

What is 'this' and what is 'that'? Pain is this and pleasure is that; hope is this and disappointment is that; life is this and death is that. When life is there, death is also happening. Life is apparent, death is not so apparent, but they both are happening simultaneously. If pleasure is there, pain too is happening; one is apparent, the other is hidden. In a while, the other will become apparent and this one will become hidden.

So, this and that are there—*always* there. You remain well-seated in your restful place. Ashtavakra says, 'You can go to your rest, complete as you are.' You remain restful. Restfulness should not turn into restiveness.

217

And this and that, they will keep existing for you because you are a person. You are spatially and temporally localized. You exist as a tiny bit in a huge fragment of your own creation. You are a tiny grain of sand in a huge universe that you yourself have painted, created, manufactured, imagined.

In this universe of your own making, this and that are integral. This universe is synonymous with this and that. You cannot have the universe without this and that. Don't ask for the impossible. If the body is there, pleasure and pain will be there. If you put even the so-called realized saints in an oven, they will experience pain, and if you bring them out of the oven into an air-conditioned room, even they will experience pleasure. It is inevitable.

In fact, the whole purpose of sweating is to give you relief from pain, and then evaporation will give you some pleasure. When it is hot and humid you sweat, and the same sweat that was a product of displeasure gives you pleasure as soon as the wind blows. Have you not experienced it? If you have been sweating, after a while you start feeling a little cool. Evaporation helps the body cool down. Pain itself has given birth to pleasure; pain is sweat and sweat is pleasure. Ah! What is what? I don't know. This is that! How do you differentiate?

They will be there. And if you don't want them to be there, then give up the body. But even that seems unlikely to solve the problem. If you give up the body, you will latch onto something else. So many people are anyway prepared to give up their bodies for the sake of pleasing some other body. Don't we see suicide bombers prepared to give up the material body in order to please their psychological body?

So, it is not as if you are irretrievably or inexorably attached to the physical body. For the sake of the mental body, sometimes you say, 'I will face bullets and let this body die, but let the psychic-self prevail. I would be called a martyr or I would have proven a point.' It won't work. This and that would remain. Don't give them too much importance.

Why am I suggesting this to you? Because it is practical. Why is it practical? Because you do have a choice. The importance that you gave to this and that didn't just happen on its own; the process had your consent. Sometimes you actively chose to give importance, sometimes the choice was passive, but nevertheless, a choice was always involved. That is bad news because the choice is often bad, but that is also the best news because we do have a choice. And if we can make a bad choice, we can make a good one as well.

Bad news is good news. This is that. Choice is bad news because so far we have been making bad choices, but even bad choices prove that good choices can be made. So, even here, this is that. Pain is pleasure. Make the right choice, and maybe then you would find that you are beyond this and that. Some people call that choicelessness. It is strange, but choicelessness comes to you via the right choice.

Before the right choice can come to you, before choicelessness can come to you, make the right choice. The scriptures put it this way: Before you can move into the guṇātīta (beyond all qualities), move into sattva-guṇa (considered highest of the three qualities of tamas, rajas and sattva in Vedanta). Before you can move into that which is beyond properties, nirguṇa (without qualities), you must first move into sattva-guṇa.

Do the right thing before you can be a non-doer. Why is it said that you must do the right thing before you can be a non-doer? That is because you are anyway used to doing, and you have been doing all the wrong things. Now that you have been doing the wrong things, wake up to your power and right to choose, and do a few things right. And then, you will slowly discover that you need not even do. That is called non-doership.

Similarly, for choicelessness to descend upon you, at least first make good choices. If you can make a choice to become engaged and involved and emotional, can't you make a choice to not become engaged and involved and emotional? Or do you have control only one way? What kind of a driver are you? You say that you are able to drive well only when you are driving on the wrong side, and when you are in the right lane you cannot drive well. You are cheating yourself.

If you ever happen to be with such a driver, what would you do? You are riding an Ola or an Uber, and the driver is constantly driving on the wrong side, and he says, 'I can drive well only when I make the wrong choice, take the wrong side.' I tell you, save your life, press the emergency button. This driver is a cheat. This driver is you.

You are very good when it comes to making all the noise and all the mischief; then you are very alert and energetic. But when it comes to doing the right thing, you say, 'You see, I am dull and foolish, and I don't understand anything!'

When it comes to creating chaos, then he knows everything. You send him to fetch a few vegetables from the market. He will say, 'I don't know where the pumpkins and potatoes are'—but he very well knows from where to get all the chemicals to assemble a bomb. Then becomes very smart. This kind of dishonesty won't do.

When it comes to all the nonsense, you see how you succeed, don't you? When you want to go and create chaos, when you want to go and satisfy your lust, just see how you find out ways. Like a rat, you find your way into the house; then you know where the hole is. And if the hole is not there, you dig a hole! But when it comes to doing something a little religious, a little less impure, then you say, 'I am such a fool! I am a duffer! I am irresponsible! I do not know which way to go! I have no intelligence, no smartness!' All the smartness is reserved only for your demonic acts. Don't you see?

Are you really so dull? You are not. In hot pursuit of your hot targets, you are able to bring the heavens down to the earth. All the energylessness, all the forgetfulness is reserved only for the right things. The right things you forget. Don't say you are forgetting. What is it actually?

L: A choice.

AP: A choice to forget. I will call your bluff. I will expose your hypocrisy. You are not so big of an idiot as you show yourself to be. In fact, you are no idiot at all; you are extremely smart. It is just that your smartness is self-destructive.

See the things that you covet and chase, and notice how you devise clever mechanisms to get what you want. But, as I said, the one thing that you cannot fetch is potatoes from the market; then you become a dodo. You say, 'What is a potato? Do they grow on trees? Do they fall from the sky? Do we manufacture them in factories? I am a dodo!'

Choice! You are not helpless. Wake up to your power. You cannot just be carried away. Nothing can happen to you without your consent. In the material sense, yes, a stone can hit you without your consent. But you cannot suffer without your consent. Restfulness is your nature. You cannot become restless without your consent.

Discover your choice. Better still, admit your choice. Admitting choice entails responsibility, and that is why you want to evade it. That, I say, is the very definition of a human being: the one with a choice. A human being is the one who always sees two paths ahead of him: one that will fetch him what he really wants, the other that would only deceive him.

Keep making the right choice. If you are a human being, you have no option but to live rightly; otherwise, there is suffering.

What is the wrong choice? Anything that involves helplessness is the wrong choice. That is the definition. Whenever you say, 'Oh, but I could not have done it! Oh, but I could not have helped it!' you are deceiving yourself, and it is bound to be the wrong choice.

Whenever you say 'it just happens', whenever you say 'I got angry', whenever you say 'I am depressed', it is a wrong choice because you are not admitting that you have *chosen* to be depressed. Dishonesty and wrong choices go together. You are not admitting that it is not happening to you; you are choosing it, admitting it. Worse still, inviting it. Worse still, manufacturing it. Worse still, nothing is happening! You are just narrating a cock-and-bull story.

When rest is your nature and the only Truth, from where has restlessness come? Obviously, it has to be a silly fabrication. It cannot exist. It is a myth. But see how you declare, 'Oh, I am so depressed!' First of all, it is a choice whether or not to be depressed; secondly, when Joy is your nature, how can depression even exist? But we not only claim that we are depressed, we also expect some sympathy, you see, a little bit at least.

You never forget. You *decide* to forget. And if you can decide to forget, you can equally well decide to not forget. No, you cannot decide to remember; remembrance is nature. You can only decide to not forget.

> " A HUMAN BEING IS THE ONE WHO ALWAYS SEES TWO PATHS AHEAD OF HIM: ONE THAT WILL FETCH HIM WHAT HE REALLY ANTS, THE OTHER THAT WOULD ONLY DECEIVE HIM. KEEP MAKING THE RIGHT CHOICE. IF YOU ARE A HUMAN BEING, YOU HAVE NO OPTION BUT TO LIVE RIGHTLY; OTHERWISE, THERE IS SUFFERING. "

(Advait BodhSthal, 2018)

33

The Secret of Unending Happiness

❝ JOY IS HAPPINESS WITHOUT A THING TO BE HAPPY ABOUT. JOY
IS HAPPINESS THAT SCOFFS AT ALL THE THINGS THAT PROMISE
TO MAKE YOU HAPPY. JOY IS HAPPINESS THAT, FIRST OF ALL,
DOES NOT REALIZE SADNESS AT ALL. ❞

किं सुखम् ।
सुखमिति च सच्चिदानन्दस्वरूपं
ज्ञात्वानन्दरूपा या स्थितिः सैव सुखम् ।

What is pleasure?
Pleasure is the blissful state that succeeds the knowledge of the essence
of Being, Intelligence and Bliss.
                                        ~Niralamba Upanishad, Verse 15

Acharya Prashant: The ego-self lives in its own little dualistic
world. In its own world, it experiences sukha and dukha, happiness
and sorrow, pleasure and pain. It knows nothing beyond happiness
and sorrow, sukha and dukha, so it is obvious that the question
cannot exceed the knowledge or experience of the questioner. And
the questioner, therefore, asks, 'What is sukha? What is happiness?'

In his own estimation, the questioner is asking about the highest state of experience that can be had—sukha, happiness. By asking about happiness, the questioner has disclosed that he takes happiness to be important, rather special, probably the most desirous and coveted state possible.

The questioner is just being honest. The questioner is not asking about conceptual states. The questioner is not probing into mythical, transcendental universes. The questioner is simply saying, 'Sir, to me, happiness is the most exalted state possible. What is it?'

The rishi, the teacher, takes it up from here. He says, 'Fine, I will tell you about happiness', and then he says that once you experience the heights of consciousness, when you realize that which normally remains hidden from you, then upon that realization the Joy that dawns upon you is called happiness.

Look at the rishi's approach. The rishi is not directly saying, 'Son, why are you caught in the dualistic paradigm of happiness and sorrow?' Instead, he takes up the word that the student, the questioner is using and elevates that word itself. He infuses that common, vulgar word, 'happiness', with a sacred meaning. He says, 'Jñātvānandarūpā. Sukhamiti ca Saccidānandasvarūpaṁ jñātvānandarūpā.'

So, starting from sukha, he takes the student to Ananda. He says real happiness is when your consciousness experiences something beyond its normal world, something that is unlikely to be eclipsed by time.

Sat—that which is sat (Truth).

Chit—that which is available only to the rarefied heights of consciousness.

Ananda—that which is beyond the dualistic happiness and sorrow polarities.

That is happiness.

Now, why doesn't the rishi simply dismiss the question and tell the student that what he is asking for is something not worthy of desire? He could have straight away rubbished the question. He could have said, 'Keep sukha aside. Let's talk of Ananda!' But he doesn't do that. Why doesn't he do that? Because even when the student is asking about happiness, the latent desire is for the highest thing possible.

It is just that the highest thing possible has so far not been available to the student. The highest has not just been within the experience of the student. After all, he is a student. He has not led a very sublime life so far. But he wants that absolute height, so what does he do? He uses the highest that has been available to him in his limited experience and asks about it.

It is almost like a kid who has never gone any higher than the flight of stairs in his house that takes him to the terrace. He is just a little kid. So, to him, in his experience, what is the highest? The terrace, the rooftop. So, the terrace, to him, becomes a synonym of height. The terrace, to him, starts symbolising height.

So, next time, whenever he has to refer to something high, he refers to it in the language of the terrace. He might, in fact, be referring to an aircraft flying high in the sky above his house, but he has no way of referring to the aircraft directly. His language is insufficient. His experience does not consist of aircrafts. So, he starts referring to the aircraft using the words 'terrace', 'roof', 'ceiling'.

That is what we always do. We want something that is beyond our imagination, beyond our experience. That is what the desirous one who sits at the centre of all desire really craves for. But how does he express what he really wants? The expression is limited by his experience and the power of his senses. The senses include the mind, the memory and the intellect as well.

You might want the highest, but your mind has no way of knowing what you really want. The mind just gathers a vague impression of a deep desire, and it expresses that vague impression in some incomplete, hazy way. The deep self is desirous of one thing, whereas the mind, thoughts and actions proceed towards something vastly inferior. And it can be quite a tragedy.

You could be desirous of the sky; sitting here in this hall, you might be desirous of the sky, and you are looking upwards. All that the mind knows of is the roof. So, the mind is trying to reach the ceiling, and the mind will be stopped, limited and barricaded by the ceiling. If you want the sky, the ceiling doesn't quite assist, or does it?

That is what happens normally to most of us. Something within you wants to rise up and up and up and up, but the entire movement has to take place via the mind, via the faculties, via the bodily experiences—and none of these have any affinity for the sky. They know their own limited province.

It is quite amusing. You want the sky, and the mind latches onto the ceiling, and in its own estimation the mind has reached a high place. And if you argue with the mind, it will say, 'Is not the ceiling a place higher than the floor? Have I not succeeded?' And you tell the mind, 'No, but this is not what I wanted.'

You are talking in dualities. The floor and the ceiling constitute a pair of dualities. So, you were at the floor, which you called as low, and now you are at the ceiling, which you call as high—and you are quite happy for yourself, gloating and proud. You say you have achieved something in life, and you also have proof. From the ceiling you look downwards, and you say, 'This is the roof and that is the floor where I started my journey. Look at the distance I have covered!' What you do not realize is that you haven't really risen; rather, you have blocked your possibility to rise beyond the ceiling.

So, that is how we operate. Really wanting one thing but targeting something totally inferior; really desirous of one thing but consoling ourselves with something totally inferior.

The rishi says, 'Fine. Let me change your very definition of happiness. Happiness, then, is not about obtaining something within the purview of your experiences. Happiness is when you move into Saccidānanda.'

Do you see the method being used here? It is almost a trick. What the rishi is saying is, 'Let the floor be where it already is—I will move the ceiling. Because if I tell you that you have to go as high as the sky, you will find my words absurd; you do not know the sky. Instead, if I tell you to rise up to the sky, you will get stuck at the ceiling—as you always do.'

What is the rishi doing, then? He has plucked the ceiling and taken it up to the sky. He is saying, 'Yes, the floor is dukha, the ceiling is sukha, the sky is Ananda. You want sukha; I will equate sukha to Ananda. You will not directly come to Ananda. You are a pleasure-seeker, you want happiness, so I am raising the bar.' The ceiling is now hanging from the skies. It is a floating ceiling. Not merely floating—it is rising constantly like a hot air balloon.

Sat. Saccidānandasvarūpam jñātvānandarūpā. Know that which time cannot destroy.

But the mind only knows that which is within the construct of time. So, what is it to know that which is Sat? It merely means to forget that which is asat (untruth). It merely means to turn oblivious to all that will be anyway no more.

At one place the Upanishad says, and it appears a very simple, rather ordinary thing to say, 'Mortals cannot become happy through wealth.' If you can understand this statement, you will know why Sat is so important and why asat has to be abjured.

Ananda

You are a mortal, which means you are constantly passing away, and wealth is something you can have at most as long as you exist. But you are a mortal. If you are mortal, your real problem cannot be that you do not have much. If you are mortal, your real problem, obviously, is that you do not have much time.

So, the Upanishad puts it so pithily: 'Mortals cannot become happy through wealth.' Because you are dying, you have to give up death itself if you are to be really happy.

How do you keep clinging to death? Death is not a thing; death is not a person. What is death? Death is a process. Death is a property. Death simply means destructibility. How does one cling to death? By clinging to things that are destructible.

The Upanishad is saying, you have to know that which is Sat. We are saying, you have to forget that which is asat. But if you want to forget the asat, we have to firstly ask how we keep clinging to asat, how we maintain our mortal identities. We maintain our mortal identities by clinging to things that are destructible, mortal, timebound.

So, happiness is when you obtain these things. Joy is when you no longer have a need to obtain these things.

Happiness is when you have something with you that makes you feel happy. Joy is when you do not need anything in particular to feel happy.

Happiness is to carry the obligation to be happy. Joy is when you are no more obligated to be happy.

That is the reason why the Upanishad discusses these ordinary questions—what is sukha, what is dukha. If these basics are not clear, it is inevitable that life will be misspent. One will be chasing stuff that one does not even want.

It is one thing to say, 'Boy, you are going after things that you do not really need'—our madness is deeper than that. We keep going after things that we do not even want; we keep desiring stuff that we are really not even desirous of. And that is why that stuff loses its sheen the moment it is obtained.

You want freedom from your mortal nightmare. How can you get freedom from that by going after and clinging to things that are all timebound in themselves?

Joy is happiness without a thing to be happy about. Joy is happiness that scoffs at all the things that promise to make you happy. Joy is happiness that, first of all, does not realize sadness at all.

Sat-Chit-Ananda.

Eternal. Conscious. Joyful.

'Sat' is often taken as existent—that which really is, in the sense that it won't disappear. It is. It does not appear—it *is*. It is not a thing that you perceive—it *is*. That is Sat.

Remember that practically the much more useful word is 'asat'. Happiness is freedom from the clutches of asat.

> **❝ HAPPINESS IS WHEN YOU HAVE SOMETHING WITH YOU THAT MAKES YOU FEEL HAPPY. JOY IS WHEN YOU DO NOT NEED ANYTHING IN PARTICULAR TO FEEL HAPPY. HAPPINESS IS TO CARRY THE OBLIGATION TO BE HAPPY. JOY IS WHEN YOU ARE NO MORE OBLIGATED TO BE HAPPY. ❞**

(Advait BodhSthal, 2020)

34

The Source of Unending Pain

> " SUKHA IS TO BE FREE FROM THE NEED TO LOOK AROUND FOR
> RELIEF. DUKHA IS TO LOOK AROUND FOR RELIEF AND INVITE
> MORE TROUBLE. "

किं दुःखम् ।
दुःखिमित अनात्मरूपः
विषयसङ्कल्प एव दुःखम् ।

What is pain?
It (dukha or pain) is the mere saṅkalpa (or the thinking) of the objects
of mundane existence (or of not-Self).
> ~Niralamba Upanishad, Verse 16

Acharya Prashant: Dukha is the mere saṅkalpa or thought of the objects of mundane existence. The thought, the desire of all that which is fleeting and ephemeral is dukha.

Why is it dukha? For whom is it dukha? A few things have to be understood.

Everything likes to be in its most stress-free state. That is what even material wants—to be in the most relaxed state possible. Given the suitable condition, everything in the universe wants to move towards its most relaxed, lowest agitation, lowest energy state, and that is what is called its natural state.

Anything which is not in its natural state will be unstable. Being unstable, it will want to do things that can relieve it of its energy, or it will want to use the environment around itself to be relieved of its excess energy, which in itself is stress. So, a system or an object which possesses excessive energy or tension tends to react with the environment. It wants to react with the environment precisely with the intention to give up its stress and settle down into a stable state.

That is what consciousness also does. Its most stable state is energyless and inert, totally non-reactive, totally at rest and peace. But somehow if it is not in its peaceful and restful state, it will look around to react with something or somebody in its vicinity so that it may come to stability and rest. If the reaction is right and suitable, consciousness will be relieved of its excess tension. But if the reaction is with an improper or unsuitable object, then instead of the tension being relieved, the tension will multiply. This tension itself is dukha.

What is the fundamental tension that consciousness has? The fundamental tension that it has is existence itself. 'Why do I exist? Why do I exist as I appear to exist? I exist in a bodily confinement'— that is how man's consciousness is: bodily. 'Why do I exist in a bodily way? Why do I exist in a temporal way? Why am I spatially limited? Why do I forget things? Why can't I know fully?' This is what the innate tension of consciousness is: 'Why am I so limited?'

Now, because of this tension, consciousness wants to react with the stuff around itself, stuff in its sensory purview. But all the stuff in the sensory purview of consciousness carries the same properties that consciousness is so stressed about.

Consciousness is saying, 'But why am I confined in a bodily cage? Why can't I know everything insightfully? Why do I look at reality through a spatial, temporal prison?' And what does consciousness see around itself? Entities which are limited, confined, and in as much bondage as consciousness itself. There is nothing around the self that exists at a higher platform compared to the self. But the self has to seek relief. It cannot remain inert or patient as it is.

How is the self, the consciousness feeling about itself? It is feeling disgusted and sick about itself. So, given its state, it has to do something. What does it do? It starts seeking the help of the stuff around itself that is as sick as itself, or probably even more sick than itself.

You are confined within this hall, and you have a strong stomach ache. There are five-six other people here, and you can see that they all have their own various sicknesses: they are groaning, moaning, crying, yelling, some are rolling on the floor clasping their stomachs. You can see that they are in no better position than you—but you are in need of help. What do you do? After a while your patience runs out, and you go to one of these people and start engaging him; you start offering to help him and you start expecting help from him. This is what the Upanishad is calling as dukha.

You are sick and tired of your worldly existence, and your sickness and tiredness force you deeper into the recesses of the world—this is dukha. You are tired of being what you have become, and you are engaging and affiliating with beings that are at the same level of becoming as you are—that is dukha or sorrow.

There are objects of mundane existence—anātmarūpa— things that are non-Self, things that are non-Truth, things that are ephemeral, things that will deceive, stuff that will simply not live up to your expectations. Thinking of these things, desiring them, targeting them, associating with them is dukha.

As they say, dukha is like trying to douse fire with oil. Why? Because you cannot spot water. 'Because I cannot find water in my vicinity, what do I do? I start using whatever I can lay my hands on. After all, I am burning. I am burning, so I need something.'

Sukha is to be free from the need to look around for relief.

Dukha is to look around for relief and invite more trouble.

What is the root cause of dukha? The idea that you are not all right.

See, the highest thing, the best thing is to not at all have the idea that you are in trouble. The second best thing—if you at all have the idea that you are in trouble—is to find something or somebody who will show to you that you are not in trouble.

The worst thing is to believe that you are in trouble and be in the company of people who attest that you are in trouble; thereby, they make you believe in your troubles all the more, and then they provide solutions, and such solutions only further exacerbate your trouble.

The best thing is probably impossible to happen on its own— to simply drop the idea that you are a troubled consciousness. So, in the questions that we now come to, the Upanishads talk of the second best thing.

'What if I do believe that I am the ego self? What if I do believe that I am the body? What if I am the questioner? What if it is practically impossible for me to drop the idea that I exist? In my own eyes I do exist, and I exist as a mass of suffering. What do I do then?'

The Upanishads answer that question now.

> ❝ THE HIGHEST THING, THE BEST THING IS TO NOT AT ALL HAVE
> THE IDEA THAT YOU ARE IN TROUBLE. THE SECOND-BEST
> THING—IF YOU AT ALL HAVE THE IDEA THAT YOU ARE IN
> TROUBLE—IS TO FIND SOMETHING OR SOMEBODY WHO WILL
> SHOW TO YOU THAT YOU ARE NOT IN TROUBLE. ❞

(Advait BodhSthal, 2020)

35

What Is Heaven and Hell?

> " HELL FOCUSES ON WHAT YOU HAVE. HEAVEN REMINDS YOU
> OF WHO YOU ARE. AND ONCE YOU CLEARLY REMEMBER WHO
> YOU ARE, YOU DON'T EVEN NEED HEAVEN; THEN WHAT YOU
> HAVE IS LIBERATION. "

कः स्वर्गः । को नरकः ।
स्वर्ग इति च सत्संसर्गः स्वर्गः ।
नरक इति च असत्संसारिविषयजनसंसर्ग एव नरकः ।

What is heaven? What is hell?
Heaven is the association with the holy.
Association with the worldly folk who are unholy alone is hell.
~Niralamba Upanishad, Verse 17

Acharya Prashant (AP): 'Heaven is association with the holy.'
The best thing would have been a non-dual state in which
no association holds any meaning—there exists nobody else to
associate with, there is nobody else at all. And that state is blissful
beyond all imaginations of the best of heavens.

Even heaven is confined by the depiction and definition of what 'heaven' means. Therefore, Liberation is a place higher and better than heaven. Heaven has a depiction and definition, and, therefore, heaven has its boundaries. And where there are boundaries, there is sorrow. Liberation has neither depiction nor definition, and Liberation is freedom from all boundaries and, therefore, all sorrow.

Here, the sages are talking of heaven. They are talking of heaven because heaven will make it possible to be liberated. Theoretically, it is possible to be liberated even from hell, but it is difficult. Therefore, this is a graded approach: Heaven, and above heaven lies...?

Listener (L): Liberation.

AP: And below heaven lies...?

L: Hell.

AP: And we live in?

L: Hell.

AP: Hell. We live in hell. We are being told how to graduate to heaven. And if you make good use of heaven, you will be liberated even from heaven.

What is heaven? The company of holiness is heaven— satsaṁsargaḥ. 'Sargaḥ' means association, coming close to something. 'Sat' means that which is indestructible, infallible, eternal. Be with someone who will not solve your problem but will demonstrate your problem to be false. That is heaven. Heaven is a place where you get no sympathies for having problems.

Hell, on the other hand, according to the sage, is association with the unholy worldly folk. Hell is a place where your problemed self is ratified.

Do not think of hell as a place where you will be cruelly dealt with. All the usual comic book depictions of hell are exactly that—a kid's fantasy or nightmare. Immense cauldrons full of boiling oil and slaves being dealt with whiplashes, monsters out to suck your blood—that is what we think hell is. Hell is not all this.

Hell is a place where you get a lot of sympathy, consolation, condolence, commiseration. You are told that 'we agree that you are in a miserable state'. Your neighbour comes to you, puts his hands on your shoulder, and with a grave face tells you that you are indeed in deep trouble. What has been done? Your belief in your problemed existence has been deepened. That is hell.

Your problem is not that you have problems. Your problem is that you think you are the one who can have problems. And these are two very different things. It is one thing to have problems. It is another thing to mistake your identity so much that you start imagining yourself as being problemed.

In hell, your belief in your problemed identity is reinforced. Hell is full of people ready to offer you a shoulder to sob on. You go to someone and tell him, 'You know, I am so weak, and I am a victim of circumstances, and I am ignorant and sick, luckless and witless!' And the other fellow will be very quick to not only accept what you are saying but also return and reflect back to you an exaggerated version of what you are saying. You tell him, 'I am feverish, I have a temperature of 101!' He will put his palm on your face and say, 'No, it is 103!' That is hell. The fact is you have 98.4.

Heaven is where your problems are not solved; heaven is where your problems are dismissed. To solve a problem is to honour a problem. Heaven is a place where problems are not admitted. Hell is the place where you are not admitted if you don't have problems.

So, heaven is the company of people who will not pay attention to what you *have* because all that you have is problems. Heaven is the company of the people who will pay attention to what you *are*. Because when you do that, you have very little respect left for what you have. And the more attention you pay to what you have, the easier it becomes for you to turn oblivious to what you are.

Hell focuses on what you have. Heaven reminds you of who you are. And once you clearly remember who you are, you don't even need heaven; then what you have is Liberation.

There are three ways of living.

The most common way of living is: 'What do I have?' Nine hundred and ninety people from a thousand constantly worry and wonder, 'What do I have? How much do I have? How long will it last? How can I have more?'

Then some nine people maybe bother to look at what they are: 'What is the quality of my mind, thought, consciousness, life?'—quality that is not measured through possessions because all possessions are ultimately sources of problems. Either they are explicitly problems, or they are problems waiting to manifest; they are lying latent, dormant. 'I am not very concerned about what I have. The more attention I pay to what I have, the more I am empowering my problems. I am rather much more concerned about what I am.'

And if you pay sufficient and honest attention to who you are, you are liberated of even the need to ask who you are. That is the fruit of constantly inquiring and wondering about your fundamental existence.

You could either worry about all the miscellaneous things— which most people do—or you could keep aside all the miscellaneous worries and focus your mind on this one question or concern or worry, which is: 'How am I doing? What is the quality of my existence? Who am I to be worrying so much?'

Needless to say, all the three are meaningful only with respect to one's mortal existence. Hell, heaven and Liberation—none of these relate to any kind of afterlife or places that one reaches after death. Hell is a way of living, heaven is another way of living, and Liberation is royal life itself.

You are not consigned to hell. You are not rewarded a heaven. Hell and heaven are both choices, your own sovereign choices. No angel, no record keeper, no god outside of you decides whether you will be in heaven or hell. Give up that excuse. You decide whether you want to be in heaven or hell.

Heaven gives you one kind of happiness; hell, too, offers you a particular kind of happiness, and what Liberation gives you is the ultimate happiness. So, it is not about forgoing happiness.

Unfortunately, the lowest kind of hellish happiness prevails and dominates so much that hellish happiness has become synonymous with happiness itself. There is a funny repercussion, therefore: those who are not in hell often start wondering whether they are happy at all. You might actually be blissful, that you can easily admit: 'Yeah, I have a silent, gentle bliss about me'. But if you are asked, 'Are you happy?' you will have a problem quickly and conclusively asserting yourself because happiness has been monopolized by the citizens of hell. Laughing, shrieking, yelling, loud, glitzy, blingy happiness.

So, it is important to realize that when you rise from hell, you don't give up happiness; you just rise to a higher level of happiness. Similarly, Liberation is not liberation from happiness; it is the ultimate level of happiness.

Why am I talking about this? I am talking about this because if you are not convinced that you are graduating to a higher level of happiness, then heaven can feel like a place with no happiness because heaven does not have happiness of the kind that is found in hell. And if your very definition of happiness gets dictated by the citizens of hell, if you start buying into and believing in the definitions they create, hell will become very attractive, and heaven will look very dull to you. And that will pose a danger. Even if you are offered heaven, even if you wisely choose heaven, even if you do gain admission to heaven, you will have an unfortunate inclination to slip back to hell. Why? Because heaven will appear quite an unhappy place.

Therefore, the one who graduates to heaven, the one who elevates himself to Liberation must be very clear that he is not forsaking happiness; he is reclaiming happiness. And reclaiming happiness is very important. You cannot allow happiness to be monopolized by the inhabitants of hell. The ones who are in heaven, they are the ones who really deserve to be happy. The ones who are liberated must be infinitely happy.

But you see what we have done? We have abandoned the word 'happy' to be used by the worldly folk, and for the liberated state, we have felt obligated to coin another word: 'bliss' or 'Joy'. What are you saying? You are saying, 'We have bliss, we have Joy'—what the hell! And who has happiness? Exactly that—hell.

You have bliss, you have Joy—but who has happiness? Hell has happiness. Indirectly, you have declared that you are not happy, that you have Joy and bliss, but you don't have happiness. It is a very puritan way of looking at things, but it is also harmful. It is not harmful when you are already liberated, but when you are in hell, it is a very harmful way of putting things.

You are in hell, so what does your ego really crave for? Happiness, right? Your ego wants happiness, and you are telling the ego, 'Happiness is found in hell. In Liberation, you can have bliss'; the ego says, 'Who wants bliss? I want happiness, so I will very happily stay put in hell!' And that is what happens.

In the hell-state of its existence, the ego has very little respect for bliss or Ananda—all that it cares for is sukha or happiness—and you are telling the ego that 'you cannot have happiness if you graduate beyond hell'. So, the ego refuses to graduate beyond hell. The ego says, 'I will stay here. I am happy because this is the only place where one can find happiness. So I will not go to heaven or Liberation.'

You have to tell yourself: 'What is found in hell is the lowest and the most polluted, the most diluted, most corrupted kind of happiness. It is no happiness at all. I really want to be happy; therefore, I am giving up this place; therefore, I am venturing out; therefore, I am rising high.'

So, those on the spiritual path must take special care to be happy. As we said, the spiritual seeker must reclaim happiness. Otherwise, you are letting happiness go to the dogs—literally. You are allowing such people to monopolize and misuse the word 'happy', people who have no right to be happy. But they are the ones who are always found happy.

Heaven is a very happy—no, *hell* is a very happy place. See? I needed to correct myself! Heaven should be a happy place; instead, all the happy ones are found in hell. All hours in hell are happy hours, and heaven is such a dry place! Why have we allowed that? All the people who are laughing and giggling are found in hell.

Somebody said that all the interesting people are found in hell. No, they are not interesting. They are sick people. It is just that the very definition of the word 'interesting' has become distorted to their advantage. People in hell are as interesting as a stinking pile of trash. It is indeed interesting—but to whom? To crows, to dogs, to various kinds of bacteria and such things. They find it very interesting. Are you a crow to accept that definition? Why must you accept that definition?

Therefore, it is important to reclaim these words—'interesting', 'happy', 'smart'. Why must you call all the nonsensical beefcakes as smart? I have never heard somebody calling a Buddha or Mahavira smart. Why not? Why have you abandoned all the interesting words to the creatures of hell? Why? By doing that, you have raised trouble for yourself.

We have come to a point where if you find a spiritual person really pleased and radiant and actually happy, you start doubting whether he is really spiritual—because the only ones who have a right to be happy are the people of hell.

'You say you are spiritual. How are you happy then? You are not supposed to be happy!'

'Then what am I supposed to be?'

'You are supposed to be gloomy, dull—de facto dead! You are supposed to be a corpse somehow in motion. You are not supposed to dance, you are not supposed to sing. You are supposed to be just regretting the fact that you are breathing; you are supposed to be wishing that you dropped dead this moment or next. Then you are a spiritual person!'

All the merrymaking is reserved for the inhabitants of hell. No wonder that place is jampacked. If all the merrymaking is supposed to happen in hell, where would you find most people? In hell. And that is what we have done. Everything that makes life worth living has been allotted to hell. Now, how is it surprising that everybody is attracted to hell?

If you are a lover of Truth, if you are in the spiritual pursuit, then you have the double responsibility to remain highly happy. And when I say 'highly happy', I do not mean the degree of happiness; I am referring to the quality of happiness. Do you get the difference? I am saying you have to be highly happy. That does not mean that you have to increase the decibel levels doubly as you guffaw out.

'Highly happy' means your happiness has to be of a high order. It is your responsibility.

Do not starve yourselves of happiness. If you are giving up on lower happiness, make sure that you provide yourself with higher happiness. That is your privilege. More than privilege—that is your dharma, that is your responsibility.

This will sound strange to you. 'Is it my dharma to be really happy?' Yes, it is your dharma to be really happy. Because if you are not really happy, then you will seek happiness, and if you do that, sooner than later you will find yourself in hell.

The only way to avoid hell-like happiness is to create heaven-like happiness for yourself. If you are living in a heaven devoid of happiness, that heaven will not be able to hold you for long; your patience will run thin, and you will find yourself attracted to hell. All said and done, hell offers happiness.

Elevating life is one thing. Giving up on life is a totally different thing. Choosing the right road compared to the wrong road is one thing, and not travelling at all is a totally different thing.

L: I have come across many such people who brag that they are living happy and satisfied lives, but it is clear that they are just suffering in ignorance. They still make these claims and do not want to confront themselves honestly.

So, if I am a spiritual seeker and I want to show them that there is something higher to be had, how should I approach them? How can I have the clarity to display to them what is really worth having?

AP: See, the resident of hell who claims that he is happy will be terribly afraid of facing someone who is really happy. That is his nightmare. So, he is always cautious. He will not want to come across a really happy person. Therefore, he will be very choosy, very selective in terms of the ones he speaks to, the ones he chooses to make claims in front of, due to fear.

You are saying there are so many residents of hell who go about bragging that they are happy and satisfied. They cannot make these claims in front of everybody. They make these claims in front of only those who would not dispute or disprove these claims.

So, if they are able to successfully make these claims in front of you, it merely means that right now you are not in a place where your very being or presence or voice reflects back to them their miserable state of existence. They think that you are a soiled mirror. You can deceive yourself by standing in front of a soiled mirror, can you not? Once they know that you reflect back honestly and accurately, they will be very afraid of making dishonest claims in front of you.

The fact that they avoid reality, the fact that they avoid Truth and spirituality itself demonstrates that they are afraid. If you say that you are indeed happy and satisfied, would you be reluctant to test the depth of your satisfaction, the depth of your life? No. But you will notice that these people are very reluctant. They are reluctant because they know they will be exposed.

So, it is not as if it is a tremendously difficult problem that some people are putting up an act. Such people are more conscious of the act and the deception than anybody else. It is just that you are still not very evolved, and hence they are able to pull a fast one and fool you, or so they think.

L: We see many cases of such seekers. They say they have experienced heavenly happiness but they have lost it and fallen back to their habituated state. So, is the claim that they experienced this higher happiness false? If they actually had a taste of it, why would they go back to lower happiness?

AP: Because Joy has to become a habit. It cannot remain a once-in-a-blue-moon kind of experience for you.

The very process of realization has been broken down into four steps: śravaṇa, manana, nididhyāsana, and samādhi or dissolution.

You get an instantaneous taste of Liberation through śravaṇa itself. In the moment of immersed listening, you are actually liberated. But the latent tendencies haven't disappeared; they haven't been burnt down. They have just retreated. They have retreated because in the moment of listening you are not empowering them. You are not empowering them, so they have just shrivelled up. Soon they will regain their size and might.

Then comes manana. You keep contemplating, thinking; your mind is full of the words that you have received even after the speaker is no longer in front of you.

Then comes nididhyāsana. Now you are letting those words become a habit with you. This requires disciplined effort. The thing is not merely intellectual or cerebral. Nididhyāsana means that now it is becoming a matter of life with you. You are not merely thinking about what has been said unto you; you are now living it. And once you start living it consistently, there is samādhi.

So, it is rather easy to get an occasional taste of Liberation, but it does not suffice. You have to pay the full price to get the licenced version. Otherwise, all that you have is a little bit of demonstration, which is quite charming—but how long will that charm last? A few seconds, a few minutes, and then you will be told to pay the price.

So, there are so many people who indeed get a glimpse of the Ultimate Joy or Freedom or samādhi. Those glimpses, as we said, are rather frequent; they aren't as rare as we assume. The very process of life is such that you will stumble upon Liberation sometime or the other even without effort.

You may want to live in your lies and fantasies continuously and consistently, but the problem is that lies and fantasies cannot be continuous or consistent. Only Truth can be consistent. Falseness, by definition, carries a certain innate inconsistency. So, those inconsistencies will frequently be exposed. You will stumble quite harshly upon the fact that your make-believe world is false.

Now, that is an opportunity. The moment when your imagination is dashed, the moment when life comes down very harshly upon you, the moment when you receive humiliating setbacks, occasions when your basic assumption about life and yourself are proven wrong—those moments are all moments of opportunity.

And such things keep happening with all of us. We keep receiving rays of sunlight when cracks inevitably show up in our dark cocoons of falseness. And cracks will show up—sometimes here, sometimes there. Why? Because the cocoon itself is false and inconsistent. It cannot hold up for long. It cannot have structural integrity that is inviolable. Only Truth is inviolable. Falseness, by definition, will keep imploding within itself.

So, those moments when your cocoon cracks up and light enters your darkness, you could either take it as a moment of remorse, or you could take it as a moment of opportunity. Most people take it as a setback. Therefore, what do they do? They seal the place from where the rays entered. Others use the incoming sunlight to clearly see what is there inside the darkness of their cocoon. And once they see that, they blast the cocoon out from within. That is Liberation.

Life will keep giving you chances, but those chances are just chances. It depends on you to turn those chances into life. That is the choice you have to make. And that is nothing automatic.

If someone says, 'I have had a glimpse of the Truth', he is probably not lying, because most of us do get several glimpses of the Truth. The question is not whether you have had those glimpses. The question is: what did you do with those glimpses? Those glimpses were an invitation. Those glimpses were a challenge. How did you respond?

L: Saints have said that even heaven is not worth having. If that is so, shouldn't it be seen as worthless right from the beginning?

AP: If you are in hell, you do not even realize the worthlessness of hell. How will you realize the worthlessness of heaven? One has to somehow keep clear of the temptation to speak from an absolutist vantage point. Heaven is worthless only from the point of absolute attainment. Otherwise, it is not.

Who has the right to say that heaven is worthless? The one who has surpassed even heaven. The liberated one alone has the right to say that heaven is worthless.

But most of us are creatures of hell. Living in hell, we borrow the words of the liberated ones who said that even heaven is worthless. The ones who are liberated, in their liberated exaltation, in their liberated frenzy, uttered, 'Oh! Even heaven is worthless!' These were the utterances of the ones who had transcended and surpassed even heaven. So, those words befit only them.

And who are we? We are living in hell. Our only hope is heaven. But we catch the words of the liberated ones, and the words tell us that heaven is worthless. So, very comfortably, we stay put in hell.

This is ridiculous. And this happens so often. People will take the words of some liberated master and say, 'See? Saint Kabir has said that there is no point in worshipping even Rama, so why should I worship Rama?' Saint Kabir can say that. How can *you* say that? He is the one who has surpassed even heaven. But how can *you* say that? You are neck-deep in the muck of hell! Who are you to quote the sages? Why are you quoting them? You should rather look at your life.

It is a favourite pastime of those who don't have the wits to make sense of the scriptures. To berate the importance of scriptures, they quote the scriptures. They quote the scriptures to prove that the scriptures are not needed. The idiot does not know that, on his own, he would not even have known that scriptures are not needed. Even to say that scriptures are not needed he needed the scriptures. So, all these are just childish manoeuvres of the ego trying to somehow escape the parent.

A three-year-old wants to hide from papa. So, what does he do? He hides behind papa! Papa is huge, and the fellow says, 'I don't want papa!'

The only little problem is that you need papa even to hide from papa. So inexorable is papa!

But the little one is quite smug: 'I don't need papa!'

" DO NOT STARVE YOURSELVES OF HAPPINESS. IF YOU ARE GIVING UP ON LOWER HAPPINESS, MAKE SURE THAT YOU PROVIDE YOURSELF WITH HIGHER HAPPINESS. THAT IS YOUR PRIVILEGE. MORE THAN PRIVILEGE—THAT IS YOUR DHARMA, THAT IS YOUR RESPONSIBILITY. "

(Advait BodhSthal, 2020)

36

Looking for Happiness without Peace?

> **“** IT IS NOT TRUE THAT WE WISH TO ACHIEVE HAPPINESS DIRECTLY.
> WE NEVER WANT HAPPINESS DIRECTLY. WE ALWAYS WANT
> MEDIATED HAPPINESS. **”**

नास्ति बुद्धिरयुक्तस्य न चायुक्तस्य भावना ।
न चाभावयतः शान्तिरशान्तस्य कुतः सुखम् ॥

*There is no intellect (buddhi), and no contemplation (bhāvanā) for
the unsteady man, and for an unmeditative man there is no peace.
How can there be happiness without peace?*
~Bhagavad Gita, Verse 2.66

Listener: What is meant by bhāvanā here, and how does it lead to
peace? Shri Krishna first talks about buddhi and bhāvanā, and then
he mentions peace and ultimately speaks of happiness. But in our
daily activities, we wish to achieve happiness directly. Does this
verse indicate a major flaw in our standard worldview?

Acharya Prashant: Let's take this question step by step. What
exactly is meant by bhāvanā here, and how does it lead to peace?

The verse says: For the unsteady there is neither buddhi nor bhāvanā. And 'buddhi' here has been translated as 'intellect', and 'bhāvanā' as 'contemplation'. They refer to two parts of the same thing.

The one who is unsteady is not steady where he must be. He is steady somewhere else; he has taken roots somewhere else. He is not centered where he must be. Instead, he has found an alternate, false and worthless centre.

When you say someone is steady or firm or rooted or unwavering, don't you want to ask where is he rooted, where is he steady, and what is he steady about? That is implicit in the word 'steadiness': you have to be *steady* in the Truth.

So, to be unsteady in Truth is really to be committed to something else. What is this something else that you are committed to? That something else is the aham-vṛtti ('I'-tendency). From vṛtti (tendency) arises bhāvanā, and from bhāvanā arises vicāra (thought). Buddhi operates through vicāra. Both are in the same dimension.

So, when the verse says that 'for the unsteady there is neither buddhi nor bhāvanā', what is being said is that when you are unsteady, both vṛtti and vicāra go wrong because your vṛtti is now on its own, separated from the Truth; therefore, vṛtti becomes rootless, uncontrolled, somewhat of an autocrat, a sovereign in itself. And from such vṛtti, the passion, the bhāvanā, the emotion that arises is directed only towards the nourishment of falseness and, therefore, the suffering of the individual. And when the underlying passion itself is directed towards falseness, all the thoughts that will arise from the passion will obviously be thoughts towards self-destruction.

Now, coming to the second part of the question. It is not as if peace is a steppingstone towards eternal or true happiness. First of all, the word used in the actual hymn is 'sukham'. When the word 'sukha' is used in a classical scripture or a spiritual text, it really refers to higher happiness, true happiness, not dualistic happiness, not the sukha-dukha (happiness-sadness) pair.

When Shri Krishna says you must have sukha, he doesn't mean ordinary happiness or pleasure. He refers to non-dualistic happiness, which is more accurately called 'Ananda'. But because the words are being spoken to Arjuna, it is probably better to use the word 'sukha'. Arjuna, due to his conditioning, would resonate more readily with sukha than Ananda. So, understand sukha as Ananda here.

Peace is not a step towards Ananda. Peace and Ananda are the same thing. Spirituality is not about creating more and more layers, structures and distinctions. We are anyway victims of the endless distinction and divisions we have created. Spirituality is not about saying that such things have eight divisions and distinctions and out of these eight, the fifth one has three types, two belong to this category, and one belongs to other that tallies with the third distinction. You often read such distinctions in spiritual texts, more frequently on commentaries on spiritual texts. Avoid these things.

Spirituality really knows only two distinctions: Truth is distinct from false. Only that distinction exists. And even that distinction doesn't really exist in non-duality, in Advaita. Advaita says that that which appears as false is really a manifestation or expression of the Truth, so even this final twoness disappears, and hence Advaita. No twoness.

So, peace, happiness, liberation, simplicity, clarity—they should not be taken as separate states. Remember that all the separate states, all the separations really exist only in the conceptual mind, only in thoughts, as ideas. And all the concepts and ideas and mentation are anyway of no avail.

When we say that on one side is silence and emptiness, and on the other side are all the ideas of the mind, then all the distinctions that you have created are clubbed together and brought under one single umbrella. What is the name of that umbrella? Mind.

So, there is the mind, and then there is the mother of the mind, that which is beyond the mind; that you can call as the 'full mind' or the 'no-mind'. Only these two distinctions are there. Do not bother for other distinctions.

You know, a lot of this so-called spiritual scholarliness is based on mugging up those distinctions. 'What are the twelve types of such and such thing?' Someone says, 'I know all the twelve types!' and then he is taken as some kind of a great spiritual scholar. Nonsense! Putting something in memory—how does that have anything to do with freedom from memory?

Spirituality is freedom from the little self. By adding some concept to memory, how are you gaining freedom from memory itself? Rather, you are glorifying the value of memory, are you not? By putting something in your memory and de facto attaching your ego to it, your identity to it, are you not glorifying memory itself? And if you are glorifying memory, then how will you be liberated from memory?

Memory, to always remember something, is such a burden, is it not? To remember something is to think about it. And if the mind is constantly thinking, where is relief? Where is freedom?

It is not true that we wish to achieve happiness directly. We never want happiness directly. We always want mediated happiness. Don't you say, 'I will get happiness by doing this', 'I will get happiness through him or her', 'When I achieve that, I will allow myself to be happy', 'When I reach there, I will be happy'?

So, our happiness is not meditated; it is mediated. Between us and happiness there always stands something—a condition or a mediator.

'How will I achieve happiness? Through my wife.' The wife is the mediator.

'How will I achieve happiness? Through my new car.' The car is the mediator.

So, you are obviously not very attentive or conscious when you are writing this question. 'In our daily activities, we wish to achieve happiness directly'—no, don't even try that.

In fact, that is the central problem. We always bring in the world as the mediator; we always want some middleman in between. 'I will get the Truth through this. Through the world, I will get the Truth.' Now the Truth actually becomes unimportant; the world becomes very, very important. The Truth is de facto forgotten, the real thing goes for a toss, and the worthless mediator gains all the importance.

See whether it is necessary to be Joyful through something. Even before that, see whether the medium you are using is of any avail. Once you see that all these media that you have used have actually been useless, then you say, 'What is the point in using an intermediary? Let me try something a little more directly.'

And the moment you say that, you discover that the Truth really didn't need to be achieved. It didn't need to be achieved through a mediator. It does not even need to be achieved *without* a mediator. It is just that when there is a mediator, the fact that the Truth doesn't need to be achieved at all remains hidden in the shadow of the mediator. Remove the mediator and then there is no need to achieve the Truth.

The very need to achieve the Truth through the mediator is created by the mediator itself. The mediator says, 'Use me, bribe me, worship me, I will deliver you the Truth.' The fact is otherwise: the Truth is already there. The mediator exists to hide it from you.

The mediator will not give you happiness.
The mediator is blocking your real happiness.

> THE VERY NEED TO ACHIEVE THE TRUTH THROUGH THE
> MEDIATOR IS CREATED BY THE MEDIATOR ITSELF. THE MEDIATOR
> SAYS, 'USE ME, BRIBE ME, WORSHIP ME, I WILL DELIVER YOU
> THE TRUTH.' THE FACT IS OTHERWISE: THE TRUTH IS ALREADY
> THERE. THE MEDIATOR EXISTS TO HIDE IT FROM YOU.

(Advait BodhSthal, 2020)

37

Truth Is Not for Those Who Want Pleasure

❝ IF THE SPIRITUAL MAN NO MORE CARES FOR HAPPINESS OR
REGULAR PLEASURES, IT IS BECAUSE NOW HE HAS A DEEPER
AND HIGHER PLEASURE—A PLEASURE THAT ABIDES, A
PLEASURE THAT DOES NOT COME ALONG WITH DISPLEASURE, A
HAPPINESS THAT DOES NOT COME ALONG WITH SORROW. ❞

वाग्मिप्राज्ञमहोद्योगं जनं मूकजडालसम् ।
करोति तत्त्वबोधोऽयमतस्त्यक्तो बुभुक्षुभिः ॥

*This awareness of the Truth makes an eloquent, clever and energetic
man dumb, stupid and lazy, and therefore Truth is avoided by those
whose aim is pleasure.*

~Ashtavakra Gita, Verse 15.3

Listener (L): Please help me understand this verse from the
Ashtavakra Gita.

Acharya Prashant (AP): Ashtavakra is saying the Truth makes the
eloquent man dumb, the clever man stupid and the energetic man

lazy, and therefore those whose aim is happiness in life avoid the Truth.

If you have been eloquent, you talk too much, then Truth puts a lid on your mouth because you start seeing the foolishness of your words. You used to talk so much, and a little touch of the Truth left you awestruck. What to say? The words have been stolen away. It feels stupid to express the nonsense within.

Similarly, if you have been clever, Truth makes you see how stupid your cleverness is, so you give up on cleverness. Giving up on cleverness is not stupidity. But in the eyes of the world, only two states exist: cleverness and the opposite of cleverness, cleverness and the absence of cleverness, which the world defines as stupidity.

The spiritual one is certainly not clever. The saints have said and repeatedly emphasized that even a moron can reach there but not a clever mind. The ones who have a lot of belief in their tricks and methods and personal wisdom and intellectual strength are never, ever going to reach there. Truth is for the innocent ones.

Similarly, the one who keeps running about here and there starts seeing the futility of his efforts. Incessant movement ceases. In the eyes of the world, the energetic man has become lazy. He has not become lazy; he has actually become just restful. But the world does not know rest; the world will call rest laziness, which does not mean that rest and laziness are one. There is laziness that is very, very restless, and there is rest that looks like laziness. These two should not be conflated; they are not one. But if you do not have discretion, you may conflate these two. You may start talking of the relaxed person as lazy.

So, when the world looks at the disappearance of eloquence, the disappearance of cleverness and the disappearance of the running around, the world says, 'Oh, terrible! Spirituality has left this fellow totally useless! Earlier he was in fine fettle: he was an impressive speaker, he was a sharp thinker, and a high achiever. Surely in fine fettle. We looked up to him. But this thing called "spiritual realization" has made him totally worthless, useless! Now he doesn't talk too much. Now he doesn't come up with clever ideas to win the world or gain pleasure or prestige or riches, and now he is not seen making frantic efforts to rise up the social ladder. He has become absolutely worthless!'

And having seen and concluded that spirituality turns a fellow worthless, the worshippers of happiness and pleasure start abhorring spirituality even more. They were already scared of the scriptures and the teachers; now they may actively start hating the scriptures and the teachers. They will say, 'Don't talk to me of Ashtavakra. You know what he did to my brother? My brother was such a nice man, and now he is of no use to anybody!'

Do you see what the society wants? That you remain useful. Useful to…?

L: Society.

AP: And spirituality liberates you from being a useful slave to others. Therefore, the others will really dislike it when you turn spiritual.

The spiritual man is not of much worldly use to others. The fact is that now he becomes *really* useful to others. But the real use is not what the world wants from you; the world wants from you a worldly use, and this worldly use you will now refuse to provide. Therefore, the world will get angry.

L: Does it mean that the spiritual man is incapable of enjoying the pleasures of life?

AP: He is now incapable of committing himself to stupid pleasures. He now has deep and high pleasures.

Don't be scared. There are pleasures beyond pleasures. I did not speak on this to scare you away!

If the spiritual man no more cares for happiness or regular pleasures, it is because now he has a deeper and higher pleasure—a pleasure that abides, a pleasure that does not come along with displeasure, a happiness that does not come along with sorrow.

What do you want, a small pleasure that comes along with displeasure, or a huge pleasure that comes only with itself? What do you want, a plus one that comes with a minus one, or a plus hundred that does not come with a minus hundred?

L: Sir, I have received a lot of things, and I am grateful for that. At the same time, I feel indebted because I keep on receiving. What do I do about this indebtedness?

AP: Settle the debt.

L: It is like an ever-increasing debt.

AP: Settle as much as you can.

L: Jesus mentioned very clearly that only those who are innocent like children will enter the Lord's land. What is the meaning of real innocence?

AP: You know of one guilty act from the Bible. What was the guilt of Adam and Eve?

L: They took the apple.

AP: If guilt is to do what Adam and Eve did, what is guilt?

L: Taking the fruit of knowledge, the apple.

AP: And not following the instructions. So, now you know what innocence is.

'Innocence' and 'guilt' are related words, right? Innocence is freedom from guilt. So, the same source from where you are quoting about innocence also gives you the definition of guilt. What was the guilt? To not listen to the one who is your Father, to not follow His instructions; to be tempted by the apple, to give more credence to the words of the snake. And then you know what happened after the guilt? They started getting civilized. Eve demanded some designer dresses, and God came and asked, 'Who taught you to wear all these clothes? I left you naked!' And then He said, 'Oh! So, you have *knowledge* now.' Now you know what guilt is.

Avoid guilt. That is innocence. You remain innocent with Him. By being guilty, you consider yourself as earthly beings.

They were subjected to Earth, banished from Heaven. The innocent ones continue to remain in Heaven. The guilty ones are banished to Earth, and they think of themselves as earthly beings.

L: Sir, I am not attached to pleasures, but if they come my way, I do not see any problem in enjoying them. So, if I am living in a five-star hotel, it is fine. I won't have any resistance to it. And if I am living in a hut, with some other amenities, that too is perfectly fine for me.

AP: You don't accidentally stray into a five-star hotel, do you? You are saying, 'If providence brings me to a five-star hotel, it is okay. And if I have to live in some rag-tag place, even that is fine.' Are these acts of providence, or do you book your hotel two months in advance? You choose where you will stay and you actively pay for it. Is that the best use of your money? No. But you are devoting your resources to pleasure.

It is a choice. It is not an accident. Providence didn't bring pleasure to you; you arranged for pleasure. But you talk as if pleasure accidentally came your way. It didn't—you paid for it.

L: But I can afford it, that's why.

AP: The thing is you have limited resources, and we have talked of the best use of your resources. What is the best use of one's resources in life? Liberation. Now, have your resources gone towards Liberation? No. You found something higher than Liberation—that is pleasure.

L: I am obviously choosing.

AP: Obviously it is a choice. But your question, see how deceptively it presents the situation. Where could the same money have gone? Pleasures are hardly ever accidental. And if accidental pleasures do come to you, fine. But these are pleasures that we pay for with our life; these are very costly pleasures. Very costly. The chirping of the bird is an accidental pleasure. Unexpected rain might be an accidental pleasure.

L: So, the 'I'-tendency is still attached to pleasure.

AP: Obviously it is. It is not merely attached to pleasure; it is also not accepting something higher in life. That something higher is more pleasurable than pleasure. Come to it. It is an invitation.

" THE ONES WHO HAVE A LOT OF BELIEF IN THEIR TRICKS
AND METHODS AND PERSONAL WISDOM AND INTELLECTUAL
STRENGTH ARE NEVER, EVER GOING TO REACH THERE. TRUTH
IS FOR THE INNOCENT ONES. "

(Advait BodhSthal, 2020)

38

When All Desires Vanish

"BEING ABLE TO WORK HARD IS A PRIVILEGE. VERY FEW PEOPLE
CAN AFFORD TO WORK HARD. IT IS NOT A DECISION, IT IS YOUR
BEING. UNLESS YOUR BEING IS ILLUMINATED, UNLESS YOUR
VERY EXISTENCE IS RIGHT, YOU JUST CANNOT WORK HARD EVEN
IF YOU WANT TO."

कामान्यः कामयते मन्यमानः स कामभिर्जायते तत्र तत्र ।
पर्याप्तकामस्य कृतात्मनस्विहैव सर्वे प्रविलीयन्ति कामाः ॥

*He who cherishes desires and his mind dwells with his longings, is by
his desires born again wherever they lead him, but the man who has
won all his desire and has found his soul, for him, even here in this
world, vanish away all desires.*

~Mundaka Upanishad, Verse 3.2.2

Listener (L): Who is the one who has won his desire? What is
meant by being born again by desires?

Acharya Prashant (AP): This verse has to be read with a lot
of care. Otherwise it will feed into the conceptual mess and

misinterpretation which already exists since long and in a great proportion of the population.

'He who remains involved in desire, whose mind remains immersed in desires, is by his desires born again wherever they lead him.'

What is the meaning of being born again, here? For this, we have to understand what the *current* birth is like, because the verse says that if you are lost in your desires then you will be born again where your desires are. So, a particular place is being talked of; you will be born again where your desires are. The question is: What is the current birth? Where are you right now?

If you look purely in a bodily sense, then you are where you are sitting, where your body is. But human beings are more mind-identified than body-identified. Animals are purely body-identified. Most human beings would not mind being called ugly as much as they would mind being called stupid. It is the mind, the consciousness, the level of the consciousness, whatever the level is, which defines a human being. And if the mind defines a human being and the body defines an animal, then an animal is where his body is, and the human being is where his mind is.

Remember, you are not where your body is. You are where your mind is. That is the reason why in any activity of any importance just being physically present does not mean much; what matters is where your mind is. And there might be situations when you cannot be physically present at a place, but if your mind is there, then it is more or less all right.

So, when it is said that you will be born where your desires are, it simply means that your mind will be where your desires are. You would start a new story where your desires are, and that is a new birth. You would open a new thread where your desires are, and that is a new birth. New birth, here, does not refer to physical birth, the birth of the body. New birth, here, refers to mental birth, and the mind keeps on taking several births and rebirths every hour.

And there is ample proof in the Upanishads to conclude that the rebirth they talk of, when it comes to the lifespan of an individual, is the rebirth of the mind. And when they talk of the rebirths of the body, then they are not referring to the individual; then what they are saying is that bodies keep coming and going, the body keeps taking rebirth, in the sense that there are bodies today and there will be bodies tomorrow. So, bodies are born again and again.

So, if you apply a little attention, it will be quite obvious. Fifty of us might be sitting in a hall, but actually we are at our respective mental places. And what are those places? Those places are where our desires are. You are your mind and the mind is where its desires are, so you are where your desires are. That obviously does not mean that if you keep desiring to live in the USA—with the money, the luxury, the pomp, the lifestyle that it offers—you will be reborn in the USA, or you will take your next birth in the USA. Kindly do not interpret this verse to mean that kind of a juvenile thing. Or that if you keep thinking of the moon always, you will take birth on the moon next. That is not going to happen. It merely means that rebirth happens in the mental sense, which is the only sense that counts as far as our existence is concerned. If the mind vanishes, are we even called alive?

Look at a patient in coma. His body might be functioning more or less normally, but the mind is gone, the consciousness has ebbed. After a while, even the doctors say that there is not much sense in keeping him alive; they start calling such a person a vegetable. Physically healthy, mentally no more existent—he is considered next to dead. He is considered next to dead because in human beings life is defined not so much by physical activity but by mental activity. So much so that as long as your brain is functioning, you are not declared dead, and if your brain is gone, then you are surely dead. Not even the heart, but the brain.

So, as long as the mind stays desirous, you will keep starting new stories, and a new story is a new birth. Each story starts with a certain act of doership and wants to end, consummate in an act of consumption. You sow something, and then you want to harvest. You invest at some place, and then you want to reap the profits. You begin a relationship, and then you want the right results, happiness, pleasure, etc.

Unfortunately, this story rarely proceeds as per the desire. Desire will impel you to initiate a new story, and that much desire can surely do. If you are desirous you will start something. So, desire will start a story, but the story will not move as per the desire. You can start something that you like but cannot make it move as per your likes; its movement is governed by other laws, laws that just do not respect your desire.

Therefore, you are free—in a very limited sense of the word 'free'—to do what you want. A desire arises in you—and of course it is a conditioned desire, so the word 'free' or 'freedom' does not accurately apply here, but I am using the word 'free' here in the common sense of the word. So, you are free to do what you want, but you have no freedom in deciding the results of what you do. Go begin a new story as per your desire, but the story, the moment it begins, takes a life of its own, and its life will not be governed by your desire. The story will grow in its own way, and more often than not you will not like that way. It will not be the way you had desired or imagined. Therein lies suffering, and that is the reason why the verse now proposes a better option.

What is the first option? Keep desiring, and with each desire that you patronize you will begin a new story. You will have certain expectations from the story and those expectations are not going to be fulfilled. That is the first scenario. Now the Upanishads propose an alternate, superior scenario, which is:

'The man who has won all his desires and has found his Self, for him even here in this world vanish away all desires.'

Now, this has to be understood. What does 'this world' mean? This world means the world of facts, not where imaginations are but where reality is. You might keep imagining this and that. You might keep regaling yourself with flattering illusions about your condition. Living in a dilapidated hut, you might have convinced yourself that you live in a great palace. Do you understand the difference between fact and imagination?

The rishi is saying that for the one who has found the Atma (the Self)—he uses the word 'kṛtātma'—all desires vanish exactly where he is. What does that mean? Suppose you are in a hut. What does it mean to be beyond desires even in a hut? Suppose you are in a jail; suppose you are in captivity; suppose you are surrounded by ill-meaning enemies; suppose you are in a position where there is a lot of injustice all around you, and you are someone who has found his Self. Would you still have no desires? Yes, you will have no desires. What would you have, then? You would have clarity. You would know what to do.

Understand the difference between acting out of clarity and acting out of desire. Desire keeps the future first, and then from the future it decides a course of action for the present. What does desire say? It says, 'This is what I want to achieve, that is where I want to be. A distant place and a distant time, that is what I am looking at. And if I want to be there tomorrow, then I project what I must do today.' That is the common mode of thinking, right? 'Tomorrow I want to be there, and if that is where I want to be tomorrow, I need to figure out what I need to do today to be there tomorrow.' That is the way of desire. That is action born out of desire. It keeps the future first. At its centre is an imagination. When you proceed from desire then at your centre is an imagination: 'that is where I want to reach'.

Whereas the kṛtātma, the illuminated man, the person of the Self, great true Self, keeps the fact at the centre, the present at the centre, the reality at the centre. That is what concerns him and that tells him what to do. He is not working to reach somewhere. Wherever he had to reach he has already reached because he is kṛtātma. The man of imagination is working to reach somewhere; kṛtātma has no place to reach. All journeying and running and arrivals are now behind him. How does he act then? He acts from the fact. He acts from reality. He does not act to reach anywhere. He acts just because he must, not because he desires a certain result but because he must.

Now, this is something that will not be very comprehensible to us. What is this 'mustness'? Desire we very well know. We know what it means to be impelled by the pull of desire. What we do not know is action, strong action, vigorous action, determined action which does not come from a desire for results but from an appreciation and understanding of reality. We are not really acquainted with the kind of person who says, 'I know how things are, I know the facts of the situation. And because the situation is this way, therefore it needs redressal. I will act not because I want to achieve something but because there is an impersonal need for action, which is called Dharma.

'Not that I am lacking something which I need to gain through my action; no, I am not personally lacking anything. My actions might bring me any kind of result; I am not bothered about the result. But being alive, I must act. I have to act. Life is action. Even if I choose not to act, that is an action. I have to act and I know what reality is like. Therefore, I will act in the right way. I will do what I must. I am not acting because I want some fruit and some result from the action. No, not that. I am acting because there is no alternative. I am acting because action is indispensable.

'One has to act, and if I have to act I will act rightly. It is as simple as this. Something will be done through me this moment, the next moment, the next moment, and the next moment. And I understand, I have clarity, so I will do the right thing. I will do just the right thing, not the thing that fetches me rewards, but just the right thing. Rewards I need none. Not that I am so great that I am spurning rewards; it is just that I don't need any rewards from action. What I need is of a much higher value and I have acted rightly to satisfy that need already. That was my first project. Before I undertake any other work, I completed the first work that every individual must. I am kṛtātma: I am done. I am kṛtkṛtya: I am done. I am done with all that which is needed to be done for my personal self. I am done.

'So, that part of my journey is already over. I have arrived at the destination. Now, being at the destination, I see that I still need to move because life is movement. Life in Prakriti is a continuous movement. Inwardly, now I do not need any movement, I have arrived. But outwardly movement is compulsory till the body lasts. There is no option. There is no alternative. Because the body is there, action has to be there. Inwardly I have come to a standstill; I am okay, finished, done. You could call me completely alive or you could call me completely dead, but I am complete. Outwardly there has to be movement, so I move. How do I move? Without desire. But I move with a lot of energy, with determination and dedication'—and that kind of energy and dedication can actually be possible only in desirelessness.

We obviously know the great force of desire. We know how people are greatly motivated when they have something to covet, to go after, to lust. We have seen that, right? We have seen that when a person is hugely desirous then he is hugely energetic. We know all that. What we have not seen is the energy of the man who acts without desire. There is a great difference there. What is the difference? When the fellow who acts from a centre of imagination, from a centre of desire finds that his desire is not being fulfilled for long, he is frustrated. His energy drops because he is acting on hope, and when hope dwindles his energy dwindles. Whereas the other person is not acting from hope, he is acting from mustness, he is acting from Dharma, so he can carry on for very long in a very high energy state. He can sprint a marathon because he does not want anything. He is running because he must run, so there is no question of disappointment.

You could say, 'But sir, you have said earlier that people who are still alive in the bodily sense are never really perfect. You have said that there is nothing called a final enlightenment, that one has to be constantly vigilant, and that imperfections are never too far away, the bodily tendencies are never fully gone.' Well, yes. So? Now you will say, 'So, you know, some disappointment will be there, but right now you said there will be no disappointments.'

All right, point taken. He will be doing his marathon and in between there will be disappointment and fatigue and many other things that happen to all of us, but he will relatively very quickly get over all of that. That is the advantage. Now, this statement will not only satisfy you but also make this story much more relatable, because perfection is something that you can have no relationship with. Perfection is just a good ideal, and what does ideal mean? Something that exists only in ideas.

So, this person who acts not from a centre of desire will be able to overcome his disappointments very easily, very smoothly. He will remind himself that an outcome was anyway never the first thing, that the work in the first place was never for a particular result. The work was for the sake of the work itself. So, if the results are sour, if results are unsavoury, it is irrelevant because the work was never anyway done for the sake of results.

So, he will have setbacks. He will have his frustrations and all those things, but none of that will be powerful enough to stop him in his tracks. Maybe he will pause for a while, maybe he will deviate for a while, maybe he will be stranded or lost for a while, but then he will again pick up the speed, pick up the threads. Relatively, compared to the person who acts from the centre of desire, this fellow will be far more focused and much less susceptible to distraction.

'The man who has won all his desires and has found the Self, for him, even here in this world, vanish away all desires.'

To him exists only this world, the world of reality. He does not live in illusions. Most of us do not live in the real world. We live in illusions, like the backbencher in the classroom who is constantly looking out of the window. Is he in the classroom at all? Where is he living? He is peeping into the other classroom across the corridor, he is staring at the football ground, and if the window opens over a road, he is counting the vehicles. Where is he? In the classroom? Not at all. He is not living in the fact; he is living elsewhere. Even when he is looking at the vehicles he is imagining that one of those vehicles would soon be near him to take him away to his home. Is he living in the fact? Most of us live like that, like a backbencher.

Our association with reality is very weak. We live in our very imaginary universes. The man who has conquered his desire understands that his mind does not need to live in desire. He knows how things are. Things might be great, things might be bad. To him things are neither good nor bad; to him things are as they are. And knowing perfectly how things are, he knows perfectly what his actions must be like.

Why does he act at all? Well, all that we can say is he does not act for himself. He has no personal self left to act for. What does he act for, then? Well, as long as this universe exists there would be plenty of reasons, plenty of causes that would demand action. He acts for those causes. I repeat, his personal needs are all met already. His personal story finished long back. Now he exists to restore order wherever he is. Now he exists to restore Dharma wherever he is.

But what if he is at a place where there is nothing wrong at all? What will this person do then? He will relax. He will relax because he has no inner compulsion to act. He is anyway always relaxing within. And if the situations do not really merit or demand any action, he will be very, very comfortable not acting at all. That will be the right action. So, he will then display what is very difficult for most people: an ability to unconditionally and unapologetically relax.

The condition of the commoner is that when action is demanded out of him he is found short of energy. You demand action and he will not be able to act in the way that is required. And if there is a situation where he can fully relax, you will find that he is not able to relax either. That is the commoner's situation. When he needs to act he cannot act. When he needs to relax he cannot relax. Isn't that how most of us are? In the office you are scolded because you are not diligent enough, because you don't work, because you can't keep the laptop or the phone away. Your boss is scolding you because when you are in the office you cannot keep the wife away, and your wife is scolding you because when you are on the vacation you cannot keep the boss away. We neither work nor relax. That is the punishment for lack of self-knowledge.

The kṛtātma can lie as actionless as a python. There is an entire gita devoted to the kṛtātma, it is called the *Ajagar Gita*, the Python Gita. When he relaxes he will be totally unapologetic; when he works he will be unstoppable. Most of us, because we do not work deeply enough, therefore we remain apologetic about our relaxation. We carry what you can call a guilty conscience. Because our work is not yet complete, our sleep is interrupted by nightmares involving the work which you didn't complete in the day. So, at night you are having bad dreams about the incomplete work. Had the work not been left incomplete, you would have had no dreams about the incomplete work. So, the day is bad because you didn't work hard enough, and the night is bad because the day is bad.

You think it is today that you have come upon the cool catchphrase, 'work hard, party hard'. The rishis were the first to coin it and they knew the real essence of this. To you it is just a cool catchphrase; to them it was something arising out of realization. Remember that only the kṛtātma can work hard and then sleep hard. The one who has little self-knowledge, very little realization, shallow attention, no spiritual orientation, such a person can neither work hard nor party hard. He will be a middling fellow, a mediocre thing in everything that he does. And the world is full of such beings who belong neither here nor there. When they are working they are sleeping, when they are sleeping they are trying to work. At the end of their life they discover they have neither worked nor slept and the time has come for the final long sleep.

Being able to work hard is a privilege. Very, very few people can afford to work hard. It is not a decision, mind you. It is your being. Unless your being is illuminated, unless your very existence is right, you just cannot work hard even if you want to. You may decide at 7 a.m. in the morning, 'Today, I will work very, very hard', as most people do. You are supposed to have morning resolutions. You want to belong to the 5 a.m. club, so you say, 'I too will get up and do this thing and that thing.' Fine. Try! You will soon be found authoring an alternate book, 'The 8 a.m. club', which will tell how everything that you decide at 5 a.m. gets shattered by 8 a.m. And this club will have a huge membership. Even those who belong to the 5 a.m. club will be secretly enrolling in the 8 a.m. club. Do you think they are all illuminated fellows? It is just that it is cool to act like the poster boy and make others jealous of you, you know.

Working hard does not come from your decisions, it comes from your being. You have to be the right person to work rightly. This might not go down well with most people. They will say, 'No, it is just that we have not chosen to work hard till now. Tomorrow we will decide to work hard, and we will work hard!' Please do decide and test. Please do decide, at least once, to work hard and then see whether you can. It is like the obese person very confidently declaring that tomorrow morning he will work out on the treadmill for forty-five minutes. He says, 'I could have done it any day I wanted. It is just that I didn't choose to. Tomorrow, if I choose to, of course I can!' Well, for forty-five minutes, you can at most stand on the treadmill, sir—that too if your legs can afford that. But we remain confident: 'No, no, it is a matter of deciding. The moment I decide I want to do this, I will do this!'

You are incapable. You *cannot* work hard. It is not that you have chosen the right life till this moment; you are *incapable* of making the right decisions. Try and test. It is a challenge. Try! But you won't even try because somewhere you know it would expose your self-deception. So you will say, 'No, no, there is no need to test, I know in advance. My old Ambassador car can do 250 kilometres an hour any day if I want it to, any day. It is just that I choose to drive it at 25 kilometres an hour. It is a choice, you know. It is a choice!' It is not a choice, it is a compulsion. Try taking it beyond sixty, it won't accelerate; it will disintegrate. I hope the difference is clear.

That is our life: it moves at 25 and we pompously keep assuming and declaring that any day we want it can move at 250. We want to call our compulsions our choices. There is no choice there. There is just bondage.

L: These descriptions about the kṛtātma throw light on our sorry state and generate a desire to be like him, and the actions we must undertake to reach his stature could be called as sadhana. But seemingly, even this sadhana is future-oriented and therefore associated with all the perils of the desire-powered action described by you. Please help us understand how these descriptions should be made use of.

AP: You see, there is one thing the Upanishads are very clear about, and that is the most important thing that we too must have clarity on.

Right action does not arise from a vision of the future. It is just that since long in popular culture there has been just too much undue respect for visionaries. That is because Vedanta hardly ever became the mainstream thing at any time, for various reasons. So, we keep thinking that the greatest kind of action is when you have the greatest imagination in your vision. This thinking is so deeply ingrained in our culture here and elsewhere across the world that it appears intuitive to everybody. Set a goal, go after it; decide where you want to be and choose a road accordingly; have a target. Such things. Because these things are so deeply prevalent in culture, therefore they penetrate spirituality as well. Not true spirituality but pop-spirituality, the common kind of spirituality.

So, the common kind of spirituality is borrowing from culture, it leans on culture. It does not correct the culture or purify the culture or give birth to culture; instead, it is a slave to culture, it is a slave to the going conditions. Therefore, you will find the wrong kinds of spiritual teachers talking a lot about culture. What does spirituality have to do with culture? But they find a great need to talk of culture because their spirituality is nothing but a slave to culture. All that they know is culture and conditioning, and they want to uphold the cultural conditioning.

So, they allow culture to dominate their brand of spirituality, which means that if culture says that you must have a vision, they will say that your sadhana must have a vision, because their spirituality is following popular culture. In popular culture, every action must follow a vision; therefore, the pop-spirituality also follows a vision. They will say your sadhana will have this kind of target, and a lot of people will be lured towards that kind of sadhana. They say, 'If you do this sadhana, then you will get such results.'

So, the results are told in advance. It is like a company luring prospective employees: the salary is told in advance. 'You come and you will get such a thing!' Or a shopkeeper attracting buyers. He will not say, 'You come here and you will be desireless.' Will he say that? No, he will say, 'If you come here, this is what you will get.' The vision is sold in advance, and then the real sale happens. The vision is given for free, and then the customer is charged. The vision is free, the thing is charged. And the thing can be charged only when the vision is given for free because if the vision is not there, the thing will not sell. That thing will not sell if, first of all, the shopkeeper doesn't disperse the vision for free. That is how it happens in popular culture, and then that takes in its fold the shallow kind of spirituality as well.

So, one fellow is asking, 'What kind of sadhana do I need to do so that I can read others' minds?' The vision is already clear to him, so he asks, 'Please tell me what kind of sadhana enables the seeker to read others' minds.' Somebody must have told him all this. Actually, you do not need somebody to tell this to you; eight kinds of siddhis are popularly known to exist. And if you do not know the exact

meaning of those siddhis—anima, laghima, garima and all those—
then you can easily misinterpret them to mean these kind of things,
that some siddhi will be there and you will be able to read the other's
mind and such things. But we are right now not talking about the
real meanings of those ashta-siddhi. We are talking about sadhana
that proceeds from a vision. The beginning point itself is desire: 'If I
do this sadhana, I will reach such a place. If I do this sadhana, I will
acquire such powers.' It is obviously quite nonsensical.

Sadhana must not proceed with a vision in the eye. It must start
with a realization of your current state. All that you have is your
reality, this one life. Imaginations are just fluff. Keep them away.
Please look at how things really are with you. Don't shy away from
the facts. And if you are looking honestly at the facts and what
needs to be set right, nobody will need to come to you and tell you
a particular course of action. You will just know, *just* know. That is
the power of facts.

> ❝ THE MAN WHO HAS CONQUERED HIS DESIRE UNDERSTANDS
> THAT HIS MIND DOES NOT NEED TO LIVE IN DESIRE. HE
> KNOWS HOW THINGS ARE. THINGS MIGHT BE GREAT, THINGS
> MIGHT BE BAD. TO HIM THINGS ARE NEITHER GOOD NOR
> BAD; TO HIM THINGS ARE AS THEY ARE. ❞

(Advait BodhSthal, 2021)

39

What Lies at the End of the Story of Knowledge

> *THE EGO IS NOT A SIMPLE, INNOCENT, OBEDIENT CHILD.
> THE EGO IS A TRUANT, MISCHIEF-MAKER; IT RUNS AWAY
> HITHER-THITHER. AND WHEN IT GETS BEATEN UP, THRASHED
> FROM ALL SIDES, ONLY THEN IT WANTS TO SEEK REFUGE IN
> THE SCHOOL.*

यः सर्वज्ञः सर्वविद्यस्यैष महिमा भुवि ।
दिव्येब्रह्मपुरे ह्येष व्योम्न्यात्मा प्रतिष्ठितः ॥

The Omniscient, the All-wise, whose is this might and majesty upon the earth, is this Self enthroned in the divine city of the Brahm, in his ethereal heaven.

~Mundaka Upanishad, Verse 2.2.7

Acharya Prashant (AP): What is meant when it is said 'whose is this majesty on this earth or 'who is the mightiest on this earth'? What is 'this earth' referring to? The consciousness of those inhabiting the earth. So, it is referring to the mind of man; it is not referring to trees or mountains or things like that.

'This Self (Atma) enthroned in the divine city of Brahm, Brahmapuri, in his ethereal heaven, in his mighty space, vyom.'

No, dear ego, you do not know much. No, dear ego, you do not see much. Atma is omniscient, Atma is sarvajñaḥ, sarvavid; you are not. Have some humility. Don't be so confident of yourself. That which you know of is just foolish, and the proof is that you continue to know much. Had you really known much, all your knowledge would have disappeared; you would have moved into a spontaneous sahajāta (ease). That hardly requires any knowledge. But you continue to know much; you continue to live and operate from a point of knowledge, and that itself is sufficient to prove that you do not know much.

When real knowledge comes to you, then the centre of knowledge disappears; then you are left with the centre of Atma. When you have false knowledge, then you continue to operate from knowledge. Is it too paradoxical to understand?

When you have false knowledge, then you live from knowledge itself.

When you have real knowledge, then you stop living from knowledge.

There is this story of a man who was sitting in a group, and they were having a nice chat post dinner. And then they all decided to share the most interesting things that they knew about themselves and others. A bit similar to the truth-or-dare kind of games that we play.

So, this man went on to narrate an extremely interesting story. He said, 'You know, I went to Paris and I was living in a room, and that room had a damp patch on one of its walls, and the damp patch used to keep changing shape, and as it would change shape, I would know how my destiny is going to proceed that day.' A lot of interesting things he said.

When he began to tell the story, he said, 'There are three very interesting things about the story I would narrate.' So, the first interesting thing he said was, 'It is very uncommon to have a damp patch on the wall in a room in Paris. It is not so humid there.' And then it came to the second interesting thing, and he said, 'You know what the second interesting thing is? All of you would agree that mine is the most interesting experience. Among all the stories that have been told tonight here at this place, you would all believe that mine is the most interesting experience', and people agreed.

After he had just finished the story there was a deep silence, and somebody said, 'In the beginning you had said that there are three interesting things you would tell us. You told only two. Could you tell the third one as well?' He said, 'The third interesting thing is that I made this story up twenty minutes ago!'

That is the thing about knowledge. You would know that it is false only when you go right till its end. If you stop somewhere in between, you will keep believing in its authenticity. It is a long story, you stopped somewhere in the middle. Or if you stop anywhere before the end, you will keep thinking that the story is real. Only those who go right till the end of knowledge realize that knowledge is a very unreal story, and then they laugh at the story.

They do not hate the story, by the way; they enjoy the story. They enjoy the story as a story. Don't we read stories? Don't we read fairy tales? We do. Don't we read fiction? Great fiction has been written, and we read. Don't we read our epics? They often contain a lot of fiction, but still, it is lovely to read.

The one who goes right till the end of the knowledge story realizes that it is just fiction—nice fiction maybe, useful fiction maybe;

nevertheless, just fiction. If someone is sticking to knowledge, that itself is proof that he has not gone till the end of the knowledge story; he has become a knowledgeable person. Knowledge is not a story for that fellow, knowledge is a reality.

When knowledge is a reality for you, then you become knowledgeable, you start calling yourselves jñānī (knower), whereas the mark of the real jñānī is that he has been liberated from jñāna (knowledge). He has navigated the entire territory, he has cut through the entire landscape, he knows every bit about it. Not that he doesn't know knowledge, he knows knowledge, but he doesn't live in it. He knows knowledge, he might have knowledge, but he does not become knowledgeable, because it is far more joyful to live in sahajāta. It is far easier—you know, easy: it requires far less effort, it requires far less conflict and struggle. You don't have to eat out of your memory. Is that not a blessing?

Otherwise, we are such beggars in front of memory. Life comes to us with a question and we go begging to memory, 'Please tell us some old rehashed answer!' And what if memory is in a bad mood that day? Then you get no answers to the questions that life poses. Does that not happen? Sometimes you want to remember something and you are saying, 'Argh! Why am I forgetting?' and that day you recall nothing. Next day, the thing comes to you; memory was in a bad mood the previous day.

Why should you depend so much on a foolish and unconscious aggregation of experiences? That is what memory is. The man who lives in sahajāta is liberated from this dependence on memory. The false jñānī has a great dependence on memory. The real jñānī, again, it is not that he does not have knowledge; he does not eat out of knowledge, he does not find it necessary to operate from knowledge. Knowledge is his handkerchief; he sometimes picks it up, sometimes drops it; he does not even carry it always.

So, Atma is all-knowing, all-seeing, omniscient. What does that mean for us? — because all meanings are for us. To Atma nothing means anything. All meanings are with respect to the ego. So, when we say that there is completeness, when there is complete knowledge, that is fulfilment. In other words, what is it that we are saying?

Fulfilment is when you are liberated of knowledge. Complete knowledge is liberation from knowledge.

Complete knowledge does not mean a lot of information; complete knowledge does not mean that you have become a super Google. Complete knowledge is a different centre of life altogether. When it comes to information, you will never have total, whole, and absolute information; not possible. But when it comes to living totally, wholly, absolutely, it is possible.

Therefore, if your absolute life depends on absolute knowledge, you will never get an absolute life because you cannot get absolute knowledge. Hence, it is important to de-link your existence from your knowledge—and I am not talking of biological existence, I am talking of mental, psychic experience.

Learn to be without thoughts; thoughts feed on knowledge. Learn to enjoy uncertainty; certainty feeds on knowledge. Learn to be comfortable without any assurances about the future. Learn to be faithful without answers. Learn to be committed without guarantees. That is liberation from knowledge.

In that sense the pure Self knows everything. It knows everything because it has no need to know anything. Even without knowing anything it is Joyful, and that is what you have to learn. Because if you link your joy to assurances and certainties and information, you are never too far from slipping into depression. Life can throw very unsettling uncertainties at you, and you said, 'I would be comfortable only when I am certain'—and certainty basically means knowledge, right? 'Now I am certain that such a thing is going to happen, I know.' But that certainty you will not get; you will start trembling within.

Be unreasonably sassy. You look very spritely! Any reason? In fact, you got spanked just an hour back. Oh, I am sorry—it was me who spanked you an hour back! So, nobody knows better than me how you have received the wrong end of the stick by my own hands. But still you are just so cheerful! The answer is: unreasonable spunk. The fellow has a spring in his feet. I am just wondering, how is it possible? Nothing especially good is happening to him—in fact, nothing at all is going right for him—still, look at him! That's the way. Even if you don't physically do this, mentally that's the way.

Don't depend on guarantees, certainties, beliefs, thoughts for your well-being. Just be all right—just be more than all right. I repeat, why not have some fun? Why be satisfied with just alrightness? Let's transcend from well-being into something a little more. The spiritual man is sometimes called blissfully foolish—foolish not in the sense of having wrong knowledge; foolish in the sense of being contemptuous of knowledge. This is the spiritual connotation of foolishness.

In the world, we call someone foolish when the fellow has wrong knowledge or no knowledge. In fact, if someone has wrong knowledge, he is called even more foolish. If I ask you what is the score in the India-New Zealand cricket match and you say 'India made 700', you are foolish. But if you say 'three goals to one', then you are super foolish.

The spiritual man is foolish in the sense that he is contemptuous of the story. He won't throw the story book away; he would just know the story book as a story book. He won't take it any more seriously than a fairy tale.

The verse says, 'whose is this might and majesty upon the earth'.

The one who is to be accorded the highest value is neither the ego nor anything the ego deems to be valuable. The lower state of consciousness is not valuable, lesson one. Lesson two: anything that the lower state of consciousness considers valuable is not valuable.

It is not enough to say, 'I do not value myself much, but I value that.' You yourself are a very lowly ego, so whatever you value has no value at all. People say, 'I don't value myself much, I know I am nobody. But I value that thing greatly.' But you value that thing from your own lowly centre, don't you? And from this lowly centre, whatever you value would be lowly.

So, stop valuing the world or yourself. First of all, invest yourself in raising your centre.

Why does the sage have to return to this question of raising yourself? Because the entire game of spirituality is not about this or that, good or bad, right or wrong; the entire game is about seeing that we are two. And that is very difficult to remember for a beginner. Why? Because both of them carry the same name. What is the common name for the two within you? 'I'. Only in one discipline, only in the discipline of spirituality, are the two given different names; otherwise, the name is common: 'I'.

You say 'I am joyful' and then you say 'I am miserable'. It appears you are referring to the same entity, right? At one point this 'I' was joyful, and then at another point it was miserable. The fact is, these are not the same people. You are two, and within the two centres that you have lies a long range of possibilities. You are these two and possibly everything between these two. You are not one. And that is what spirituality constantly keeps reminding you.

Where are you coming from? Who are you at this point? Koham (Who am I)? Who are you? Even as you do this, even as you say this, who are you? You hate this thing as what? You are hating this *while being what*? In what capacity are you hating this? From which identity are you hating this? From which centre are you hating this? Are you coming from your real point or from the false point? And you have both and the option to be at either.

'I love this, I want that'—which centre of you loves that? Don't you want to ask that question? It is such an obvious one. 'I love that.' You can love that in two ways: like a Bhagat Singh loves freedom or like Champulal loves chicken. Both of them use quite the same words, 'I love'. But because the 'I' is very different, therefore look at the difference in implications. When Bhagat Singh says 'I love freedom' and when you say 'I love chicken', do you see the difference? When Bhagat Singh loves freedom, he gives up his own life for it, and when you love chicken, you take the chicken's life for yourself. That is the difference.

But these two statements are so frighteningly similar, 'I love freedom' and 'I love chicken'. The 'I' is different, but language conceals that. When you say 'I love freedom' and when you say 'I love chicken', language encourages you to use the same 'I'. Different 'I's should be used. If ever there is a spiritual language, it will ask you to use different pointers for different states of consciousness. What is coming from a high state of consciousness should not be expressed using the same subjective pointer; it has to be a different 'I'. Just as in spiritual books the self is written sometimes with a small 's' and sometimes a capital 'S', similarly there should be a small 'i' and a capital 'I'. When you are talking nonsense, you should use a small 'i'; when you are talking utter nonsense, then you should use just the dot in the 'i'. And it should be obvious, then, what you are coming as, where you are coming from. And then you will not be able to so blatantly assert 'I love chicken' and 'I love freedom'.

The highest on this earth is the highest within you. Would you remember this? Nothing else is more valuable anywhere. The highest within you is the most valuable anywhere.

So the verse goes: 'whose is this might and majesty upon the earth is this Self enthroned in the divine city of the Brahm, in his ethereal heaven'.

In a poetic way, this is pointing towards the identity of Brahm and Atma. Atma is fully established in Brahm.

What is Brahm? The Truth in all that you perceive. What is Atma? The Truth in the perceiver. There is you, there is the world. When you ask, 'What is the Truth of the universe?' the answer is Brahm, because you are coming from the side of the universe, you are coming from that end of the scale. When you come from that end of the scale, the answer that is given to you is Brahm. And when you ask, 'What is my own Truth?' then you are coming from the inner end of the scale; then the answer that is given to you is Atma. And the Upanishads say these two are one.

Atma and Brahm are one. Your own Truth is the Truth of the universe; your own falseness is the falseness of the universe. But the perceiver or the questioner or the sufferer is not the universe, it is you. Therefore, if you perceive falseness in the universe, it is your own falseness. And if in a moment of relative innocence, you want to ask, 'Where did the falseness in me come at all in the very first place?' then the answer is: it came from the universe. Your falseness is the falseness of the universe; your Truth is the Truth of the universe. The Maya that you see outside is the aham (I am) within you, and the Truth of the universe, Brahm, is your own inner Truth.

Therefore, when you come up with a question like, 'How do I know whether a person is Truthful?' the only honest answer can be: for that *you* will have to be Truthful, because the falseness in the world is your own falseness. If you want to see Truth anywhere, first of all you will have to be Truthful.

The punishment of being false within is that you will only be treated with falseness everywhere. Now, don't come and complain that 'people deceive me and this happens and that happens'. It is only because of something within you. Had you been operating from a point of Truth, nobody would have been able to deceive you, or rather people's deceptions wouldn't have left you scarred. You would have remained healthy in spite of all the deceptions and things that happen in the world.

Listener: You mentioned that one can either have faith in the sage, or one can suffer a lot. Are faith and suffering exclusive, or can they come together? Can they lead to each other?

AP: In general, to be blessed with faith without having gone through suffering is quite rare. But that is the way the ego is. It does not want to take the dignified road to the school. The school bus comes, it is a proper school bus, and the kid can opt to wilfully board the bus, reach the school, sit on his chair, and learn what is being taught. But that is not the way of the ego.

The ego is not a simple, innocent, obedient child. The ego is a truant, mischief-maker; it runs away hither-thither. And when it gets beaten up, thrashed from all sides, only then it wants to seek refuge in the school. It goes to seek refuge in the school only because some bully outside the school walls is waiting to thrash this one really hard. So, he says, 'Just to, you know, save my own backside, I will go to the classroom.' That is the way of the ego, unfortunately.

So, to have faith in the teacher without having gone through suffering is rare. The question is, how much suffering do you want to opt for? Some suffering obviously you will have to go through. Choose to minimize it. That is my request.

The second part of the question is: Would faith in the teacher bring about suffering? No, because your suffering, in general, would have already peaked when you go to the teacher; otherwise, you wouldn't have gone. That is the way we are. Yes, one thing might probably happen: that when you go to the teacher, he might reveal to you that your suffering is deeper than what you take it to be.

See, you don't go to a doctor because you are feeling fit as a fiddle; you go to the doctor because you are already suffering. What is possible is that the doctor diagnoses you and tells you that your disease is deeper than what you imagine. That is possible, but there would always first of all be an underlying suffering; otherwise, you won't step into the hospital in the first place.

Does faith increase suffering? No, it doesn't really increase suffering, but it may reveal to you that your suffering is deeper than your assessment or experience of it.

> " LEARN TO BE WITHOUT THOUGHTS; THOUGHTS FEED ON KNOWLEDGE. LEARN TO ENJOY UNCERTAINTY; CERTAINTY FEEDS ON KNOWLEDGE. LEARN TO BE COMFORTABLE WITHOUT ANY ASSURANCES ABOUT THE FUTURE. LEARN TO BE FAITHFUL WITHOUT ANSWERS. LEARN TO BE COMMITTED WITHOUT GUARANTEES. THAT IS LIBERATION FROM KNOWLEDGE. "

(Advait BodhSthal, 2020)

40

Why the Wise Call Atma the 'Enjoyer'

> " WHEN YOU ARE BEING THE MOST SERIOUS, THE TRUTH
> POKES FUN AT YOU. IN FACT, YOUR SERIOUSNESS IS THE
> BIGGEST JOKE. "

इन्द्रियाणि हयानाहुर्विषयांस्तेषु गोचरान् ।
आत्मेन्द्रियमनोयुक्तं भोक्तेत्याहुर्मनीषिणः ॥

The senses are called the horses, the objects of the senses are their paths. The wise call the Atma—united with the body, the senses and the mind—the enjoyer.

~Katha Upanishad, Verse 1.3.4

Listener (L): Sir, why do the wise call Atma the 'enjoyer'?

Acharya Prashant (AP): Enjoyer in the sense of being the watcher, just as you enjoy a show in the cinema hall. How do you enjoy the show? By leaping into the screen? You enjoy the show by relaxing in your seat. That is what the Atma does. It keeps relaxing in its seat.

L: Does that mean the Atma is enjoying our sufferings?

AP: Yes. Don't you enjoy even tragic scenes on the screen? That is what the Atma does. For the Atma, there is no tragedy. All suffering is

This reminds me of my college days. You know how young students are—brash, hard, mocking everything that appears sentimental. That is the environment in hostels. Nobody likes weaklings there. If you are a mama's boy, if you display a lot of emotions, you end up becoming butt of a lot of jokes.

So, there was an inter-hostel dramatics competition, and one of the hostels was trying to enact a sentimental play in which one of the characters was particularly sentimental. With due respect, the student crowd tolerated that play and that expressive actor for about a minute, and then we all, as part of the audience, came into our own. Now this sentimental actor, playing an even more sentimental character, is wailing, weeping and sobbing his heart out. And the more he cries on the stage, the more the audience laughs! Can you visualize? He is screaming with pain, and the public is going mad with laughter; people are rolling down the aisle. And hearing a lot of commotion in the audience, he thinks he is being applauded, so he beats his chest even more ferociously! And now the public has started throwing their clothes and stuff! After three or four minutes of such rioting, the actor finally realized that something was wrong.

That is how the Atma probably watches us. That is why the *Katha Upanishad* says that the Atma enjoys. We are such stupid actors. It becomes obvious that the suffering we are displaying on the stage is a false suffering. How can any intelligent watcher empathize with us? The more you cry, weep and shriek, the more the Atma enjoys!

That is why all the Buddhas of the world have a great time. That is why the first thing Buddha said was, 'The world is suffering.' What you missed seeing was his faint smile when he said that. Why else do you think he is smiling all the time? When the world is suffering, why else would he smile? Because even your suffering is so imperfect, fake, superficial.

The actor on the screen is beating his chest—and the audience, too, are beating their chests! That is how the Atma enjoys.

L: Does the Atma have no compassion?

AP: No. In fact, there is only compassion, but no mercy, no sympathy. A lot of empathy, but no sympathy. Only compassion, no mercy.

L: Why is this drama set?

AP: Because you like it! Talking about the hostel days again, there used to be some nights when parties were assured. Somebody's girlfriend ditched him, or somebody got rejected at an interview, and now it is certain that somebody would throw a party, in which the dumped one, the rejected one would be the chief guest.

That is how the Atma enjoys. You could even say that the Atma is a little self-centred. Or should I go to the extent of calling it a sadist?

L: What if one breaks his leg? Is there no mercy or sympathy even then?

AP: Yes. You break your leg, you get that big white plaster, and that becomes a canvas for all kinds of erotic expression. The fellow is sleeping, and two or three would gather to vent out their heart and other organs on it, and he cannot erase it! Plaster of Paris, if you write something on that with a sketch pen, it is immortal now and you have to carry it around!

L: If you bear some load, you will get even more load!

AP: Well said. That is what Christ has said. 'Those who do not have shall find themselves robbed of even the little that they have, and those who have, they shall be blessed with more.'

That is how the Atma operates. Do you think of it as sympathetic? It is not sympathetic. It is not socialist or communist; it does not believe in equal distribution. If you think that you don't have grace, even the little grace that you think you have shall be snatched away; whereas if you feel blessed with grace, then you shall receive even more blessings.

Complain, and you lose even what you already have. Be grateful, and you shall get more than what you are grateful for.

Atma is very peculiar. Very peculiar. It has no soft corner for weaklings. Complaints don't work. Atma has no regard for any kind of occasion, no regard even for the camera. Totally disregardful, even contemptuous. Atma takes as dirt even that which you think of as the holiest of the holies. Atma, in that sense, desecrates, spoils. Atma has no regard for your temples, churches, mosques. Atma treats them as jokes.

When you are being the most serious, the Truth pokes fun at you. In fact, your seriousness is the biggest joke.

Visualize it. You are sitting with all your seriousness and your graveyard-like face with two dead bodies popping out from somewhere, and against your graveyard-like face sits an old man and a child—and both are dying of laughter. That is the Atma.

Even your highest sadness gets no response from the Atma. Somebody has died and you are wailing, 'Rama naam satya hai' (Rama's name is the only Truth; religious chant often heard in funeral processions in India). The Atma is responding, 'Murda badaa mast hai!' (The dead body is happy!)

That is why saints have laughed at death. That is why in the *Katha Upanishad*, Nachiketa returns with deathlessness. That is why there is the story of the three monks who lived together and laughed together. When one of them died, he put all kinds of stuff under his clothes, crackers and such things, so that when he was being burnt, everyone would get something to laugh at.

That is the Atma—even death is a joke. Even death is not significant enough to make you heavy, to make you feel mortal, limited, contained. When the Atma is immortal, how can you be sad at death?

> **COMPLAIN, AND YOU LOSE EVEN WHAT YOU ALREADY HAVE. BE GRATEFUL, AND YOU SHALL GET MORE THAN WHAT YOU ARE GRATEFUL FOR.**

(Uttarakhand, 2017)

Acharya Prashant

The Vedas are the oldest religious documents known to man. And Vedanta is the crown jewel, the absolute peak, of the Vedic essence.

The world today finds itself grappling with problems unseen in history. The problems of the past were mostly related to poverty, disease, hunger, illiteracy, lack of knowledge and lack of technology. In short, the challenge was external, the enemy—whether in the form of a microbe or lack of resources—was outside. It was about man struggling against the tyranny of his external circumstances.

The last hundred years, however, have been different. The spectre of man's conflicts has risen to a very different and difficult theatre in this century. The secrets of the atom and the universe have more or less yielded to man's relentless investigation. Poverty, illiteracy and disease are no more the invincible monsters they used to be. Today, matter is at man's beck and call, and there is ambition to colonize the universe, and even beat death.

It should then sound like the best of times. The current period should be the best one in the history of our species. Far from that, we find ourselves staring at, as we said, a very different dimension of challenge in the inner theatre. Having conquered almost everything in the external world, man finds he is a bigger slave to himself today than he ever was. And it's an ignominious slavery—to rule all, only to find that inwardly one is a huge slave of an unknown oppressor.

Man has immense power over his environment today, but is himself controlled by his inner destructive centre he has very little knowledge about. Together, these two mean that man's tendency and ability to wreak havoc over his ecosystem is unlimited and unquestioned. Man has only one inner ruler—desire, the ever-sprawling desire to consume and experience more and more happiness. Happiness, that is experienced only to find that it evades all experience.

In this context, Vedanta, as the pure essence of spirituality, becomes more important today than it probably ever was. Vedanta asks the questions: Who is the inner one? What is his nature? What does he desire? Will fulfilment of his desires give him contentment?

As a response to the situations mankind today finds itself in, Acharya Prashant has taken on the solemn project of bringing the essence of Vedanta to the world today. His calling is to bring the pure essence of Vedantic spirituality to all, and apply it to solve today's problems. These problems of today are borne out of man's ignorance towards himself, and therefore they can be solved only by sincere self-knowledge.

Acharya Prashant has approached the matter of bringing Vedanta to the public in a two-pronged way. One, he has spoken on scores of Upanishads and Gitas and his comprehensive commentaries are available in the form of video courses and books. (solutions. acharyaprashant.org). Two, he addresses the daily mundane problems of people and demonstrates how to solve them in the light of Vedanta. His social media channels are dedicated to hosting tens of thousands of such open QnA sessions.

A BRIEF BIOGRAPHY

Prashant Tripathi was born on the auspicious day of *MahaShivratri* in 1978, at Agra, India. Eldest of three siblings, his father was a bureaucrat and mother a homemaker. His childhood was spent mostly in the state of Uttar Pradesh.

Parents and teachers found him to be a child who could often be quite mischievous, on occasions, and then suddenly, deeply contemplative. Friends too recall him as having an unfathomable temperament, often not really sure whether he was joking or serious. A brilliant student, he consistently topped his class and received the highest commendations and prizes possible to a student. His mother fondly remembers how she was honoured several times as 'Mother Queen' for the academic performance of her child. Teachers would say that never before had they seen a student who was as brilliant in Science as in Humanities, as adept in Mathematics as in languages, and as proficient in English as in Hindi. The then Governor of the state felicitated him in a public function for setting a new benchmark in the Board examinations, and for being an NTSE scholar.

The prodigal student was a voracious reader since he was five years old. His father's extensive home library consisted of some of the world's best literature, including spiritual texts like the Upanishads. For long hours, the child would be tucked away in the most silent corners of the house, immersed in stuff that was meant to be understood only by men of advanced age and maturity. Lost in reading, he would skip meals and sleep. Before he had turned ten, Prashant had read almost everything in the father's collection and was asking for more. The first signs of the mystical appeared when he started composing poetry at the age of eleven. His poems were imbued with shades of the mysterious and were asking questions that most grown-ups could not grasp.

At the age of fifteen, after being in the city of Lucknow for many years, he found himself in Ghaziabad near Delhi, owing to his father's transferable job. The particular age and the change of city accelerated the process that had already taken deep roots. He took to waking at night, and besides studying, would often be staring silently at the night sky. His poems grew in depth, a lot of them devoted to the night and the moon. Rather than academics, his attention started flowing increasingly towards the mystical.

He nevertheless continued to do well academically and gained admission to the prestigious Indian Institute of Technology, Delhi. His years at IIT were full of exploration of the world, deep involvement in student politics, and shining as a debater and an actor in nationwide events and competitions. He was a vibrant figure on the campus, a dependable student leader, and a soulful performer on the stage. He would consistently win debate and extempore speech competitions in which participants from across the country would compete, and would also win prizes for directing and acting in meaningful plays. In one of the plays, he got the 'Best Actor Award' for a performance in which he did not utter a word and moved not a single step.

He had been sensing since long that there was something fundamentally amiss in the way most people perceive the world, the way our minds are conditioned to operate, and hence something is distorted in the way the relationships between people are, the way the worldly institutions are designed, the way our societies function—basically the very way we live. He had started seeing that incomplete perception was at the root of human suffering. He was deeply disturbed by man's ignorance and cultivated inferiority, the evils of poverty, the evils of consumption, violence towards man, animals, and environment, and exploitation based on narrow ideology and self-interest. His entire being was raring to challenge the all-pervasive suffering, and as a young man, he guessed that the Indian Civil Services or the Management route might be an apt one to take.

He gained admission to the Indian Civil Services and the Indian Institute of Management (IIM), Ahmedabad in the same year. However, because the service allotted to him based on his rank was not the Indian Administrative Services – the service that he had wanted, and because he could already see that the government was not the best place where revolutionary changes could be brought about, he opted to go to IIM.

The two years at IIM were obviously rich in the academic content he absorbed. But he was not the one who would confine himself to slogging for grades and placements, as is the norm in these coveted institutions. He would regularly spend time teaching kids at an NGO that operated in a slum close to Gandhi Ashram, and would also teach Mathematics to graduates to earn to spend at the NGO. Besides, his angst at human ignorance expressed itself through theatre. He took up plays like 'Khamosh, adalat jaari hai', 'Rhinoceros', 'Pagla Ghoda', and 'The Night of January 16th' and directed them, besides acting in them. At one point, he was directing two parallel plays. The plays were performed in the IIM auditorium to packed audiences from within and outside the city. In the profit-centered and self-interest driven atmosphere of the campus, he had found himself an outsider. These existentialist and rebellious plays helped him vent out his anguish, and also prepared him for the bigger stage ahead.

The next few years were spent, as he puts it, in the wilderness. He describes this period as one of particular sorrow, longing and search. Looking for a piece of sanity in the corporate world, he kept switching jobs and industries. To gain composure, he would take time off and be away from the city and work. It was increasingly becoming clear to him that what he wanted to do, and what was crying out to be expressed through him, could not happen through any traditional route. His reading and resolve intensified, and he designed a leadership course for post-graduates and experienced professionals, based on wisdom and spiritual literature. The course was floated at some reputed institutions, and he would sometimes be teaching students elder than himself in age. The course was a success, and the way started becoming clearer to him.

At the age of twenty-eight, he bid goodbye to corporate life and founded Advait Life-Education for 'Creation of a new humanity through Intelligent Spirituality'. The method was to bring a deep transformation in human consciousness. The initial audience chosen was college students who were offered self-development courses. Wisdom from ancient literature was taken to students in the form of simplified texts and engaging activities.

While the work of Advait was great and gained appreciation from all and sundry, there were great challenges as well. The social and academic system had conditioned students to study to just clear examinations and to have a degree to secure jobs. The self-development education, the education of the Beyond, the life-education that Advait was attempting to bring to the students was so new and so different from everything that they had ever read or experienced that it would often lead to indifference towards Advait's courses, and sometimes even hostility from the system. Often, even the management body of the colleges and the parents of the students would totally fail to grasp the utter importance and immensity of what Advait was courageously trying to do. However, amidst all these difficulties, Advait continued to do well. The mission continued to expand and is touching and transforming thousands of students.

Around the age of 30, Acharya Prashant started speaking in his Samvaad, or clarity sessions. These were in the form of open discussions on critical life-issues. Soon it started becoming clear that these sessions were deeply meditative, brought the mind to a strange peace, and had a miraculously curative effect upon the psyche. Acharya Prashant's voice and videos would be recorded and uploaded on the internet. And soon a website too was developed to publish his writings and the transcriptions of his talks.

Around the same time, he started organizing Self-awareness camps. He would take true seekers with him to the Himalayas, in groups of around 30 each, for periods of around a week. These camps turned out to be deeply transformational events and the frequency of the camps increased. Hundreds of camps have been organized so far, providing immense clarity and peace in relatively short spans of time.

Acharya Prashant's unique spiritual literature is at par with the highest words that mankind has ever known. His genius is founded on Vedanta. With his broad Vedantic foundation, he is seen as the coming together of the various spiritual streams of the past, yet is someone not confined by any tradition. He attacks the mind vigorously and simultaneously calms it with love and compassion. There is a clarity that radiates from his presence and a soothing effect from his being. His style is forthright, clear, mystical and compassionate. The ego and the falseness of the mind do not find a place to hide while facing his innocent and simple questions. He plays with his audiences—taking them to the very depths of meditative silence, laughing, joking, attacking and explaining. On one hand, he appears to be somebody very close and approachable, and on the other hand, it is obvious that the words coming through him are from somewhere beyond.

Over 10,000 videos and articles uploaded by him on the Internet are freely available to all and make the world's single biggest repository of spiritual content on the internet, of which more than 20 million minutes are watched daily (as of May 2022). He has been regular speaker at IITs, IIMs, many other prestigious institutions, as well as platforms like TED. In print media, his articles get regularly published in national dailies. His discourses and interviews have been broadcasted via national TV channels too. Today, his movement has touched the lives of tens of millions of individuals. Through his direct contact with people, and through various internet-based channels, he continues to bring clarity to all.

PrashantAdvait Foundation

PrashantAdvait Foundation (PAF) is a non-profit socio-spiritual organization founded and led by Acharya Prashant. It was established with an objective to demolish falseness – both within the human being and in the society in general - and promote a scientific and spiritual attitude towards self and life.

How does the Foundation operate?

The Foundation facilitates Acharya Prashant's discourses across various platforms and organizes spiritual retreats, online courses, lectures and conferences. Over the years, Acharya Prashant has spoken on more than fifty Vedantic scriptures. Beyond the *Upanishads* and *Gitas*, Acharya Prashant has spoken on saints, sages and topics of timeless essence.

These discourses are recorded and turned into educational courses, so that they reach as many as possible in the most organised form.

Where is the content available?

a. **Mobile App:** Even as Acharya Prashant continues to generate his literature and commentaries at a prolific rate, the Foundation's role lies in collating, documenting and publishing everything in a form that preserves the original nature of the works for the centuries ahead. In the most organized form, Acharya Prashant's courses and books have been stored for public use on the Foundation's official mobile app. This app has been created as a timeless source of pure knowledge for all those who will ever seek the Truth.

b. **Website:** Acharya Prashant's courses and books are also available at the Foundation's website: www.solutions.acharyaprashant.org

c. **Social Media:** Acharya Prashant's channels on YouTube, Facebook, Instagram, Twitter etc. all carry huge volumes of educational content for all, and are managed by the Foundation.

Sections most benefitted by the Foundation's work:

a. **Non-human life forms** including animals and plants: Given that the overwhelmingly biggest threat to flora and fauna of all kind comes from the ignorance of man about his own body and self, reforming man's mind is the best way to save nature. It is estimated that millions of animals especially animals used for food – chicken, goat, sheep, cows, buffaloes, fish have been saved due to Acharya Prashant's work. Besides, a large number of wild animals too have been saved. With his efforts over the years, it is estimated that lakhs, if not millions of people have adopted vegetarianism or veganism and have chosen an awakened lifestyle involving environmental consciousness and a low carbon footprint. Many see him as the spiritual face of the vegan movement.

b. **Youth**: Youth, especially in India, face multi-directional challenges because of conditioning acquired from family, society, education, media, career challenges, dilemmas about physicality, love and relationships and deep existential questions about the meaning and purpose of life. They are in a delicate situation where the chances of making suboptimal decisions and life taking unhealthy turns are quite high. Acharya Prashant has been unique in addressing the energy and conflicts of the youth. There are so may who remain indebted to him for having received lifesaving clarity at critical junctures of decision- making.

c. **Women**: Women throughout the world, and especially in India, continue to be recognized as the largely disempowered half of mankind. While there have been concerted efforts in social, political, economic ways to instil women with due agency and power, nothing is really effective without the inner dimension of clarity and freedom. Acharya Prashant's work has been to awaken women to their true identity beyond the compulsions of the body and the conditioning of the mind. Countless women today—from the teenage schoolgirl to the septuagenarian homemaker—owe their sense of liberty, clarity and the courage to rise against external oppression and internal debilitation, to the teachings of the master.

d. **Spiritual seekers**: There is a large class of spiritual seekers for whom spirituality is mere entertainment. Then there are those for whom spirituality is a respectable name for medieval superstition. There are also those who come to spirituality to escape the bare realities of life or those who suppose that spirituality consists of esoteric rituals, methods, and exercises or those who want only superficial treatments to life's deep underlying problems. Acharya Prashant has been well known to vigorously shake all such seekers out of their self-deceptive psychological stupor. And then there is the odd genuine seeker. The one who has already tried hard to go into the recesses of his mind, and the reality of life—the one who is prepared to work hard for his liberation. One who is fed up of self-imposed bondages, and is prepared to pay the price for freedom. Acharya Prashant comes as a rare and real friend to such seekers.

Over the years, more and more volunteers from various fields of life have joined the Foundation, working relentlessly to help spread Acharya Prashant's teachings. Today, the Foundation has touched and affected the lives of more than ten million individuals, and these numbers are only going to multiply in the coming times.

To know more about the Foundation, visit acharyaprashant.org.

Information about the Foundation's courses is available at solutions.acharyaprashant.org.

Contact the Foundation at requests@advait.org.in.